PRAISE FOR *A FABULOUS THRU-HIKE*

"Reading *A Fabulous Thru-Hike* feels like hiking the Continental Divide Trail with your funniest friend; every high, every low, and all the signature quirks of thru-hiking brought to life by Derick's gift for storytelling."

—ZACH DAVIS, FOUNDER AT *THE TREK*

"*A Fabulous Thru-Hike* immerses you in a rugged journey along the Continental Divide Trail. From high altitude thunderstorms and bear encounters to sublime vistas and starry nights, Lugo's humor and adept wordsmithing brings the beauty and adventure of thru-hiking to life."

—HEATHER ANDERSON, AUTHOR OF *THIRST* AND *FARTHER*

"*Aqui en la brega*—'here in the struggle'—is one of those phrases that exemplifies the Type-Two and Type-Three Fun Adventure that Derick Lugo artfully, thoughtfully, and comedically conveys in his remarkable second book. This story reminds us on every page of raw human capability, mental and physical tenacity, our deep connection to the earth beneath our feet and the stars above, and perhaps most strikingly, the kindness and generosity of our fellow indomitable human beings."

—MIRNA VALERIO, AUTHOR OF *A BEAUTIFUL WORK IN PROGRESS* AND NATIONAL GEOGRAPHIC ADVENTURER OF THE YEAR

A FABULOUS THRU-HIKE

3,100 Miles on the Continental Divide Trail

DERICK LUGO

MOUNTAINEERS
BOOKS

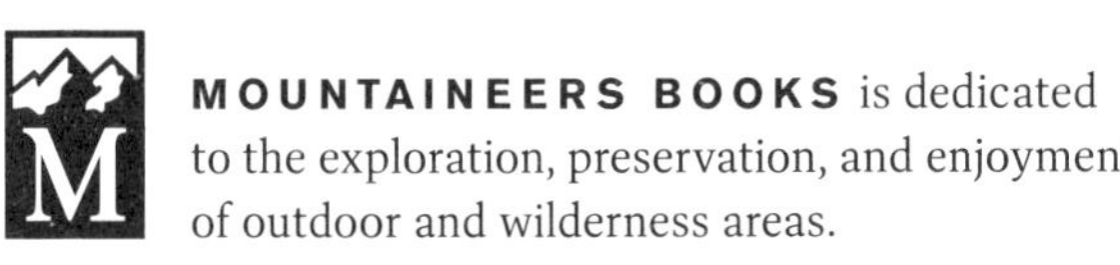

1001 SW Klickitat Way, Suite 201, Seattle, WA 98134
800-553-4453, www.mountaineersbooks.org

Copyright © 2026 by Derick Lugo

All rights reserved. No part of this book may be reproduced or utilized in any form, or by any electronic, mechanical, or other means, without the prior written permission of the publisher.

Mountaineers Books and its colophon are registered trademarks of The Mountaineers organization.

Printed in China
Distributed in the United Kingdom by Cordee, www.cordee.co.uk

29 28 27 26 1 2 3 4 5

Design, map, and layout: Melissa McFeeters
Cover illustration: Jon LaValley

Library of Congress Cataloging-in-Publication data is on file for this title at https://lccn.loc.gov/2025945356

Mountaineers Books titles may be purchased for corporate, educational, or other promotional sales, and our authors are available for a wide range of events. For information on special discounts or booking an author, contact our customer service at 800-553-4453 or mbooks@mountaineersbooks.org.

Printed on FSC-certified materials

ISBN (paperback): 978-1-68051-829-0
ISBN (ebook): 978-1-68051-830-6

An independent nonprofit publisher since 1960

To all
who seek
the outdoors

Contents

PART 3
WYOMING & IDAHO

PART 4
MONTANA

The
CONTINENTAL
DIVIDE TRAIL
Waterton Lakes National Park of Canada
CANADA
Glacier National Park
BOZEMAN
MONTANA
LIMA
Yellowstone National Park
LEADORE
WYOMING
DUBOIS
Wind River Range
LANDER
PINEDALE
IDAHO
Cirque of the Towers
RAWLINS
UTAH
COLORADO
STEAMBOAT SPRINGS
DENVER
San Luis Peak
Grays Peak
San Juan Mountains
CREEDE
CHAMA
ARIZONA
SANTA FE
CUBA
ALBUQUERQUE
PIE TOWN
Gila River Alternate
NEW MEXICO
SILVER CITY
Crazy Cook Monument
MEXICO

PROLOGUE

The Long Trail

I WAKE WITH A SHAKE, not from being shaken by another but from the vigorous tremors coursing through my body. I turn, lean over the side of the bed, hang my head above a bucket, and retch, but only spit comes out. My stomach has already emptied itself too many times. I lie back down and wait for the next episode.

When I hiccup, my chest fills with pain. I rub it, hoping to massage the pain away. Another hiccup comes, and this time it feels like fiery rivers are raging through my chest, culminating in a burst of agony. I sit up with a scream.

I can't do this much longer.

I hold my breath, hoping this old remedy will help.

"Nnnngh," I try to stifle the cry as another hiccup ignites more pain.

By 2:00 a.m., the pain has become unbearable. I lean over to the other side of the bed and knock on the wall, hard enough to alert Billy and Ann, my hosts. They picked me up at the airport before I set out on this 272-mile end-to-end hike on Vermont's Long Trail. They housed and fed me, and even hiked with me to the Massachusetts-Vermont border—the southern terminus and official start of the trail. Now, two days later, I'm back in their home.

My first day on the trail, dehydration hit hard, leaving me sick. Today, a relentless rainstorm soaked me through, leaving not a single dry stitch. Just fourteen miles into my trek, I got a text from Billy, offering to pick me up at a trailhead on Route 9 so I could dry off and recover before heading back out the next day. I gratefully accepted his offer.

"Something's wrong—I can't breathe," I say as they enter the guest room. Billy puts his hand on my chest. He's not a doctor, but something tells me he knows what he's doing.

Earlier today, it was Billy who inspected my water filter and discovered that I was missing the gasket seal that prevents contaminated water from seeping through.

Beaver waste—I was drinking beaver waste!

On my first day, I wasn't drinking enough water. By the time I reached camp, a headache had set in, only to worsen as the evening wore on. Desperate to rehydrate, I drank two liters of water last night and then three more today. But unknowingly, I hadn't properly filtered the water I drew from the nearby stream running through a beaver dam. The water had looked clear, and I'd assumed my filter was working. Now, I realize that contaminated water is most likely the source of the pain I'm experiencing.

As Billy rushes me in a fireman's carry out of the room and down the stairs, I feel shame and embarrassment, but mostly humility. This sixty-something-year-old is stronger than someone half his age. He easily takes me down the steps as I dangle, limbs useless, my mind full of loss. I'll never be the same again.

Billy and Ann drive me to the emergency room, and I struggle to make sense of my situation. My head feels foggy, and the pain in my chest persists; in my weakened state, I'm preoccupied with thoughts of how I've lost the special drive that got me through my first end-to-end hike. Back in 2012, I approached the 2,198-mile Appalachian Trail (AT) with zero experience and no idea what I was getting into, yet everything fell into place. I experienced, I learned, and I emerged from that adventure with a fresh perspective of the outdoors, people, and myself. Now, almost ten years later, I expected this Long Trail hike would not only replicate that experience but also enhance my new way of being. I was wrong.

At the ER, the doctor diagnoses me with a parasitic infection in my intestines and prescribes a week of antibiotics. The treatment will leave me weak and unable to return to the Long Trail for the foreseeable future. In my defeated state, all I can think is that it's over; I'm not cut out for this anymore. I can never attempt such a feat again. I'm done.

PART 1

NEW MEXICO

CHAPTER 1

CDT, Short for the Continental Divide Trail

BEFORE I THRU-HIKED the AT—completing the long-distance trail from start to finish in one hiking season or calendar year—I was inexperienced with the outdoors. I had never backpacked, camped, or pitched a tent. Heck, I didn't even know if I liked hiking.

Pre-2012, my entire life was spent within the limits of New York City. As a child, I played in the streets of Brooklyn, where the outdoors meant tall buildings and gum-stained sidewalks. The closest I got to nature as an adult was jogging through Central Park. My grand outings were to Yankee Stadium, Coney Island, and Rockaway Beach. A trail walk in a forest wasn't part of my metropolitan world.

It wasn't that I didn't know about outdoor activities; they just never felt as accessible as the basketball courts in Highland Park. Moreover, why would I venture out into the woods and the hills when I could be as active as I wanted closer to home, where my environment was familiar and felt much safer than out in the sticks? I didn't know what was out there. After all, the scariest movies start and end in the darkness of the rural woods. No one I knew in New York City was doing anything like that, so why should I?

That is, until a friend handed me a book and said, "Read this; it's funny." I love humor, so I figured why not?

The book was *A Walk in the Woods* by Bill Bryson. It was indeed funny, with good writing, and made for an enjoyable read. However, my friend didn't mention the AT, which the author made sound so challenging—but also intriguing.

Years passed, and I found myself searching for something beyond New York City—something outside my comfort zone, something that both scared me and dared me to discover a new perspective on the world. That's when I flashed back to Bryson's book and the AT, with all its uncertainty and challenges. And so I set out to hike, ultimately completing the journey in 183 days. Although I fell in love with the outdoors and long-distance hiking, I didn't think it would become something I would seek out again.

In fact, for years, there was no personal reason for me to try another thru-hike, especially not on what's considered to be the hardest of the United States' three north/south long-distance trails. The reputation of the Continental Divide Trail (CDT) is well earned: It stretches approximately 3,100 miles through the western United States, beginning in New Mexico at the Mexican border, and ending in Waterton Park, four miles into Canada just north from Montana. Along the way, the CDT primarily clings to the spine of the continent at elevations ranging from 4,000 to 14,000 feet. It traverses raw desert, alpine talus and tundra in the Rockies, the parched landscape of the Great Divide Basin, and the gentler but more remote mountains of Wyoming, Idaho, and Montana. The Continental Divide Trail Coalition (CDTC) estimates that only 150 to 400 people attempt the trail each year, compared with about 3,000 for the AT. However, the CDT has a completion rate of around 80 percent, while on the AT it's closer to 25 percent.

I had nothing to prove, nothing to gain, and everything to lose. Yet, with time and personal growth, subtle nudges began to wear down my firm resolve to never thru-hike again. After moving from New York City to Asheville, North Carolina, I built a life around writing, speaking, and working with outdoor companies to inspire others to connect with nature. Conversations often turned to time spent outside, and more and more, they centered on the Continental Divide.

"If there's a solid reason, adequate support, and a compelling narrative, then I could envision myself pursuing it." This was my consistent response when asked about the idea of embarking on another long-distance hike. As someone passionate about reading and storytelling, the possibility of an adventure rich with new tales to tell could be enough to get me on board—or at least, that's what I told others. Deep down, though, I was still unsure.

Much had changed since the AT, including myself. Simply picking up where I left off wasn't so straightforward. While I am an avid outdoorsman who enjoys daily hikes, the prospect of once again living on a trail for half a year raised questions. Did I still possess the resilience? Did I even desire to summon the inner strength required for such an endeavor? Most importantly, would it ultimately bring me enjoyment?

When I confide my doubts in others, their familiar chorus resounds. "You've got this, Derick. You've done it before." Yet those words don't quite resonate, so I seek the honest perspective of an old New York friend. Nina is a natural skeptic who won't hesitate to challenge my confidence.

Nina now lives in Los Angeles with her husband, and so we catch up via a Zoom call. In a way, I need her doubts, and those of others, to fuel my determination to ultimately prove them wrong. This was my motivation for not being deterred from the AT. My belief, both then and now, is that the mind is an incredible force and a formidable ally. That mindset hasn't failed me yet.

When Nina pops up on the screen, it looks like she's just finished a workout, with her short hair pulled up and her white ribbed tank top. The background is blurred, but I wouldn't be surprised if she's still at the gym—like me, she's perpetually focused on fitness, and often out for a run or pounding the treadmill or lifting weights.

Her skin is a shade lighter than mine, and people often mistake us for siblings. That's cool with us—I consider her my big sister, and she teases me like I was her little brother.

"Yeah, I heard you're going to live under a rock again" is Nina's response to my announcement that I'm considering embarking on a new thru-hiking journey.

OK, this is going in the right direction. She's going to tell me I'm nuttier than a squirrel's lunch box and that I'll never make it.

"Crazy, right?" I egg her on. I get ready to say "Ouch, that hurt" after she inevitably puts me down for being too metropolitan.

"You got this, D," she says instead.

Noooo, not you too!

"Isn't it much easier now with apps and GPS thingies?" she asks.

"Yeah, there's the Gut Hook app—well, it's now called FarOut—but I don't know, it's been ten years since my last long-distance hike. Things have changed. This is a different trail; I don't know much about it yet. I mean, it starts in the desert, for crying out loud. I've never hiked in the desert." I give her one excuse after another. "There are storms, and fires, and grizzlies, and . . ."

"What does CDT stand for?" she interrupts.

"Umm, Continental Divide Trail."

"Oh, OK, 'cause I thought it was short for Crying Derick Tears. Go wipe your snotty nose," she quips.

I touch the tip of my nose. *She's mean.*

"Did that hurt your little feelings?" she continues to tease.

"No." It did.

"Look, dude, for years you've been telling everyone how much you love the outdoors. How the AT changed your life. Man, you changed my mind about hiking. Got me to buy my first pair of hiking shoes, and off we went. Brother, you went from city-slickin' to tent-pitchin' in the rain with nothing but a bandanna, a shower curtain, and a bindle," Nina says animatedly.

She's exaggerating, but I get it. But now she's on a roll, and there's nothing I can do to slow her down.

"Didn't you wrestle a mountain borkion or something?"

"A what?"

"You know, that creature in the woods. Half bear, half unicorn or lion, goat. A borkion."

Nina smirks.

"OK, I get your point . . . I think," I say, feeling like I need a rest after all this bafflegab.

"Look, what drove you to do the AT?" she asks, suddenly more serious.

"I was discovering something new, stepping out of my comfort zone and doing something out of the ordinary," I reply.

"Well, that's not the case this time around, so what is it, Mr. Fantasy?" she says, mocking my AT trail name.

"I don't know, maybe . . ." I pause, trying to find the right words. I do have a deep affection for the outdoors, and I enjoy sharing stories that come out of it.

"I'm, I'm not doing this for me," I stammer.

"Really? If not for you, then who?"

"Others, like . . . look, I just feel like I'm supposed to do this," I force out the words, not fully understanding them myself.

"Grasping at straws," Nina says, unmoved.

"Yeah, it sounded weird out loud."

She gives me a quizzical look and waits for an answer that will satisfy her.

"Don't you think there might be someone out there who may benefit from my thru-hiking tales? I don't know . . . look, I don't have all the answers . . . but if this experience is anything like my first, I'm confident that it will all become clear once I'm done." I force a confidence I don't actually feel.

I look away from the screen and Nina's sardonic smile. If I can't voice a reason, should I even attempt this undertaking? I glance at the ceiling, half expecting the answers to be written there by a celestial being. Then I share what I *truly* feel, not just what I *think* I should say.

"I miss it . . . I miss the freedom, the simplicity of having one thing to focus on—hiking—while everything else fades into the background. I miss the connections I felt with the people I met along the way. I ache to recapture that sense of awe, and to step into a world that few can or will experience. On the AT, I felt like I was doing something special. It wasn't just an experience to check off; it transformed my way of thinking and shifted my career path. Maybe the CDT can help me build on that foundation. Oh, and dancing on mountaintops—that alone makes five months of hiking worth it."

Nina's expression softens, but not her words. "Then as a parting piece of advice, when you're using the outdoor facilities in the desert, be cautious where you bend down, because no one wants to extract rattler venom from a butt cheek."

One final snap, but she doesn't fool me. I sense that she appreciates my intent, even if I can't seem to articulate it at this moment.

"Are you going to use the same trail name, Mr. Fannypack?"

I stare at her, trying to read her neutral facial expression.

Damn, she has the best poker face.

Nina hasn't said my actual trail name in the decade I've had it, either because she finds Mr. Fabulous too grand for her little brother or because she sees it as one more thing to rib me about. Either way, I'm cool with it.

"No, and it's . . ." I pause, not wanting to give her more verbal ammunition. "You know it's . . ."

"Alright, Fab, I'll catch you later," she says and ends the Zoom call.

Wait, did she actually say my trail name? Well, sort of.

My mouth remains agape.

Fab? Well, I'll take that.

CHAPTER 2

Solo, Tie, and Sidetrack

IT'S WHEELS DOWN at Silver City, New Mexico—a moment that used to be my favorite part of a trip, as an uneasy flier. However, after years of traveling, I now find flying much more enjoyable.

This small, regional flight from Albuquerque International Sunport, shared with seven passengers and two pilots, marks my maiden voyage on such a tiny aircraft. Being so close to the cockpit, with only a thin barrier between me and the open air, gave the flight a sense of adventure. Flying lower heightened my awareness of the landscape. The gray desert spanned to the horizon, making me feel like I was touring a distant, alien planet. The sandy hills and mountains had a vintage quality, like a backdrop from an old western—not entirely realistic, but soothing to the eyes.

As I disembark, I exchange high fives with the pilots.

"That was truly thrilling. Thank you, gentlemen," I say, smiling so wide it feels like my cheeks might split.

As I approach the tiny one-room airport, I'm greeted by two thru-hiking friends: Solo, who I met when he thru-hiked the AT the same season I did, and his partner, Tie-Dye, nicknamed for the attire she wore during her own AT thru-hike, which took place a year after Solo's. Nowadays, her trail name has been shortened to Tie.

Solo and I maintained our connection throughout the years. When they heard that I was planning to hike the CDT, they both wanted to get involved—Tie offered to hike the first hundred miles with me, and considered taking on the entire trail, while Solo said he would provide support for a few weeks along the way, helping with resupplies and shuttling some of my gear, allowing me to travel lighter and cover ground more quickly.

This will be my first supported thru-hike, and I'm looking forward to easing back into it with the company and assistance of friends. An unsupported thru-hike would mean hauling everything myself, relying only on the occasional store for restocks. Supported hikes have the advantage of lightening the load and making logistics easier, which helps if speed is the goal. Going unsupported is more of a grind—it's all on you, and it forces a level of resilience. Each style brings its own set of challenges: Supported is efficient, while unsupported is all about rugged independence.

With Solo's support, I can enjoy more time in Silver City—a town the CDT passes through on the journey north—and acclimate back into a thru-hiking routine.

When I first met Solo toward the end of the AT, the then-sixty-something hiker resembled Willie Nelson, with a bandanna covering his long gray hair, a shaggy beard, and a laid-back attitude.

Today, Solo and Tie make an amusing pair. While Tie's hair matches Solo's gray, she's several years younger. They first crossed paths in the small town of Hot Springs, North Carolina, along the AT—Tie was working at the hostel at Laughing Heart Lodge when Solo stopped by. Tie's son thru-hiked the AT the same season Solo and I did. His journey along the trail inspired Tie to try it herself, and she hasn't looked back since. Solo, aptly named for his preference for hiking alone, now finds himself with a companion for his adventures.

I jokingly suggest that Solo change his trail name to Accompanied.

"We'll see how long I'll keep her around," he says, chuckling.

We jump into their new black Ford Explorer for our drive to their home. We pass through the desert landscape, with its dry prairie grass and green ephedra, suddenly overshadowed by flat platforms rising from the ground, forming a pyramidal shape. The shades of brown remind me of patchwork pants I love.

Solo informs me that these manmade mountains are tailings piles from the Chino Open Pit Copper Mine, mining waste full of leftover material from processing copper ore, which some locals are concerned may contaminate local waterways. As I ponder being back on trail again, I remember the beaver-dam-water-drinking calamity on the Long Trail. Apprehension takes hold, leaving me feeling like a tightrope walker without a safety net.

I ask, "Is the water here safe to drink?"

"Yeah, well, yeah." Solo's tone is tinged with uncertainty. Tie nods in agreement, but their half-hearted response doesn't leave me feeling warm and safe inside.

"OK, well, is it at least vegan?" I try to make light of my worry.

Solo glances at me in the rearview mirror. "Well, that's up for debate. We're not entirely sure."

Tie adds, "It does have a lot of minerals, sooo . . ." She hands me a bottled water.

I accept the water, along with the subtle message it conveys. I don't need to be knocked over the head with a glaring warning sign to realize a potential danger. I feel like a protagonist in a horror movie, told not to worry about werewolves while being handed a rifle with silver bullets, a pouch of wolfsbane, and instructions to hunker down during the full moon.

Reminder to myself: Purchase a few gallons of water for my stay in Silver City.

Thirty minutes later, we arrive at Solo and Tie's cozy apartment. As soon as we step inside, Tie shifts into high-rev host mode, unleashing a torrent of instructions, directions, and helpful tidbits for my stay, finishing with, "Be mindful of the kitchen faucet; the hot water can become scalding hot rapidly, so always run the cold water alongside it. There's a mat hanging on the shower rod; you can hang it back up when you're finished showering. In the living room, we've set up an air mattress for your sleeping comfort. Would you like a beer?"

Tie pauses to extend a beer to me. "I'll brew some coffee in the morning, and there's a café just around the corner."

I can feel her enthusiasm, which is entirely contagious. The anticipation in the air is electric—starting another thru-hike brings a swirl of excitement and doubt. I can already hear the questions in my head: *Can I endure this? How will I push through the tough days?* But this uncertainty is part of the thrill—it's a chance to prove what I'm capable of while soaking in all the sights, interacting with other hikers, and managing the challenges that come with the journey.

"Do you need to adjust your hearing aid?" Solo inquires, evidently attributing Tie's high-volume voice to her hearing aid settings.

"No, it's fine." Tie looks at me. "I just got a new pair of hearing aids."

Solo chimes in, "And not a cheap pair."

Curious, I turn to Tie.

"They're two thousand dollars each ear," she reveals.

I'm taken aback. "Wait . . . seriously? Each ear?"

Tie nods. "They come with an app to control the levels," she adds, as if that alone justifies the cost.

"Oh, I see. For that price, can you hear into the future?"

Tie laughs. "I wish."

"How about the weather? Knowing the forecast would be handy on the trail," I continue.

"I can adjust it to the TV."

"Can you change channels with it? Oh wait, Uhura from *Star Trek* had a similar earpiece, and she received signals from outer space. So, the real question is, have you heard from extraterrestrials?"

Tie chuckles and says, "I don't think so."

I suggest, "Maybe you should check the manual. You might not be using your starship communicator to its full potential."

Just then, the neighbor's dog barks.

I turn to Tie and ask, "What did that dog just say? Please tell me there's an animal interpreter mode."

Solo's friend Rick, a thru-hiking newbie, arrives a couple of days before our planned start. He's here to assist us when Solo is unavailable, driving on roads that are near the trail, reconnecting with us where we intersect or at spots where he can take a side road to us. Tie and I will each have plastic totes in the Explorer filled with extra clothes, food resupplies, energy bars, and other essentials. Rick will also have extra water, and we can text him if we think of anything else we might need. It's certainly a gradual way to ease back into the rhythm of thru-hiking.

I quickly realize that Rick, a seventy-something-year-old from Michigan, is one of those fun, charismatic people who pulls you in with an easy smile and a boisterous laugh. He's excited about thru-hiking and wants to know everything—and somehow, his questions make me feel like I'm the only one in the room. I'm looking forward to my next conversation with the guy.

Rick and Solo's friendship dates back to their days as roommates in Denver when they were in their thirties. It was Solo who introduced Rick to the wonders of the great outdoors and, subsequently, invited him on a fishing expedition at the Boundary Waters Canoe Area Wilderness in Minnesota.

"So, here was Solo, the ultimate nature boy. He could find north on a cloudy day with a stick, a leaf, and by the way plants were growing," recalls Rick as we chill at the kitchen table. "Our bromance moment happened one calm, clear evening on Lake Agnes while we were fishing from a canoe. The stars were so vivid, they reflected perfectly in the undisturbed water. One of us remarked that it felt like paddling in outer space. As we marveled at the view, a beaver startled us by slapping its tail on the water, and I nearly fell overboard." Rick laughs, the memory still vivid.

"The canoeing trip was a rite of passage for me—as iconic a memory as your AT trip."

Later, Rick reveals that he's adopting the trail name Sidetrack, bestowed upon him by his granddaughter due to his distractibility.

"Guess it's a part of old age," he muses.

"Was it 'Sideshow' or 'Sideways'?" Tie asks.

"Didn't he say 'Sideswipe'?" says Solo.

"Actually, I think he said 'Sidekick,'" I add.

We all laugh, none more so than Sidetrack.

Sidetrack is intrigued by all this talk about trail life, at times grappling with finding the right ways to convey his thoughts—akin to navigating a labyrinth, occasionally backtracking and correcting his course. He's captivated by the intricacies, terminology, and nuances of thru-hiking, in particular the tradition of receiving trail names.

"A wise man once said," he begins, "'A name is the blueprint of the thing we call character.'"

"I said that?" Solo exclaims with a grin.

"Possibly, or perhaps I read it somewhere," says Sidetrack as he heads outside to program Tie's satellite communicator with preset messages. Tie suggests they should be (1) "My knees hurt. I'm too old for this crap"; (2) "I give up. Go on without me. Let me die in pain"; and (3) "Where's Mr. Fabulous?"

"All legit messages," I say.

Sidetrack searches online for videos that can show him how to track us on his phone. I double-check my gear as Solo leans over a map on the kitchen table, plotting the first leg of our hike.

I meticulously lay everything out on the living room rug, inspecting each item I'll carry. I begin with a 60-liter backpack, adorned with a silicone hand-sanitizer holder clipped to one of its straps. Next to it sits my one-person bikepacking tent, complete with a footprint—a protective groundsheet to guard against moisture and abrasions, ensuring a clean setup area. I chose a bikepacking tent for its compact size and light weight—just about two pounds.

My three-season sleeping bag actually consists of two bags: the outer bag will be great for warmer nights, while the inner bag is perfect for cooler temps down to 35 degrees. Combined, they'll keep me warm down to 15 degrees. The outer bag wraps around my sleeping pad and includes a pillow pocket to keep my air pillow in place. And yes, I'm bringing a pillow on this hike. As someone wisely put it, "If you use a pillow for a good night's sleep at home, why not when camping?"

I glance at my camp gloves, lightweight and breathable for those chilly early mornings, atop a blue, zippered fleece hoodie. While the hood part of the hoodie is practically useless with my dreadlocks wrapped up high, it's the same fleece I used on the AT and is still in great shape. I neatly fold an extra pair of merino wool underwear, a T-shirt, and socks on top of the fleece. Next to them, I place lightweight shorts, a shirt, and socks for sleeping. Having something cleaner than my hiking clothes will make a big difference in getting a restful night's sleep after a long day on the trail.

A mini gas stove and titanium cup are essential for my morning coffee. Both are compact, and I can easily hang the cup on the outside of my backpack for quick access when I need to mix drink powder with water while hiking. I also have a rain cover for my backpack that folds into itself, ready for quick deployment.

Besides the air pillow, another piece of gear I'll be using for the first time is a compact, UV-resistant sunbrella to ward off the intense desert rays. I also have two bandannas: an orange one for wiping my drinking and eating utensils and a purple one for everything else, like cleaning my hands and wiping morning dew off the tent.

I check a small storage sack filled with wipes and toilet paper, as well as another sack containing a mini med kit with bandages, sports tape for blister treatment, tweezers, nail clippers, lip balm, a small pack of tissues, and a small mirror—not essential, but I like having it. Perhaps some of my metrosexual tendencies still cling to me; Nina would probably have a clever remark about that.

I also have a small sack of gear-repair tape for the tent footprint, sleeping bag, and anything else that might rip, along with duct tape and fishing line for repairs.

I pack my headlamp, composition book, pen, battery bank for charging my phone, and charging cords into a stuff sack just big enough to hold everything. I run my hands over two 1.5-liter collapsible water containers—one light blue, one black—both made from extra-durable silicone. I pick up the black one, which has a water filter attached. This container will be the one I use to scoop water from rivers, creeks, or any other water source along the trail. I can squeeze the water through the filter into my blue container or drink directly from the filter nozzle. I set it down next to a 3-liter reservoir that I'll definitely need for the first stretch through the New Mexico desert.

I have a lightweight food-storage bag—durable and puncture-resistant, designed to protect food and other items from bears and other wildlife.

Earlier in the day, Tie and I picked up fingerless, UV-protective sun gloves. Since I've never hiked in the desert before, I hadn't considered how my hands might age twenty years in a week from sunburn and abrasion. While hand modeling isn't exactly my dream, I don't want to close any doors of opportunity.

I locate my lightweight fabric gaiters, another item I didn't use on the AT. With all the desert sand and pebbles that might get into my shoes, I figured I'd try a purple psychedelic print pair, which adds a touch of sass to my step.

Last, I double-check for my two buffs—a versatile tubular cloth I can wear around my neck, head, or face for warmth, sun protection, and moisture wicking—and the pair of round-rimmed blue sunglasses hooked to the neck of my shirt.

"OK, I think I'm set," I say, holding my trekking poles as I glimpse over at Tie in the kitchen.

She seems to have a lot on her plate. I can't discern if she's checking her gear, preparing dinner, organizing her prepped trail meals, or perhaps doing all three. After a moment, she leans in to kiss Solo, but he's so engrossed in his task that she misses his cheek.

"You have to be quick with me, or the next lady will swoop in," he jests, leaning in to offer his cheek for her to try again.

She begins to respond, but then turns to the front door, and says, "Oh my gosh, Rick. I'm getting the video you're watching in my hearing aid."

She heads outside to the front porch, where Sidetrack is on his laptop. I add computer hacking to my mental list of her hearing aid capacities.

She comes back in and resumes juggling tasks in the kitchen. I make my way over, grasping the doorframe. I'm sporting a new pair of flip-flops, which will serve as my camp shoes, and for some peculiar reason, they have a slippery insole. If I walk too briskly, I slide right off them.

"These *chancletas* are gliding me into the kitchen like James Brown," I remark to Tie, catching myself from falling, but she doesn't hear me, seemingly preoccupied or still listening to Sidetrack's video.

Solo, Tie, and Sidetrack—my support team, my hiking companions, and my CDT family. All three born in the 1950s, each possessing a great sense of humor and limited hearing acuity. The beginning of my CDT is bound to be quite interesting with this merry band of septuagenarians.

CHAPTER 3

UnFabulousness

WE SET OUT for the southern terminus of the CDT at 4:30 a.m. on April 12. Our route will end at the Crazy Cook Monument, near the New Mexico-Mexico border.

Sidetrack drives along New Mexico State Road 81, while Tie navigates from the passenger seat. Despite getting little sleep, I'm fueled by the anticipation of finally setting off. I'm in the back with Kenny, a photographer and filmmaker from Oboz Footwear, who arrived in Silver City yesterday. He's joining us for the first hundred miles of the CDT—a stretch known to be one of the toughest—to capture the start of my thru-hike for a short film he's producing for Oboz, and he seems game for the challenge.

Sidetrack is expressing his genuine excitement for the adventure with every word he speaks. Tie exudes a calm demeanor. As for me, despite appearing ready on the surface, internal doubts persist.

It's been ten years. Am I truly prepared for another five- to six-month hike? Is my physical condition up to the challenge, and is my mental focus where it needs to be? What if I get severely dehydrated again?

My setback on the Long Trail a few months earlier was a humbling experience that may be prompting me to now overreact: I down two liters of water in the first hour and aim to finish three more before stepping onto the CDT desert floor. I'm "cameling up"—drinking large amounts of water before heading out where water may be scarce, similar to why a camel stores water.

Despite my past susceptibility to dehydration, with its severe headaches and other ailments, I find myself questioning my apprehension. Am I exaggerating the significance of our water situation? I mean, there are five water caches spread out along the initial eighty-five miles. There will be five-gallon military-style water containers stored in bear-resistant food-storage lockers at each. And Sidetrack has two full five-gallon containers in the SUV. There's clearly nothing to worry about. Plus, the others seem way more chill, not chugging buckets of water like their mouths are on fire.

Have I let my water concerns get the best of me? Nah, I'm fine, I conclude as I guzzle another liter of water.

After two and a half hours, we come to a halt just before a cattle-guard turnoff. A street sign reads Hatchet Road. I make my way off to the side of the road to relieve myself—the inevitable result of all that water intake. As I pivot back toward the SUV, Tie points out a roadrunner.

Its tiny stature catches me off guard. My Looney Tunes education and the trusty ACME encyclopedia led me to believe that a roadrunner was towering at six feet tall, like an ostrich. However, what I'm seeing is more in line with an average-sized bird, measured in inches, not in feet. Yet if this swift and feathered bird in front of me is smaller than his animated counterpart, am I to infer that Wile E. Coyote is also pint sized? *Am I going to see mini-coyotes scampering around the desert? And why haven't I heard the roadrunner beep-beeping as it does in the cartoons?* Instead of sounding like a malfunctioning R2-D2, it gives off coos and a series of clucks.

Has my childhood understanding of reality distorted my adult reasoning?

I climb back into the SUV. Sidetrack begins navigating the rugged dirt road like a pro. The terrain is uneven, filled with bumps and large rocks. This drive to Crazy Cook Monument would be challenging for standard cars, which might get stuck or break an axle or the oil pan. With Sidetrack's patience, and this sturdy Explorer, he's managing to get us there.

As we bounce along, I gaze out the window. Desert plants—what Tie calls creosote bushes—dot the landscape in every direction, low and scrappy, yet resilient against the tough conditions in this vast open space. Their branches are thin, almost spindly, with clusters of small deep-green leaves that seem darker against the pale sand and dust. The bushes are growing in isolated clumps, reminding me of good neighbors respecting each other's space in some unspoken understanding. They look ancient, survivors against sun and drought, with tiny yellow flowers that hint at life in even the harshest terrain.

This desert is a strange, new environment for me. I wonder how I'll fare. Will I be able to adapt quickly, or will it be difficult? I'll find out soon enough.

After over two hours on this rugged road, it's 9:40 a.m., and we're finally at Crazy Cook Monument.

"Hey, Tie, could you do me a favor and tap your hearing aid to unlock the back doors?" I flash a mischievous grin.

"Oh, hold on, wait." She laughs and then taps her left ear. "There you go."

The doors unlock. There must have been something amazed in my expression, because Tie and Sidetrack start laughing, and I see what they did.

"Haha, thanks, Sidetrack," I say as I step out.

We're parked about fifty yards from the CDT starting monument, waiting our turn while a group of thru-hikers spill out of a Crazy Cook shuttle van, grab their gear, pose for photos, and then set off on their long-distance trek.

Meanwhile, Tie spots another stone monument, which has been weathered into the shape of a tombstone. The letters are slowly wearing away.

FRANK EVANS BO
JUNE 12 1865 KILLE
HERE MAY 1 1907 BY
CRAZY COOK MURDE
IN COLD BLOOD WITH A
AX MARK BY DEAE

Tie reads aloud, "Frank Evans, born June 12, 1865. Killed here, May 1, 1907, by Crazy Cook. Murdered in cold blood with an ax. Marked by . . ." The rest is lost to time, the edges of the tombstone broken away, taking the letters with it.

Tie adds that from what she heard, Frank Evans was a member of a survey team who got into an argument with the crew's cook. The "crazy" cook swung an axe at him and killed him on the spot.

Wow, talk about taking "Don't make me angry" to a whole new level. I guess Frank should have picked his battles—or at least his cooks.

Just then, a message from Verizon lights up my phone:

Welcome to Mexico.
As talk, text and data
is included in your

domestic plan, you'll
have no additional
charges while roaming.
Enjoy your trip.

Standing here at the border, the weight of that message sinks in. It's astonishing to think about how close I am to another country, at a threshold between worlds. My service provider taps into cell towers from Mexico, but it's comforting to know I won't be charged extra for kicking off my thru-hike. I take a moment to absorb the atmosphere—the air feels electric with possibility.

The hikers ahead of us finally secure their packs, clutch their trekking poles, and set off. Sidetrack, Tie, Kenny, and I take our turn posing in front of a four-foot stone obelisk set on a two-foot square base. This symbolic marker signifies the southern terminus of the CDT—the starting point for northbound, or NOBO, thru-hikers and the finish line for southbound, or SOBO, thru-hikers.

The sun here hits differently than in New York City; there are no buildings to block its rays. Today, temperatures are in the mid-eighties, but it feels much hotter. I slip on my light-gray sun gloves, grab my trekking poles, and follow Tie, with Kenny trailing behind me.

Sidetrack wishes us clear skies and smooth trails, mentioning that he'll meet us in a couple of miles at the junction of a dirt road and the trail. Our next rendezvous after that will be at the first water cache, fourteen miles ahead, where we'll make our first camp.

It's 10:30 a.m., and as we embark on our hike, I see a US Customs and Border Protection cruiser racing along the dirt road toward the monument, leaving a trail of dust like the Looney Tunes roadrunner. Perhaps they've spotted us from a concealed tower in the sky, and now they're double-checking that Sidetrack hasn't decided to take a quick detour across the border.

As we take our first steps along the dirt trail, the desert engulfs us with its unyielding heat and gusting wind. Amid this unforgiving terrain, a quote I encountered days ago resurfaces: "Walk as if you are kissing the earth with your feet."

I strive to uphold Thich Nhat Hanh's wisdom, which guides me to tread this path with reverence and deep connection. In truth, I am seeking practical strategies to alleviate the physical discomfort I'm sure will be forthcoming.

"Wait, why is Tie up there?" I say to Kenny, pointing just ahead, to our right and up an incline.

I've been on the CDT for only ten minutes, and I'm already misplaced. There are no white blazes out here to mark our path, like on the AT. Some CDT signs are on U-channel posts, but they're not as frequent. They're more like indicators that we're on CDT land. I pull up FarOut on my cell. The red line, representing the CDT, is to the right of the blue arrow indicating my location. (On FarOut, alternate trails are assigned other distinct colors, to provide clarity for hikers.)

"Yup, we're off the trail," I tell Kenny. We head toward the red line, where Tie is, yet moments later, we're off the trail again.

"This is some undercover bull-doodle," I remark.

Prior to arriving in New Mexico, I read an article suggesting that being lost for about an hour each day on the CDT was to be expected. Initially, I dismissed the idea, thinking it must be a relic from a time when hikers relied solely on paper maps and a compass. However, even with our modern navigation tools, I'm starting to reconsider. The CDT—with its multiple route options, varying trail conditions, land-ownership complexities, and ongoing trail development—is not a continuous, well-defined trail. Hiking it requires thorough preparation, extensive trail research, and flexibility in route choices. I've consciously prioritized flexibility in my route planning; while it might not be the most prudent approach, I tend to avoid overloading my mind with excessive details. Although I carried and used a guidebook on the AT, I didn't bother studying it beforehand. Just point me to the trail, and I'll set off—the rest will unfold as it's meant to. Now I acknowledge the need to improve preparedness and to research as I move forward.

While I won't keep my phone glued to my face during this long hike—doing so would defeat the purpose of being out here—it is clear to me that navigation is going to be made simpler by using FarOut, my only CDT guide source. I could have gone with a guidebook or a map and compass, but my brain aches just at the thought of it.

Still, no matter how hard I try to stick to the red line, it's baffling how, within just a few minutes, I go from following it perfectly to veering several yards off course.

I recognized that depending solely on an app is risky; numerous things could go awry, such as a drained battery or a wet or overheated phone. Nevertheless, I have a portable power bank, and I'm hiking with two other people with phones of their own. What could possibly go wrong?

Somewhere in there, there's a joke.

I contemplate this, keeping my gaze fixed on the trail to avoid any more detours. Minutes later, as we navigate yet another course correction, I remember the joke: The reason the hiker refused to carry a paper map was because he wanted to be completely lost in the moment.

I share the joke with Kenny, but his laughter doesn't reach my ears. Maybe the wind carried it off. Nonetheless, a mediocre joke is preferable to dwelling on our constant missteps. Internally, I make a pact: From now on, when I find myself disoriented or off course, I won't be lost or misplaced; instead, I'll be "lost in the moment"—while expeditiously working to find the red line.

We've started late for a desert hike, and as the day rolls on, the sun shines brighter. Hiking during midafternoon may not be our brightest move, a fact made abundantly clear when the sun decides to tap my shoulder and breathe its hot breath on my face.

"Ah, spatial awareness, *sol*," I meekly whisper.

I'm feeling lightheaded, I'm weak, and a mild headache is creeping in—clear signs of dehydration. I don't understand how. I drank five and a half liters of water before I even started hiking, and twelve miles in, I've had almost five more liters during our nearly fourteen-mile first day. The rule of thumb is to drink a liter for every five miles. I've had two more than that, and I'm still dehydrated.

What is wrong with me?

Tie asks if I ate. I began on an empty stomach, had one energy bar, and now eating is the last thing I want to do.

"It's not just water; you have to eat, Mr. Fabulous. Also, drinking too much water can actually cause hyponatremia, where your blood's sodium levels drop too low," Tie emphasizes.

I'm frustrated with myself for focusing so much on water intake that I neglected food. To make things worse, the wind is too strong to open my sunbrella, leaving my head exposed to the sun and adding to my headache. I thought since I was peeing a lot, I was hydrated, but it doesn't seem to be the case. I'm starting to feel exhausted and disoriented. I follow Tie and Kenny, who are now several yards ahead, yet I have no sense of direction.

Upon reaching our designated campsite for the night, I find myself floundering mentally. My head throbs incessantly, as though something is attempting to break free through my forehead and eye sockets.

Sidetrack greets us happily. I stalk over to the Explorer, rip off my backpack, and sit on the ground, hugging my knees. I rest my head on my knees in hopes of alleviating this headache.

Despite not feeling thirsty, I still drink excessively. I persist in the struggle, but I'm losing the battle. In an open area not far from the water caches, I spew up all the water I've consumed. With this type of heat sickness, once it kicks in, it's already too late; my body starts to reject any attempts to keep water down.

I'm embarrassed to be dealing with heat exhaustion on my first day. Still, I count my blessings that it's not heat stroke, a more severe and terrifying medical emergency that involves a significant rise in body temperature that requires immediate treatment.

Regardless, I'm a hot, buttery mess, and though the expulsion has eased my headache, I'm still feeling weak. This, combined with the wind, turns my attempt to pitch my tent into a comedy of errors. The fabric blows onto my face, and I find myself twisted in its gray nylon folds. I imagine that with my moaning and arms flailing, I must resemble a ghost from the *Scooby-Doo* cartoon.

Today, I'm a textbook example of how not to hike in the desert.

Sidetrack comes to my aid, unraveling my snafu. I lie in my tent with feet sticking out and arms over my face, hoping to muster the strength to at least remove my shoes and pull out my sleeping bag.

Kenny approaches with his camera in hand, recording as I remain sprawled on the bare floor, capturing the unfolding drama. Earlier, sensing a descent into the pits of illness, I granted Kenny permission to document both the fabulous and unfabulous moments.

"If you care to, capture the good and the bad," I asked of him.

"And the Fab," he adds with a smile.

Yes indeed—the good, the bad, and the Fab.

CHAPTER 4

Here in the Struggle

THERE'S A PUERTO RICAN term *la brega*, meaning "the struggle." *La brega* signifies a challenging situation without an easy fix, demanding a proactive approach and creative solutions. When I was growing up in a low-income neighborhood with a single mother raising three energetic kids—me and my sister and brother—*la brega* felt as constant as breathing.

It wasn't until I was an adult that I truly understood how intricately *la brega* must have been woven into my mother's daily life, an unspoken rhythm guiding her every decision and compromise. Her resilience and ingenuity ran deep: working multiple jobs that often kept her away on weekends, cooking meals from a pantry that barely seemed to hold enough for one, and finding ways to stretch whatever little cash she had.

She showed me the value of pushing forward even when the path ahead seemed tangled and unforgiving. It was through *la brega* that I learned some of the strongest foundations are built not from ease but from the will to persist.

So, on my third day—following a less eventful day two—in this derrière-scorching desert, when Kenny asks how I'm feeling, I reply with "*Aquí en la brega*": "Here in the struggle."

Roughly thirty-five miles into this thru-hike, I'm making only minor strides at adapting. The wind ceased yesterday, giving me the chance to unfurl my sunbrella, a relief from the sun's touch, but I'm still feeling drained and lightheaded from getting heat sickness.

In this sprawling, flat, sandy terrain, the respite of shade is elusive, so you can imagine my surprise when I look up and see a lone desert willow, offering not just shade but several gallons of bottled water at its foot, left by someone who understands our desperate need to stay hydrated.

Beneath the tree sits a hiker in his fifties, with straight black hair and skin that suggest a Native American heritage. He sports a mesh trucker hat and a black leather choker around his neck adorned with a vintage-looking sterling silver pendant that hangs below a black buff. He greets us with a smile, his socks drying on the branches of a smaller willow behind him. His long-sleeved blue shirt hangs loosely over his stocky frame as he proudly declares this the trail's premier rest stop, having, he says, spent the past hour soaking in its cool respite.

I recline beneath the tree, using my backpack as a makeshift pillow. My head spins, and closing my eyes provides minimal relief. I endure my discomfort in silence while Kenny and Tie talk with the easygoing hiker.

More hikers join, all bursting with contagious enthusiasm. One I recognize from my first day, before I got sick. She's short—only five feet tall—but her big, friendly smile suggests she's ready to share a story she's been eager to tell all day. She removes a backpack that looks far too large for her petite frame and sets it down effortlessly.

Her trail name is Dysfengshuinal, but I prefer calling her Dysfengswayze because it's more fun to say; at times, I'll give nicknames to the trail names.

"Dysfengshuinal is sort of a morph of 'dysfunctional' and 'feng shui,'" she shares. "I was on the PCT—I forget exactly where; it might have been north of Big Bear—but anyway, I had, like, a pack explosion. I'd gotten in my little baby tent and emptied out my pack, and then somebody walked by who was camped near me, and he said, 'Well, that's not very feng shui,' and I said, 'Well, I don't give a rat's ass about feng shui; in fact, I'm Dysfengshuinal.' It just kinda stuck."

I like her defiant attitude. She continues, "I was thinking of going by DF, but then people would think it was short for Dumb F***."

It's nice to see DF again, but I'm not up for much conversation right now. My arm covers my face, and I hope it somehow relieves my illness. Words from conversations meld into a blur, echoing with a muted, trombone-like "wah-wah," like the adults speaking in the *Peanuts* cartoons.

"Wah-wah, wah-wah, wah-wah, wah-wah, wah-wah."

Then I pick out, "My name is Fausto." It's the Native American hiker.

"Oh, like from the play," remarks Kenny.

"Yes, I get that a lot."

"Doctor Faust, that should be your trail name," suggests Kenny.

"Alright, then it is."

"What the further, Kenny? You can't just come up in here, droppin' trail names like that. You ain't even thru-hiking. You should be banned from such things," I interject.

Kenny chuckles.

"I like it," remarks Doctor Faust.

It's all good. I genuinely don't mind Kenny joining in this thru-hiking tradition. I derive pleasure from assigning trail names to my fellow hikers. Unfortunately, I haven't been healthy or alert enough yet to give anyone a name that sticks on the CDT. I decide my priority is to bestow a trail name upon Kenny, the infiltrator. Well, perhaps I should prioritize hydrating myself first.

I'm uncertain if the rest under the tree has made a significant difference, but we're back on the move, now accompanied by Doctor Faust. We have another five miles left to reach a dirt crossroad around mile 40, but Tie notices my struggle and suggests we can set up camp at any point. Unlike the AT, where there are shelters, lean-tos, or campsites to aim for every day, the CDT desert offers few such conveniences. The camping on the CDT is dispersed, whenever and wherever the day allows, though people will often camp in areas near water caches. Hikers, unless they're part of a group, aren't forced to be joined at the hip by shared destinations; each follows their own unique path.

After we cover two more miles, fatigue sets in, and my headache worsens, prompting a stop. As the trail begins to incline to the left, our group notices a spacious clearing, perfect for setting up our tents. Without asking, my three trail mates jump in to help assemble my tent. Once it's up, I gratefully lie down inside to rest.

It's always astonishing to witness the solidarity among hikers when adversity strikes on the trail. In moments of need, we band together, aiding, encouraging, and sharing resources without hesitation. Today reminds me of my early days on the AT, when I was new to backpacking, pitching a tent, and using camping gear. The other, more experienced hikers offered no judgment—only a genuine desire to help make my experience the best it could be.

While I deeply appreciate my CDT trail mates' collective support and camaraderie, I feel frustrated at the thought of holding them back. However, Doctor Faust says he was prepared to camp a few miles back under the tree where we met him, and Kenny appears to be going with the flow. Surprisingly, Tie, whom I feared would be discontent with stopping, insisted that we do so. Perhaps it's time to set aside my insecurities and focus on recuperating for tomorrow's hike.

Tie suggests I try an unconventional approach by sucking on an entire electrolyte tablet instead of dissolving it in water. It's like a Pop Rocks candy for a fleeting moment. Then a fizzy tornado ensues, generating an intense sensation in my mouth. The carbonation proves too overwhelming, and I spit the tablet onto my hand. After a brief wait, I gather the courage to try again. Gradually, it becomes more manageable.

In search of fresh air, I attempt to exit my tent but inadvertently lean against something sharp outside. When I look down, my arm is entangled in a small, prickly, shrub-shaped cactus. I pull away, seeing a drop of blood suspended from one of the needle-like spines, just before a sudden jolt of pain surges through my forearm.

I plop back inside my tent like a toddler abruptly landing on his diaper-clad bottom and gingerly rub my arm, which is swiftly developing a bruise. My focus oscillates between my dehydration, my heat-induced debility, and the persistent throbbing in my pierced forearm. I shake my head, realizing that my "slip, block, bob, and weave" isn't swift enough to dodge these desert punches. The most I can hope for is that my resilience can endure these desert miles. I'm eager for the Gila River section starting around mile 170; I've heard it offers a cooler environment with plenty of water.

A couple of yards from my tent, I hear Doctor Faust telling Kenny that he lives in El Paso. Although he's primarily of Mexican American heritage, my assumption about him having Native American roots proves correct. His grandfather, an Apache, hailed from a tribe that migrated from Oklahoma to northern Mexico. During Doctor Faust's time out here, he intends to delve deeper into his heritage.

Their talk shifts to web development. Doctor Faust, the entrepreneur, is working on a social media app tailored for trail hiking. I'd like to join their conversation, but my strength is barely enough to inflate my air pad, shed my clothes, and squirm into my sleeping bag.

"*La brega*," I whisper to myself.

Both my arm and my head ache in unison, acknowledging my statement with throbbing pain.

"*Aquí en la brega*, but not for long. Tomorrow promises a brighter day," I murmur as I ease into slumber, leaving the struggle behind.

CHAPTER 5

It's All Coming Back

LAO TZU, the Chinese philosopher, famously stated, "The journey of a thousand miles begins with one step." Building upon his wisdom, it's important to recognize that the journey can only continue when the next step is taken.

There's an important difference between pooping in the woods and pooping out here in the desert. When I'm in the forest, I do a normal wipe when finished, but in the desert, I lean to the side, to stay low enough so as not to be detected, since there aren't large plants or trees to cover my actions. Additionally, with a sense of caution drawn from the character Phil Berquist (played by Daniel Stern) in the *City Slickers* movies, I adopt the practice of squatting facing bushes or trees. In the second movie, Phil goes behind a rock to attend to nature's call. Upon squatting—and unintentionally sitting on a cactus—he believes he's been bitten by a rattlesnake. It's a humorous scene, especially when Phil fears going blind from what he perceives as snake poison, but the idea of encountering either a snake or cactus near my bare buttocks is not personally appealing. That's why I remain alert, scanning the ground and nearby plants and trees when in such a vulnerable position. I might be overreacting, but let's be honest: Even with this amazing outdoor community, I doubt there's anyone out here willing to suck poison out of my butt cheeks.

Having finished my morning routine, we set off for a brief seven-mile hike to where Sidetrack is waiting to take us to a recreation center, transformed into a hostel, in the tiny outpost of Hachita, New Mexico. I'm feeling somewhat better, especially after our decision to rest at the hostel for the day before embarking on a night hike. Given my tendency to fall ill while hiking in the desert, my new solution is to avoid the sun altogether.

We reach the Hachita hostel at 1:00 p.m., rest for the remainder of the afternoon, and resume on the CDT at 6:30 p.m. for a thirteen-mile night hike. Sidetrack will pick us up at Highway 9 and drive us back to the Hachita hostel. Several roads intersect the CDT, so with Sidekick's help we can return to the hostel multiple times while still hiking north. It's a necessary move to get me through this desert section. I didn't need this sort of support on the AT, with its ample tree cover. Desert hiking just isn't my strength, and, like most thru-hikers, I adapt my journey to keep it fulfilling, not draining, while staying true to why many of us are out here: to connect deeply with the wild, find strength within, and enjoy the adventure.

We're a couple of hours into our new night-hiking approach, and it's odd to witness the sun set while still on the move. Even so, the moment marks the first time I truly believe I can successfully hike this desert without falling ill. I feel a newfound confidence.

As the sun sets and the full moon casts its ethereal glow across the landscape, it doesn't fully illuminate our path; we need to use our headlamps to prevent potential mishaps, like tripping or stumbling into prickly cacti. Tie warns me about jumping cholla, cacti with easily detachable segments that can inadvertently latch (jump) onto passing animals or people.

"Do they jump more like a long jump or a triple jump? I need to gauge my escape strategy," I joke.

Reflecting on my experience in New York City dodging urban hazards like reckless, speeding cab drivers and unsolicited strangers asking for money in the subways, I feel confident that avoiding mere plants should be manageable—until I glance down at the bruise on my forearm from trying to use a cactus as an armrest.

"Who do you look up to most as a photographer?" I ask Kenny.

"Sebastião Salgado."

"OK, why?"

"Well, he traveled to the most remote, beautiful, and dark parts of the world to expose environmental and humanitarian crises and to highlight the natural beauty of the untouched world." He explains, with a boyish enthusiasm, more about the legendary Brazilian photographer.

"Very cool. I like that noise. How about Salgado as your trail name?"

I'm pleased when he instantly accepts it.

After two more night hikes, this thru-hiking undertaking is all starting to feel familiar again. Following our second night, we opt to camp in the desert instead of hitching a ride from Sidetrack back to the hostel. I plan to cowboy camp—sleep out exposed, with no tent—for the first time, but after spotting a scorpion near a cattle watering trough earlier, I decide against it. While Tie and Salgado show no fear and easily lay their sleeping bags on the ground, I compromise by leaving off my tent fly, allowing me a clear view of any would-be campsite-invading scorpions, with whom I am certain my companions will have to contend with at some point during the night.

The next morning, I'm relieved to see that everyone is still alive.

We set out on a short hike to the road, where Sidetrack will drive us to Silver City to rest for the remainder of the day before another night hike. However, this morning's hike finds me desperately darting toward any bush every fifteen minutes. I'm unconcerned about being hidden, because I can't stop experiencing diarrhea. It's possible I took too many salt tablets to alleviate the headaches, which they did, but the side effects manifest in uncontrollable bowel movements.

I'm vexed by how the desert challenges me but impressed by its inventive ways.

We pass someone resting under a juniper, making use of a small patch of shade. He remarks on the absurdity of flies choosing to land on him instead of the cow dung nearby. I chuckle, but quickly stifle it, fearing I might experience another eruption right there in front of everyone.

After I make three more urgent trips to the bushes, we finally reach Lordsburg. The CDT passes through this gritty desert town, and it's often the first rest town for thru-hikers seeking a break from the harsh, arid terrain of the New Mexico bootheel. Its few motels, small grocery stores, and dusty streets offer a dose of civilization, though amenities are sparse, and hikers find themselves recharged by the simple comforts of shade and a bed.

Despite a discomforted bottom, I optimistically believe the worst is "behind" me, only to find myself seated on the toilet at the Lordsburg McDonald's minutes later. I'm "relieved" that we have the rest of the day off.

At Solo and Tie's place in Silver City, I prepare my backpack with essentials to combat heat sickness. I pack more electrolyte tablets, which I now easily bite into instead of dissolving them in water. I also order vegan magnesium tablets to help regulate my fluid balance and improve my heat tolerance. I still need to find the right balance in using magnesium, as I learned the hard way with the salt tablets. In the meantime, I've discovered a different and more subtle way to replace some of my sodium: I hike with a mouthful of sunflower seeds. As I work the seeds out of their shells, the salt on them is enough without being excessive for my body. Plus, the seeds are a good source of protein.

Back on the trail that night, I no longer feel like I consumed an entire chocolate bar of extra-strength laxatives. Everything is back to normal as we begin at 8:00 p.m., later than usual due to the heat.

As we step out of the black Explorer at the trailhead, three other hikers are walking toward the trailhead, having spent the day at Lordsburg. Dysfengshuinal, who I haven't seen since the water-jug oasis under the lonely tree, joins us. With her are two other thru-hikers. One is Cutie, whom I initially assume is named for his appearance but turns out to have an affinity for clementines. He's a good-looking guy sporting a wide-brimmed safari hat, and his long blond hair is braided into two strands that settle over his shoulders. His semi-rimless glasses frame gray eyes, and he wears wooden disc stud earrings, along with a long-sleeved flannel shirt and black running shorts—not your typical hiking attire. I dig that he has a look all his own. Aaron, his hiking companion, has yet to acquire a trail name, kicking my trail-name-generator instincts into search mode, awaiting further data. He seems shy and is shorter and stockier than Cutie. Dressed in a tie-dye long-sleeved shirt and gaiters, he has short gray hair that hints at his age, but his quiet demeanor gives him a youthful aura.

The six of us set out together as the sun sets. Not long after, Cutie and Aaron decide to camp in the middle of an open field. Their goal had been to avoid staying in town, not to hike most of the night. Within an hour, we lose sight of Dysfengshuinal behind us. She tends to hike alone, but she shows up often enough to remind us she's still in our hiker bubble.

At 3:00 a.m., we approach a collection of rocks carefully arranged by previous hikers to resemble the number "100," marking the milestone of one hundred miles into our journey. Delighted, we unanimously agree that it's the perfect area to camp for the night. This time, I brave cowboy camping, but only with my hiking companions on either side of me and my backpack by my head. I realize that these are merely mental barriers of protection—if some nocturnal critter really wants to get to me, it can easily do so, but not without going through another human or my backpack first.

Silver City always feels like discovering a hidden treasure amid the rugged beauty of the Southwest. Every time I'm here, its inviting, small-town vibe, combined with the surrounding wild landscapes, makes it feel both peaceful and adventurous. With its welcoming community and a slow pace of life that suits my spirit, I can easily see myself settling down here once I've finished the trail. The historic downtown, with its vibrant storefronts and diverse shops and cafés, offers a comforting touch for this New Yorker.

With its strategic location along the trail, Silver City is a perfect venue for CDT Trail Days, an annual gathering of CDT enthusiasts including hikers, supporters, gear brands, and trail advocates. The event features workshops, gear demos, storytelling sessions, and social activities, fostering camaraderie and the sharing of invaluable trail knowledge.

Tie, Salgado, and I take the late April weekend off so that we can attend. After immersing ourselves in the festivities for the first day, Sidetrack, Salgado, and I unwind at a brewery and contemplate what lies ahead.

"Are you feeling good about your time out here and what's to come, Fab?" Sidetrack asks.

"I do—it's starting to come back to me. I can see myself . . . " I start, but our conversation is interrupted.

"Excuse me, your hair is so long. Can I touch it?" someone says behind me.

I turn to face a brunette woman in her thirties, with a broad grin and eyes wide in an expectant expression. Behind her, two people I assume are her friends sit on barstools and watch her, eager smiles plastered on their faces, anticipating a performance, perhaps familiar with past such antics.

The woman's hand reaches out right away, before I have a chance to respond.

Don't let her touch your hair, Derick. Say NO!

"Well, I suppose," I reply.

Why do I do this to myself?

I'm caught off guard. It shouldn't surprise me—this has happened before, ironically during my AT thru-hike at an event in Virginia also called Trail Days. There, a big, burly guy asked to touch my hair. Inside, I wanted to say "No, thank you," but outwardly I allowed it, and he ran his thick fingers through my hair as if we were dating. It's always uncomfortable and awkward, but a common occurrence, yet today I'm still bewildered as she grabs hold of my hair, which was trailing under my right arm and over my lap. I normally wrap my dreadlocks away from my shoulders and neck while hiking; it's much cooler in the heat and less cumbersome. But in towns, I let them hang down to my calves, which can draw attention.

She grips my hair like one might hold a toddler under their arms. She fixes her gaze on my locks, her eyes tracing their intricate patterns and forms as if she's unraveling a cryptic language spoken solely by my hair.

Oh, this is interesting. Is she a fortune teller?

Finally, she looks up at me, her eyes shimmering with wonder. I'm bracing myself for some profound words of wisdom. Here it comes; she's about to share a gem.

"Your hair," she says, almost breathless.

"Yes?" I try not to appear too eager, but I feel myself tensing up.

"Your hair is simply . . . beautiful," she says, swaying from left to right, like a teenager trying on a dress in front of the mirror at Forever 21.

Disappointment floods over me like a crashing wave. I had hoped for something transformative—a revelation that would alter the course of my thoughts, my thru-hike, my life. But not this. "You're dismissed," I want to declare. In truth, what I truly desire is to hex her, to strip away any joy she might find in a stranger's hair. I wish for her hands to recoil as if struck by lightning every time she seductively reaches out for not only my locks but any luscious locks she may encounter in the future. I want her to feel the weight of my disappointment, to experience the letdown of a prophecy that never materialized. Would that not be fair recompense?

"Oh, thank you. That's very kind of you," I say instead.

She looks at me as if she's done me a favor, placing my locks over my shoulder before sauntering back to her friends with an air of accomplishment. I remove my hair from my shoulder—it's not a scarf—and place it back on my lap. I'm starting to question whether wearing my hair down is a good idea anymore. Glancing at my companions, I see Sidetrack smiling, while Salgado has a look of disbelief.

I shake my head slowly and declare, "She's a terrible hair psychic."

CHAPTER 6

Choose Your Own Adventure

THE GILA RIVER ALTERNATE marks the first of numerous trail options to choose from on the CDT. According to FarOut, the Gila River Alternate winds 106 miles through the dramatic canyons and lush forests of the Gila National Forest. With hundreds of river crossings, the Gila serves up jaw-dropping scenery—narrow canyons, welded tuff cliffs, and constant water sources, a gift after the CDT's first eighty-five miles of dusty desert. I'm more than ready for the Gila's lush, green, scenic abundance, even if it means soaked feet and trickier navigation.

Unlike typical long-distance trails, the CDT isn't a single footpath. Instead, there are several options to explore, providing thru-hikers with the opportunity to "choose your own adventure," as the saying goes, recalling the old children's books with branching storylines that let readers decide where to go next. On the CDT, it's difficult to be a purist who is adamant about adhering to a single path. It's impractical due to incomplete sections, wildfire closures, and personal choices, such as which southern terminus to start from: Antelope Wells, Columbus, or Crazy Cook. Also, there's a northern terminus at Waterton Lake in the Waterton-Glacier International Peace Park and another at the Chief Mountain Border Crossing.

I appreciate the numerous options this trail provides. Frankly, knowing that no two CDT thru-hikers will tread an identical trail also makes this long trek a bit more personal and special.

At the start of the Gila River section, I find myself hiking only with Nature, a sixty-three-year-old who has completed the AT, the PCT, and is now attempting the CDT. Salgado had left the trail in Silver City, as planned, and Tie was taking a few days off due to prior travel plans.

Nature shares with me that if successful, she will have completed the three longest and most challenging long-distance trails in the US. The

Triple Crown, as it's known, is a significant achievement in the hiking community, a dream for many. Personally, I wouldn't pursue such a title unless it came with a real gold crown adorned with diamonds, sapphires, rubies, and pearls—complete with a high arch, a love symbol, and a velvet cap akin to Saint Edward's Crown. In that case, I'd make it a lifelong mission to achieve that Triple Crown, with its regal allure.

Nature has also traipsed trails in New Zealand and Japan, as well as numerous trails in New England, like the Metacomet-Monadnock. Despite her extensive hiking experience, when Solo drove past her a few days ago, she was slumped over at a turn toward a trailhead—dehydrated and disheveled. Solo turned back, picked her up, and brought her to town.

Now Nature shares with me that her start on the CDT was rough. She began with a cold, and by the time she reached Lordsburg, she was quite sick. She initially refused help until a fellow hiker insisted he would rather carry her pack than have to carry her. They encountered a rancher who offered to take her to a medical center in Lordsburg, where she was diagnosed with pneumonia and advised to take time off. Just two days later, she hit the trail again with strong antibiotics but barely made it to Silver City. That's where Solo and Sidetrack stepped in to assist her. The antibiotics upset her stomach, forcing her to take another day off to recover. Now she's back on the trail, still on antibiotics and dealing with an unsettled stomach.

My first impression of her when we met in town was that she was struggling with the heat and seemed defeated. I understood—desert hiking wore me down too. Still, I feel conflicted seeing her here. I'm eager to get back on the trail after a few days off, and I'm concerned that my pace may be affected by a hiker who is older and facing health challenges. I want to make sure she's doing well, but that's not easy when I'm already grappling with my own dehydration issues.

Yet, when Nature puts on her wide-brimmed sun hat, covering her long, knotless, braided gray hair, and swings on her backpack, she looks experienced, stronger, and even taller than her five-foot-eight height. She is transformed into a super-hiker. Adding to her costume, she wears dark, fit-over sunglasses, large enough to cover her prescription glasses and provide side blinders, like those worn by the visually impaired.

Solo drives us to a junction where the CDT, the Walnut Creek Alternate, and the Gila River Alternate converge. The area is thick with trees—more than I've seen in the past two weeks of hot, exposed hiking. Without a CDT sign, I'd have missed where the trail picked up again, even though the day before, I covered thirteen miles to this point, before Solo scooped me up for a much-needed shower, meal, and rest at their place.

Nature and I bid farewell to Solo, who assures us he'll meet us in a couple of days, about forty miles up the trail at Doc Campbell's Post, a country store nestled in the Gila Wilderness where we can shower, pick up resupply, and camp.

Our hike begins at 6:30 a.m. and follows the forest road for about two miles before reconnecting with the trail. We start a gradual ascent of a few hundred feet. It's not too demanding, but after weeks of flat desert, it takes some effort. Nature forewarns me of her heavy breathing, expressing hope that it won't bother me.

Initially, I am not bothered, but Nature continues apologizing during the climb, diverting my focus from my own breathing, leaving me annoyed. I'm disappointed for feeling this way, especially when she reveals her severe anemia is the cause for her loud panting. Damn, it's like being annoyed at someone for bumping into you, only to discover that that person is blind—I've just unleashed bad karma on my ass.

Fine.

I resign myself to the role of the designated emergency caller if she falls off the mountain.

How did she manage the other trails?

We press on without incident. Ten miles in, we pause by a streambed just off the trail. The water is low but flowing steadily from Sycamore Creek, where the trail eventually leads. Natural running water is a significant change and a relief. I can feel an encouraging shift in my CDT experience.

Be that as it may, this is my first use of a water filter since my fiasco on the Long Trail last year, and I dread drinking filtered water. It's going to take some time to get used to trusting river, stream, lake, and various other water sources that aren't treated water from indoor faucets.

I've changed the portable water filtration system I'm using. It's significantly lighter than the pump I used on the AT and filters water much faster, hopefully with the same clean results. I cautiously filter enough water for the rest of my day's hike, dinner, and breakfast in the morning.

Here's to hoping my gut doesn't explode.

I raise the water bottle to my face. Despite my steady hands, my mind shakes. With a moment of hesitation, I close my eyes and take a sip. By morning, I'll know whether the filter did its job or if I'll need to backtrack to Silver City.

I stash my freshly filled bottles in the mesh side pockets of my backpack, then sling it over my shoulders and set off down the trail. After only a few steps, a rapid buzzing interrupts the quiet, coming from a clearing beneath a rock formation. The rattlesnake's warning echoes through the air as I cautiously proceed along the trail. I finally see about three feet of the snake; the rest is hidden under a low rock overhang. The dark crossbands on its tan body look like tornadoes—wide across its back and funneled smaller toward its belly. It's just inches from the trail, only a half yard from me, and I'm suddenly wondering if it's too late to take up indoor hobbies.

I realize I can't risk passing that close to the snake. Reluctantly, I retrace my steps, veering alongside the stream until I've safely bypassed the rattler.

Contaminated water? That's so last season. Besides the water filtration system, I need a rattlesnake-repellent spray or a snake-charmer flute.

Later at camp, I share the rattlesnake encounter with Nature, who fervently admits her fear of snakes. As she vividly describes her ophidiophobia, I'm more puzzled at how she managed her previous thru-hiking escapades in the wilderness. A mix of perplexity and admiration swirls within me.

There is something nifty about Nature's achievements. Despite her fears and health challenges, she's accomplished a great deal. Out here on the trail, we encounter countless obstacles that threaten to derail our thru-hike. But it's not what we face—it's how we face it that defines the outcome.

I think I read that on a fortune cookie somewhere.

"So, Nature, what's the story behind your trail name?" I inquire.

"Well, I was with a close friend, a wise woman, about thirty years ago, and she read my tarot cards. 'You are Mother Nature's Daughter,' she told me. Her words have stayed with me. Years later, when I started my first AT thru-hike, a group of us were in a shelter discussing trail names. When I shared that I was Mother Nature's Daughter, one hiker said, 'Well, that's too long, so I'm gonna call you 'Mother.' To which I replied, 'Umm, no, I am not anyone's mother on trail, nor am I anyone's daughter. So, I guess you should just call me 'Nature.'"

"So, not 'Mother'?" I prod.

"Absolutely not," she says resolutely.

As morning breaks, I leisurely pack up camp, oblivious to the passing time. It's not until 9:00 a.m. that I'm finally ready to hit the trail. Meanwhile, Nature has already been on the move for hours. I wonder if I'll see her again.

Even with the late start, I'm beaming with relief that my stomach didn't rebel against the filtered water.

Could it be? Have I crossed that dreadful hurdle?

I skip along the trail until I encounter a different hurdle: my first crossing of the Gila River, which stretches about thirty feet wide here. From FarOut, I know there will be a few hundred crossings throughout this alternate section—more than I've ever attempted before.

I'm determined to keep my shoes dry. At this first crossing, the water appears clear, revealing rocks beneath the surface, indicating roughly ankle-high depth. The river flows gently, posing no immediate threat, beckoning me to proceed. I scan the near and far shorelines for indications of previous crossings and spot four hikers on the other side. They explain they're adjusting their route after a wrong turn. I smile with a shrug, as if to say, "We all get turned around sometimes." I wave before slipping off my shoes and into my clogs.

After a smooth crossing, I slip back into my hiking shoes and press onward. Before I can even take a full stride, however, another expanse of water looms ahead. If I had known it was this close, I would have kept my clogs on. I switch between shoes and clogs several more times before I decide I'll stick with the clogs—meaning I'll hike in them even when I'm not crossing rivers.

How bad could it be?

Why do I tempt the trail gods like this? After seventeen crossings of the Gila River and seven miles of hiking uneven terrain in clogs, the tops and sides of my feet burn. The discomfort of wet clogs chafing against my bare skin intensifies. My ankles lack support, and my stubborn desire to keep my hiking shoes dry begins to feel foolish. I come to another crossing.

I could set up camp on this near side, but I opt to take my chances and cross to the other side. The strong current seems daunting enough to give pause to even this knuckleheaded thru-hiker. I carefully examine the river.

The fast-moving current splashes against the rocky bank to my right. I follow a rock wall, and as I draw nearer to a side pool of water, I notice footprints, indicating that other hikers have crossed here. The water barely reaches my ankles, but when I cautiously use my trekking pole to test the depth in front of me, it sinks halfway into mud.

I'm so close now.

I take a moment to consider my options, then capriciously leap toward what I believe to be firmer ground. Despite what I assume are my keen senses, I plummet like an anchor, sinking into mud up to my knees and water to my waist. Desperately, I clutch onto the edge of the dry land, gripping it like a ropeless climber clinging to a cliff for dear life.

My clogs are engulfed by the mud. The left one slides off my foot, lost in the ooze, and the right clog dangles from one toe. Perhaps due to my exhausted delirium, I attempt to retrieve the solitary clog still on my toe, but it's futile. The mud sucks it down. I abandon it, reasoning that it's useless without its mate. I heave my chest up onto solid ground, with the lower half of my body—along with half of my backpack and my once-dry hiking shoes—still submerged.

How on earth did I land in this situation? I must look like Pitfall Harry.

"Hey!" someone yells, their voice faint over the roaring water.

Great, now I have an audience.

Amid the trees and bushes across the river, there is the silhouette of someone watching.

"I'm fine, just taking a moment," I call out, trying to sound casual.Then, to myself, I mutter, "Alright, Fab, time to salvage whatever dignity remains."

Determined to extricate myself from this soggy predicament, I hoist myself up onto dry land, until only my legs dangle over the water's surface. I lie there in disbelief at my foolish blunder. Glancing over, I notice the hiker still observing me intently, hands on his knees, trying to comprehend the spectacle before him.

I stand, barefoot, on the sandy expanse of the riverbank amid large, sharp rocks. Staring blankly at the site of my ill-fated attempt to cross, I wonder why I chose that spot, other than the fact that the water was calmer. Crossing the side pool didn't even take me to the desired side of the river.

Exhausted and disheartened, I want to set up my tent right where I stand. However, the sandy terrain and scattered rocks offer little hope for a smooth surface, and so I focus on collecting myself.

After diligently keeping my shoes dry all day, I finally put them on for this last crossing. In hindsight, my efforts to preserve them may have been the most futile act of this adventure. I take a deep breath, hoist my damp pack onto my shoulders, and with some guidance from the hiker who witnessed my *America Has No Talent* blooper reel, navigate across to the opposite bank.

Whenever I'm embarrassed, I tend to chatter incessantly. So I make a beeline to the hiker's campsite, where he and a friend have set up their tents.

"Hey, you. Good to see you again," I say as I approach the hiker who watched my comical crossing.

He wears all black and has long, dark hair and a full beard, both slightly disheveled, which gives him a casual, friendly appearance. As I stop a few feet away and drop my damp and cumbersome backpack, he pushes his black-rimmed glasses up under his boonie hat. Another hiker, shorter and fuller-bodied, with short dirty-blond hair, emerges from a tent. I recognize these two from previous encounters along the trail. I know they're both British, but I can't quite remember their trail names.

Is the tall one Buccaneer, or Bootlegger?

"I'm Pirate," the taller thru-hiker announces.

"Ah, yes, of course," I respond. He's what you imagine a pirate would look like.

"I'm Dan," adds his hiking companion.

"Dan—no trail name?" I inquire.

He nods and then shakes his head. "Not yet."

"Dude, we've got to fix that," I exclaim.

Giving people trail names is, you'll recall, my favorite pastime.

We chat a bit more before I unpack. I'm relieved to find that all my belongings remain dry, thanks to the fifty-five-gallon trash bag serving as a liner. However, the clothes I'm wearing tell a different tale. I hang them on a nearby tree to air-dry.

What a day it's been. I've reached the two-hundred-mile mark and traversed the Gila River more times than necessary. While in my tent, it dawns on me that, without my clogs, I lack camp shoes, which could pose a dilemma if nature calls during the night.

I'll manage until I get my chancletas from Solo tomorrow, I reason.

Minutes later, I reluctantly slip my cold, damp shoes back on, heeding my less-than-stellar bladder control.

CHAPTER 7

Fab Fam

WITH MY CLOGS stuck six feet deep in mud, I'm forced to do the next day's river crossings in my trusty hiking shoes. I realize it's liberating not pausing to remove and then put my shoes back on. No need for the cumbersome shoe shuffle—just splash 'n' go, saving time and finding some joy in the soggy adventure.

Pirate and Dan are totally hip to crossing rivers with their shoes on. Interestingly, I realize all the hikers I bumped into yesterday kept their shoes on, too, but not one mentioned my clogs—I mean, not even a playful, "Hey, Fab, seriously? You know you're gonna trash your feet."

"I imagine those neon-green clogs will be unearthed in a millennium, showcased in a museum alongside other artifacts," Dan comments.

"Ha, I suppose you're right. I was feeling guilty about leaving a trace, but when you put it that way, I guess I did adhere to the Leave No Trace principle, because no one will find a trace of those shoes for a long time. Thanks, Dan."

"Happy to help," he says.

It's a short, 8.8-mile hike to Doc Campbell's Post, a family-run general store stocked with groceries, trail supplies, and local goods, where Solo and Sidetrack are set to meet up and camp with me for a few days. A hot shower is all I can think of.

By 2:00 p.m., the three of us approach a structure that reminds me of those old general stores in spaghetti westerns. The false front, which gives it a grand façade, is adorned with a Doc Campbell's Post sign. The store, part of the Gila Hot Springs Ranch, has a fascinating history: It's all that remains of an 1880s ranching community and was once a military camp, established to protect the homesteaders who ventured into this wilderness.

In 1930, a seventeen-year-old named Dawson "Doc" Campbell came to the Gila Wilderness looking for adventure. He became a trapper, a ranch hand, a smokechaser for the US Forest Service, and eventually, the protector of the Gila Cliff Dwellings—cliffside caves where people lived over seven hundred years ago—turning it from a forgotten site into a national monument. In 1964, he opened Doc Campbell's Post, the general store still cherished by thru-hikers and locals alike.

Under the covered storefront, I see a group of familiar faces at a picnic table.

"What took you so long?" Solo hollers.

I didn't expect Solo and Sidetrack to arrive until the evening, so it's a pleasant surprise. Sitting with them are Nature, Dysfengshuinal, a hiker who introduces himself as Slow Poke, and a couple with a dog.

After some catching up and my exaggerated retelling of my quicksand-mud-river-crossing adventure, I settle in with Solo, Sidetrack, and Nature at Upper Scorpion Campground, just four miles from Doc Campbell's Post. Solo and Sidetrack put out a spread of food and begin to barbecue. The thru-hiker's insatiable appetite has yet to kick in for me. Nonetheless, I eat my fill, only to find myself succumbing to an early drowsiness, what you might call a "food coma" or what my friends and I humorously refer to as "the itis."

In the morning, it feels like the ideal opportunity to seize an impromptu rest day, cherishing the company of Solo and Sidetrack.

We venture toward the Gila Cliff Dwellings National Monument, a mile from our campground. At the office, a ranger explains that the dwellings were built in the thirteenth century by the Mogollon people—also known by their tribal name, the Southern Ancestral Puebloans. Their name comes from the nearby mountain ranges, which, in turn, were named after Juan Ignacio Flores Mogollon, a colonial governor of New Spain. This territory of the Spanish Empire included the southwestern United States, Florida, and present-day Mexico, Central America, and the Caribbean, from the sixteenth to the nineteenth century.

I'm really drawn to this history, especially since my last name, Lugo, ties me to both a city and province in Spain. That country's influence in Puerto Rico—the island of my ancestors—started in 1493, when they claimed the island and set the stage for generations of cultural and linguistic transformation. Spanish became Puerto Rico's main language, blended with the influence of the island's Indigenous Taíno. Even after the United States took over the island in 1898, Spanish language and culture stayed front and center in our Puerto Rican identity.

As we walk through the area, I'm fascinated by this glimpse into the lives of the ancient inhabitants. The cliff dwellings were hewn from the welded tuff, are spacious and cool, with walls several feet high dividing rooms into a layout almost identical to modern houses. Every room seems to have served a specific purpose. While there's no signage, it's not hard for me to imagine their uses—a room with a firepit might be a kitchen, and another, where rocks are laid in a rectangular shape, I imagine may have been a bed with soft foliage added for bedding. There are smaller rooms with narrow openings that likely served as storerooms. Windows in the rock walls offer a bird's-eye view of the surrounding area. All of this reflects the creativity and resourcefulness of the people who once lived here.

"What happened to the Mogollon people?" I ask a nearby ranger.

"Well, it's still a bit of a mystery," she tells me. "They thrived in the American Southwest for centuries, but around the fourteenth century, they started to decline. Some scholars think it could've been due to environmental factors like drought, dwindling resources, and changes in farming practices. There's also evidence of conflicts with the neighboring Apache, which likely didn't help. Eventually, the Mogollon people either dispersed or joined forces with other Indigenous groups in the area, such as the Puebloans. But their story lives on through these dwellings."

While I understand that what I'm experiencing on my mega-hike—equipped with modern comforts and safety nets like my iPhone—is incomparable to the challenges of the Mogollon people, who were constantly searching for the survival basics of water and shelter, I feel a connection to them. With their resilience and adaptability, the Mogollon people were, in many ways, the ultimate thru-hikers of their time.

The next day, a group of us begin our final section of the alternate trail. Although Dysfengshuinal hikes ahead of us, she still feels part of this new troop that also includes Doctor Faust, Nature, Pirate, and Dan. Is this my new trail family—or, as we say out here, "tramily"? Time will tell.

This is our last day of river crossings. The morning is cold, my feet are freezing, and the tops of my shoes are covered in a thin layer of ice. Not long after we start hiking, we approach streams emitting steam. These are my first hot springs, not just here on the CDT, but in life. I step into an ankle-deep pool in my already wet shoes, soaked from the morning's frigid river crossings, and enjoy the relief of the warm water.

The warmth of the springs lingers as we leave them behind, stepping into a canyon lined with reddish-brown-clay-colored cliffs, their towering, two-hundred-foot-high faces standing like ancient sentinels, worn by time and the elements. Layers upon layers of sedimentary rock tell the story of the river's enduring presence as it cuts through the landscape, and I can feel the people who left petroglyphs and pictographs so many centuries ago, and who carved their homes in the porous rock.

We pause for a break shortly after passing another popular hot springs pool. It's a longer break than I prefer, but Doctor Faust enjoys these extended hourly pit stops. Lately, he's been accommodating us by taking fewer and shorter breaks, so I don't mind this one, especially once some members of our group drop their packs and head to the springs.

"Everyone, heads-up: Dan's going for a buck-naked dip," I tease, knowing full well that Dan is too shy and self-conscious to ever do such a thing.

Dysfengshuinal, who we've caught up with at the hot springs, suggests to Dan, "You should take the trail name Buck Wild. Wouldn't that be hilarious?"

Dan chuckles and strides toward the springs, fully clothed. Faust, Nature, and Pirate delve into far weightier matters, discussing the existential crisis triggered by the depletion of one's delicious trail mix on day one after a resupply.

On his return, Dan declares, "You know what? I think I'll take it."

"Take what?" Pirate inquires.

"I'm going to take the Buck Wild trail name," Dan says confidently.

This is hilariously out of character for the introverted Dan, who exudes an apologetic air whenever he speaks.

"Man, I wanted to give you a trail name. Curses, I moved too slow," I say, with arms crossed and giving my best faux-peeved look.

Dan reverts back to character, nervously wringing his hands. "Well, since you were the one spreading the hot springs skinny-dipping rumor, you can be Buck Wild's co-parent," Dan says.

"Pass." I quickly add, "It's fine—I don't care."

"Buck Wild it is," he says proudly, walking to his backpack.

We prepare to head back on the trail and I hear Dan say, "Ready, my Buckaroonies," while looking directly in my direction.

Oh boy, he's really going to milk this whole Buck Wild thing.

"Dan, it's not going to happen," I tell him. To be honest, I can't believe Dysfengshuinal beat me to Dan's trail name. I've been brainstorming for days, and she just swoops in and claims one, and Dan immediately goes for it. Now he's even trying to name our group after *himself*!

"How about we slow down, think this through. Don't you all think Fab Fam sounds better?" I counter.

"Buckaroonies has flair to it," he insists.

"It's kinda cartoonish. Buckaroonies? What are we, your minions? Sounds like a '70s British band, Buckwild and the Buckaroonies. Move aside Beatles. This new group name better come with a flashy costume." I swing on my backpack.

Despite my playful annoyance at Dysfengshuinal for christening my next trail-name beneficiary, we find a moment of connection while trekking. Or rather, she opens up to me in a surprisingly personal manner.

"Two weeks before I was done on the AT," she begins, "my husband emailed me that he'd moved out. Just like that. No conversation, just a sucker punch after thirty-seven years of marriage. Since I had limited phone signal on the trail, several of my friends found out before I did. I was completely devastated, but I dragged my sorry ass down the trail, braving 20- to 16-degree nights but unable to talk to anyone without having a major meltdown." Dysfengshuinal finished the AT without the usual thru-hiker's joyful sense of accomplishment, and she'd felt unmoored ever since her divorce. I understand why she's so chatty on the trail: She's rudderless and isolated.

We settle into a gem of a campsite a couple of acres wide, dotted with pine trees standing amid tall, dry grass flattened in patches from past tents. I announce that we've conquered a grand total of 249 river crossings.

"I can't believe you counted them all," Nature remarks, impressed.

"I read on the app that there were a few hundred crossings, and I had to see if it was true. Plus, I think my inner Virgo—or my OCD tendencies—might have played a part." I slip off my hiking shoes in favor of my chancletas.

"Why only one long purple sock? Is that OCD as well?" Doctor Faust's tone is snarky.

"Ha. Not really, though purple is my vibe. This is actually a compression calf sleeve. I wear it for extra support whenever my calf feels tight, which happens when I'm not drinking enough water. And with all the hiking we're doing, it helps prevent shin splints."

"Oh, OK. I thought you were trying to look cool or something."

"I guess I could have gone with a different color, but why would I waste an opportunity to wear purple?"

We all settle in our tents after dinner. Nature eats her nightly gummies to help her sleep—she claims she'll be up all night reading if she doesn't.

"Put those dreadful things away," Pirate says to Dan, who has his dirty feet outside his tent, near Pirate's tent.

"I was contemplating if I wanted to leave them out all night," responds Dan. But then he wipes the dirt off one foot with a bandanna. "In you go," he says, before placing his foot back in his tent.

"Are you giving your foot permission to enter your tent?" Pirate says.

Dan ignores the question, instead continuing his conversation with his feet.

"Now your turn," he says to the other foot. "But don't touch anything. What did I tell you?"

Since adopting the trail name Buck Wild, Dan seems to have embraced a newfound confidence, as though it has unlocked a different side of his personality. During dinner, he spoke about his new trail name as if it were a distinct entity. When questioned about this behavior, he simply shrugged. "Buck Wild prefers his quotes in the third person."

I shake my head.

This guy.

CHAPTER 8

The Forest Is on Fire

SNOW LAKE CAMPGROUND marks the conclusion of our hike together along the Gila River. Doctor Faust and I bid farewell to Nature, the Brits, and a hiker named Buffalo Chicken. Although I'd prefer to be hiking alongside them, my depleted food supply leaves me with no choice but to wait for Solo, Tie, and Sidetrack's arrival with my resupply. While I'm uncertain if we'll see them again, Faust assures me there will be a reunion. He has graciously volunteered to stay with me, offering companionship until my food delivery arrives.

I sit as patiently as I can, like a high-energy dog shaking in anticipation of a treat and a walk. The campground is nice, especially compared to what we usually find out here, which is just ground that's flat enough for tents and, ideally, near a water source. This campground has multiple campsites, most with picnic tables, potable water, and vault toilets—a luxurious find. It's likely why Faust agreed to wait here with me.

We're chilling at the picnic table, our confab ranging from Faust's planned business ventures—his hiking app, his energy drink—to his twenty-year-old daughter. His face lights up when he talks about her. I recognize that look—the one that conveys that her happiness is the most important thing in the world to him.

I'm not a parent and probably never will be, partly because I haven't stayed in one place. I've moved every year for the past eleven years, ever since my first thru-hike. I'm living like a nomad, seeking answers to unvoiced questions, always turning to the next chapter in my life's story. Plus, if I'm being honest, being responsible for another human is terrifying—I wouldn't want to mess that up. Raising Derick is hard enough.

That said, two things never fail to warm my heart: hearing a couple share the story of how they met and seeing the joy in a parent's face when they talk about their child. Some might call me a hopeless romantic for that, while others might just say I'm hopeless.

Just as I'm about to crack a joke about how sappy Doctor Faust is being, Dysfengshuinal appears out of nowhere in her Cheshire Cat–like way. One day she's hiking with us, the next she's gone. I worried about her when we first met; she was moving slowly, and I feared the heat would overwhelm her as it did me. However, I've learned that Dysfengshuinal is well-versed in thru-hiking. Despite her small stature, she has a lot of oomph, and a strong will in a small package.

Dysfengshuinal sits at our table and explains that even though she hiked with us yesterday, she didn't want to camp with us because she's had bronchitis since Silver City and is still coughing all night. Then she starts sharing stories from her past thru-journeys, one after another. There's the PCT tale of how she fought off a cougar with just a headlamp and a sunbrella, and then another PCT story about a guy she helped after finding him on the ground. He'd been bucked off his horse when the pack mule behind the horse got spooked. The accident left the man with multiple pelvic fractures.

It could be that I'm hungry, having eaten only an energy bar that Faust gave me, but I lose focus on Dysfengshuinal's stories. I partially snap out of it when I hear her say, "At this point, I consider pizza to be medicinal."

It sounds like a punch line, so I laugh. She continues with another anecdote while I continue thinking about food.

"Somebody said something like, 'Yeah, those guys, one of them didn't have any teeth,' and he goes, 'You know, we call that summer teeth where I'm from.' And I'm like, 'Summer teeth?' And he goes, 'Yep. Some are there and some are gone,'" she finishes with a smile.

Yeah, that one was definitely a punch line. I give a courtesy laugh, then catch a welcome sight of a familiar black Explorer approaching us down the dusty road.

"There they are!" I exclaim, like a child spotting the ice cream truck.

I walk to the Explorer as it pulls up to our campsite, ecstatic not only because they have my resupply but also because Tie will be rejoining us after ten days off the trail.

My excitement is short-lived. "Fab, I'm done hiking" are Tie's first words as she steps out of the car.

I try not to voice or even think anything discouraging, fearing that Tie can hear my thoughts. Yet, I'm sure my face says it all. She doesn't want to talk about why she's bailing, so I let it go.

“Will you guys still meet me at Pie Town?” I hadn’t planned a drop there, since Sidetrack and Solo said they’d be there with my resupply.

“We can’t make it,” she says.

I get it. I always knew their support wasn’t going to last throughout the entire CDT. I understand that personal situations come up, and I don’t hold it against them. I never want to be a burden or a hindrance to anyone, but this is hard to process. I wish I’d had more of a heads-up.

I collect my resupply and we make small talk, then say our goodbyes. Faust, Dysfengshuinal, and I begin our six-day hike to Pie Town. I try not to think about what will happen there.

Two days later, we find ourselves on a forest road where a wildfire, burning for days, is finally under control. Sidetrack had texted me earlier, saying a hiker called and reported he was surrounded by fire and needed a ride out. Sidetrack couldn’t get the Explorer to him, but fortunately, the hiker managed to find a safe way out on his own.

As we approach a white US Forest Service pickup truck, I wonder if we’re going to be rerouted. A forest worker steps out and informs us that the next two miles will take us through an area affected by fire, and we should not stop as we hike through. His name is Alonzo, and he mentions that he’s Navajo, which piques Faust’s interest. The two start talking about how Faust can trace his Apache lineage.

We decide to take our lunch break now. Since Alonzo is spending all day telling thru-hikers not to stop, he offers to collect our trash and top off our water bottles from the five-gallon containers in his truck.

I fill my two 1.5-liter bottles and a 3-liter reservoir. Faust mentions that 1 liter of water weighs 2.2 pounds. So, by his calculations, I’m carrying an additional 13.2 pounds.

I have a love-hate relationship with the particulars of a thru-hike like water and pack weight, anticipated elevation gain, and the remaining miles for the day. If I could just set aside those details, I think, maybe my hike would feel a bit simpler. For obvious reasons, I cannot avoid such details, but I could have done without knowing the weight of the water I’m carrying. I’m satisfied with thinking of it as a simple saying: “My water weight is as heavy as forgotten promises.”

As Faust straps on his pack after our break, he grunts, "How much are we getting paid for this?"

He again jests, as we start hiking, that there must be some payment involved; otherwise, why would we subject ourselves to the rigors of hiking every day for months? It's a rhetorical question. Each of us has our own motivations, all equally valid, all worth more than any kind of payment.

As we make our way through the two nonstop miles, we scan the burned patches of forest, spot smoke rising as from campfires, and even see flames flickering a few yards to either side of the dirt road.

Doctor Faust considers whether we should backtrack and inform Alonzo about the small spot fires. Dysfengshuinal suggests that Alonzo might already be aware, which could be why he discouraged us from stopping. After a pause, the three of us conclude that there's no cause for concern.

By 3:30 p.m., we're out of the fire-danger zone but also away from the shelter of the tree-lined path. Exposed to the open sun, with no shade in sight, we all agree that the next cluster of trees will be our camping spot.

An hour later, we discover a shaded area, though it's accompanied by scattered dried cow dung, which I nudge aside with my trekking poles and feet.

With our tents pitched, we settle onto logs and begin preparing dinner.

"Looks like another fingernail moon," remarks Dysfengshuinal.

I lift my eyes and observe the crescent moon, which is indeed curved like the outline of a fingernail. It's a description I've never thought of before, but one I'll adopt from now on.

"DF, how much vitamin I is too much?" Doctor Faust inquires.

Due to an ankle issue, Doctor Faust has been consuming ibuprofen tablets like they were tasty Flintstone vitamins. Dysfengshuinal is a retired sports medicine physician; throughout her career, she worked at several universities in orthopedic clinics. She's the right person to ask, not just because of her medical expertise, but because I have a feeling that even if she were a professional bubble-wrap popper, she would still freely voice her opinion—and it would likely be well informed. She's just that type of person.

"Normally there's a certain dose you can take," she begins, "spaced every six hours. So, you could take four doses in a day."

Hmm, have I seen him take a handful at a time, several times a day?

"You also can't mix ibuprofen and other anti-inflammatories like aspirin," she continues. "You can take Tylenol on top of that, but my biggest concern is that ibuprofen is hard on the kidneys. If you're not well hydrated, you're going to strain your kidneys. Or you could potentially cause damage if you start out dehydrated and then take a bunch of ibuprofen on top of that. And if you're doing this on an empty stomach, you can develop an ulcer, or even a bleeding ulcer."

Faust and I exchange a glance. I wonder if he regrets asking. Personally, I take everything Dysfengshuinal said seriously. While vitamin I can be beneficial for hurting hikers, like any medication, I exercise caution and responsibility in its usage.

"In other words, don't overdose, Faust," I remark.

Faust smirks, glancing at the electrolyte tablet I'm gnawing on. "Uh-huh," he says, stuffing the plastic bag of vitamin I into his pack. "I'll be sure to pace myself—just like you."

We both laugh.

One of the things I admire about Doctor Faust is that he's unapologetically approaching this long-haul hike in his own unique way. He enjoys taking breaks every hour and covering shorter distances; for him, ten miles is a significant day. It might be unconventional and it might not lead him all the way to Canada, but who's to say that Canada must be his ultimate destination? It's his journey, and he sets the rules.

I appreciate his approach even if some of his habits, like consuming excessive caffeine, could potentially disrupt his hike. Unlike me, who cuts myself off after my morning cup, Doctor Faust drinks coffee anytime—including after dinner as his evening digestif.

"Will it not keep you up?" I inquire as Doctor Faust boils water for his evening instant coffee.

"Not at all. I sleep like a baby."

"Oh, you mean lots of crying until someone rocks you to sleep?"

"Haha. No, I only wake up at night to relieve myself. And with my trusty pee bottle, I don't have to leave the tent," he says rather proudly.

I can't wrap my brain around carrying a bottle to pee in. "What if you get it mixed up with your drinking water?" I ask.

"It's marked with duct tape."

"Really? I think I saw you drinking from that marked bottle," I say, with dramatically raised brows.

He waves my quip away and continues brewing his coffee.

And that's how it goes with the three of us. We engage in playful banter that takes on a life of its own, often leaving others bewildered.

After spending hours hiking together in the heat, we sometimes get a bit slapsticky. Doctor Faust calls Dysfengshuinal "DF," Dysfengshuinal calls Doctor Faust "DF," and there are times when she calls me "MF," but she feels that one is a little loaded. I don't mind; it's just another bit of hiker lingo. I find it amusing, especially when there are people around who know nothing about trail names and she starts swinging her trekking poles at me while yelling, "What's up, MF?"

The next day, Dysfengshuinal takes a shuttle from a trailhead to the town of Reserve, where the rest of the Fab Fam ended up a couple of days ago because Dan didn't have enough food and became weak. They all agreed to stick together with Dan while he resupplied. This highlights a common concern when thru-hiking with a group: Someone else's problems can become your own. If someone becomes sick or injured, it can impact the entire group.

Doctor Faust and I both have other schedules and commitments, so while we wish Dan well, we choose to hike on. As we walk, he reveals more of his deepest thru-hiking desires.

"I'd like to try an Islamic toilet etiquette," Faust shares.

"A what?" I ask.

"An Islamic toilet etiquette. It's cleaning with water instead of toilet paper."

"Huh."

He must be kidding.

"There's the Tushy portable bidet," he continues.

"Tushy . . . ha, nah, you're trying to pull one over on me, aren't you?"

"It's the truth," he insists.

"How does it work?"

"There's an attachment you add to your water bottle, and it squirts water in the right area," he explains, gesturing toward his bottom.

"Faust, first the pee bottle, and now a water bottle for your bumhole? That's too many drinking bottles used in ways that mean you can never bring them near your mouth. It's too easy to mix them up."

I respect Faust's outdoor ingenuity, and I love him for it, but I've decided that shaking his hand—or taking a swig of his water—is officially off the table.

CHAPTER 9

The Unlikely Vegan Thru-Hiker

DOCTOR FAUST and I take a zero day (a day with no hiking) at Davila Ranch CDT Rest Facility, allowing the rest of the Fab Fam to catch up. The Davila Ranch, at mile 26 on the Pie Town Road Walk Alternate, is a donation-based rest spot about fourteen miles south of Pie Town, with an L-shaped, five-hundred-square-foot, dirt-floored shelter framed in galvanized metal sheets. Inside, there's a cozy canopy sleeping area, a fridge stocked with eggs and potatoes, and a cooking shed with gas burners and shelves lined with cans of beans—all thanks to the owner's generosity. The place even has a quirky, makeshift shower, a flushing toilet, washer/dryer, electricity, Wi-Fi, and a spot for camping and picnics. It's compact but just right for us to recharge.

The next morning, Dysfengshuinal and I are the last to leave the ranch, heading back out onto the gravel Ed Jones Road. It looks like it's going to be a chatty hike.

"I know I probably crossed a line by nagging him about his 'running with the bulls' dream," Dysfengshuinal begins about Doctor Faust. "After years of advising patients, especially knowing the risks of orthopedic injuries, I sometimes blurt things out, and it can come off as insensitive. When I get talking, especially if I haven't hiked with anyone in a while, I bet other hikers wonder where the off switch is."

"Yeah, brevity might not be your strong suit," I remark.

Well, isn't that the trail orator himself accusing another hiker of talking too much?

I'm cut to the quick by my inner voice, and it's justified, considering I never shy away from a chance to share a good story. I often get caught up in the thrill of telling them, but sometimes I forget that not everyone is eager to listen. It's a reminder that knowing when to speak is just as important as knowing what to say.

"To be honest, I would probably get chatty too if I hadn't hiked with someone for a while, and from what I've seen, you've hiked alone quite a bit," I add.

As Dysfengshuinal and I continue on, we dive into a deep discussion about veganism. Continuing my vegan lifestyle on this thru-hike has been smooth so far; I've figured out how to pack delicious, nutrient-dense foods that fuel my adventures without straying from my values.

All my adult life, including on the AT, I followed a pescatarian diet, relying on tuna and salmon packets for protein. I had considered adopting a vegan diet before I started that journey, I tell her, but jumping into something so unfamiliar and restrictive didn't seem practical while taking on a new, challenging activity. My path of total veganism began soon after I returned to New York City, nearly ten years ago now. Initially, my motivation was driven by the potential health benefits associated with a plant-based diet. As I gained more knowledge and grew more comfortable with the vegan lifestyle, concerns about animal treatment and the eco-friendly aspects of veganism became important factors as well.

"What is veganism?" I've been asked.

I've lost track of how many times a restaurant insists they can cater to vegan preferences, only to serve a dish smothered in butter or cheese. The specifics can evade some, so I usually sum it up simply: I steer clear of anything sourced from anything that used to poop.

Many consider thru-hiking the CDT without consuming any animal-produced food inconceivable, due to the trail's physical demands and limited food options. Hikers burn thousands of calories a day and require protein-rich foods. Resupply points along the CDT are, at times, sparse and carry mostly nonvegan options; additionally, animal-based products are lightweight, shelf-stable, and easy to carry, making them seem like the practical choice for long stretches between resupplies.

I've heard tales of vegan thru-hikers bravely setting out on the CDT, only to surrender to the siren song of sizzling bacon somewhere along the trail, or to the ease of carrying convenient beef jerky, string cheese, or Spam in their food bag. Or they give in to an irresistible diner breakfast of old-fashioned pancakes made with milk, butter, and eggs, paired with a side of scrambled eggs. Or after a grueling twenty-mile day, they reach town and succumb to the temptation of pepperoni pizza. The calories burned are untold, the temptations are many. I imagine a group of determined vegans, armed with kale chips and quinoa, ready to conquer the wilderness, until Mother Nature plays her carnivorous card and, suddenly, the call of the wild becomes the call of the barbecue.

There was never much mention of anyone who successfully completed the CDT without giving in to omnivorism.

When I first started a vegetarian diet at age nineteen, my Hispanic mother couldn't grasp why I would shame her by refusing her delicious, meat-filled Puerto Rican *arroz con gandules*. She was utterly convinced that I needed saving, and she prayed that my abstention from meat wouldn't land me in purgatory in the afterlife.

"*Que Dios te perdone*," she would spout. "I raised you better than this. Don't you like my cooking? Do you know how many kids are starving in Jersey?" Like many New Yorkers, my mother thought New Jersey was a third-world country compared to the Empire State.

For quite some time, Mom resisted my new dietary choice, treating it as merely a passing phase.

"Mom, I'm nineteen; I know what's best for me," I'd insist.

"Alright, alright," she would say, but her actions painted a different picture. She would meticulously dice chicken and blend it into her vibrant rice and beans, thinking I wouldn't notice its presence.

"Mom, I can spot the meat in this rice." Did she believe I'd mistake white meat for pink beans?

"Chicken is fine. You can have it," she'd persist.

Her Puerto Rican rationalizing always left me perplexed.

On the trail, being a nonmeat eater may be less challenging than in my mother's kitchen, though maintaining a healthy diet poses a challenge for any hungry thru-hiker. Dried instant foods, ideal for lightweight backpacking, sometimes lack optimal nutrition, while vegan staples like ramen noodles, oatmeal, and rice sides often contain processed ingredients. But few hikers dehydrate their own food, a practice I aspire to but find daunting given my procrastinator's tendencies.

Most of my daily meals so far on the CDT have followed the same pattern: organic, sprouted rolled oats with peanut butter for breakfast; a flour-tortilla wrap with peanut butter and occasionally fruit preserves for lunch; and organic millet or brown-rice ramen noodles for dinner. I also rely on Knorr rice side packets and other vegan ready-to-eat meals, and throughout the day, I snack on vegan energy bars and sometimes indulge in dark chocolate.

One of my less healthy weaknesses is Oreos, preferably Double Stuf Oreos. Yes, Oreos are vegan, but they also have high sugar and fat content, highly processed ingredients, calorie density, and additives and preservatives. However, I can't resist including these in every resupply. They've become almost an addiction.

Dysfengshuinal tells me about a study suggesting that Oreo cookies could be as addictive as cocaine or morphine, at least when it comes to lab rats.

Of course she would know that.

The research, she goes on, explored how high-fat, high-sugar foods contribute to the obesity epidemic. Rats were given Oreos on one side of a maze and a control food (rice cakes) on the other. They spent similar amounts of time on the Oreo side as rats conditioned with addictive drugs did on the drug-associated side. The study also observed rats consuming Oreos had increased neural stimulation in the pleasure centers of their brain that was comparable to the rats with cocaine or morphine, suggesting that food addiction parallels substance dependence.

"Does that make me an Oreo junkie? A Double Stuf fiend?" I ask.

"Well, here's a surefire way to find out," Dysfengshuinal says. On her phone, she pulls up a list of typical indications and symptoms of addiction. She reads each one out loud, replacing "cocaine" with "Oreos":

One: Intense cravings for Oreos.

Two: Increased tolerance, requiring larger quantities of Oreos to satisfy cravings and achieve the desired effects.

Three: Failed attempts to quit or reduce Oreo consumption.

Four: Spending a significant amount of time and money on obtaining and using Oreos.

Five: Restlessness, anxiety, and irritability when unable to eat Oreos.

Six: Noticeable weight gain or fluctuation due to consuming excessive amounts of Oreos.

Seven: Changes in sleep patterns, such as insomnia or irregular sleep, due to Oreo cravings.

Eight: Engaging in behaviors like hiding or hoarding Oreos or consuming them in secret.

Damn, who put a spy cam on my backpack?

"Any of this sound like you?" Dysfengshuinal asks with a smile, already knowing the answer.

"Absolutely not," I reply.

I'm certainly not fooling someone who has witnessed me sporting an Oreo-covered smile, with black chocolate wafer coating my teeth like debris on the front grill of an old steam engine.

As we reach Pie Town—a place with a slim chance of having vegan provisions, let alone my coveted Oreos—I cling to the possibility that trail magic, the benevolence of the trail gods, or any stroke of trail serendipity might provide me with something to sustain me until the next resupply town, nearly one hundred miles and four or five days away.

CHAPTER 10

Road Walkin'

PIE TOWN, FOUNDED in the 1920s in remote Catron County, New Mexico, and named for its homemade pies, is a small community of about 180 people. It became a beloved stop for travelers on US Highway 60, thanks to Clyde Norman's famous apple pies. During the Great Depression, the town drew Dust Bowl migrants and homesteaders, and to this day is still known as a destination for pie lovers, with its three cozy pie cafés and restaurants, its annual Pie Festival, and the opportunity to savor a wide variety of delicious homemade pies.

"They're all out of pies," a hiker staying at the Toaster House hostel, with its quirky array of toasters lined up on the front fence, divulges upon our arrival.

"Out of pies? But it's literally in the town's name. They can't just run out," I remark, though I'm not too bothered. I doubt they have vegan options anyway, and it's not like I can easily take a pie with me on the trail as resupply food.

Yet this town is a beacon for thru-hikers for its namesake treat. It's akin to a child rushing to an ice cream truck only to find it devoid of ice cream. It feels downright unfair. Talk about being a false "pie-d" piper.

I'm certain this town—well, settlement—with its handful of homes on dirt streets (Custard Lane, Berry Boulevard) depends heavily on revenue generated by those pies. Heads will roll for this mishap. In a place this tiny, the mayor likely wears multiple hats—sheriff, mailperson, and perhaps even the pie maker. Someone needs to rouse them before hikers decide on eating snickerdoodles instead. In a town where pie is practically a religion, this is blasphemy.

For me, pie is the least of my concerns. Scavenging anything I can for my resupply is my top priority. I approach the front porch of the Toaster House to contemplate my predicament. As I sit down on the old car seat on the porch, I'm instantly swallowed by its springless, worn-out embrace. My legs stick straight up like an old TV antenna, wobbling with every attempt to free myself. I squirm and shift, feeling like a kid who sat too far back on the toilet and is now stuck. Each wiggle pulls me in further, and I resign myself to my new identity as the person who got eaten by a chair. Finally, with one good push, I break free.

I sit cautiously on the edge of the dastardly seat and take in my surroundings. Behind me, the wall is covered in old hiking shoes retired from the trail and repurposed as abstract art. In the middle of the porch stands an antique dining table with legs carved into decorative shapes, a strangely elegant centerpiece amid the scattered garage-sale finds. However, perhaps to help the table fit in with all the other kitsch, it's covered with a gaudy Thanksgiving tablecloth that hides its true beauty.

Around me, everyone is sorting through their resupply boxes, filling their food bags with breakfasts, lunches, dinners, energy bars, and all the snacks they shipped to the hostel. The table is strewn with carefully packed provisions. Inside the front entryway, stacks of resupply boxes await, sent by thru-hikers weeks before their arrival. If I'd known my resupply wouldn't be waiting for me in the black Ford Explorer, I'd certainly have done the same.

It'll work out—somehow.

"Hey, Fab, here's my box. I've taken what I need, so you can have whatever you can use. I'm not vegan, but I try to eat healthy, which sometimes means vegan food," a fellow thru-hiker says, placing a box on the porch table.

"Really? Ah, thank you," I say, giving her a grateful hug.

This generous gesture starts a domino effect. Others start leaving what they have on the table for me. I fight the urge to get emotional. Just then, Nita, the owner of Toaster House, arrives. When she hears my story, she walks me inside. Next to the kitchen is a six-foot-tall storage cabinet filled with extra trail food left by hikers who had shipped too much in their resupply. This cabinet might be the biggest hiker box—a repository of excess stuff thru-hikers leave for their compatriots—I have ever seen. It's stocked with dehydrated meals, ramen, peanut butter, oatmeal, energy bars, and canned foods (which, being heavy, must be for eating at the hostel). With this and the generosity of kind souls, I quickly have enough food to make it to the next town, Grants.

As always, thru-hikers unite, this time to resupply a vegan. The solidarity of my outdoor peeps knows no limits. I couldn't be more humbled and grateful.

I thank everyone who's kept me in the game of thru-hiking and head to Jackson Park Campground, a free campsite in a scrubby area on the edge of town. Doctor Faust, Nature, and Dan—whom I haven't come around to calling Buck Wild yet—join me, while Dysfengshuinal books a bunk at the hostel with Aaron, whom I last saw hiking with Cutie at Lordsburg. Aaron now goes by the trail name Lowrider, a nod to his slower-than-average hiking pace. Pirate decides to camp outside the hostel, likely influenced by the abundant beer supply in the fridge out back.

While walking to the campground, I notice more than a few abandoned and boarded-up homes, hemmed in by unkempt, trashed yards. This outpost town has a messy, haunted feel to it. It seems to lack something besides pies—perhaps the energy of happy townspeople, but there's something more.

What is it?

"Hey, have you guys seen any kids?" I ask my tramily.

"Hmm, actually no," says Dan.

Everyone is worried about the absence of pie, but what about the children? Are they kept locked up somewhere, away from pie-deprived thru-hikers? Is there a connection between the missing pies and missing children? It's a bit eerie, and come to think of it, I haven't seen any dogs either.

"Arf! Arf!"

Never mind. A dog barks from a yard two houses ahead of us. And perhaps the kids are just at school, since it is, after all, a Wednesday.

The next morning, one month after the start of my CDT thru-hike, Nature, Dan, Pirate, and I set off for Grants. Doctor Faust caught wind of a possible pie shipment arriving around 9:00 a.m. and stays behind. The idea that pies not being made locally in a town named for them is baffling to me, but numerous other hikers opt to stay, drawn not just by the promise of pie but also by the cozy amenities of the hostel. This is what we refer to as getting "sucked into the vortex"—the irresistible allure of town that makes you postpone your hike an extra day or two.

We follow the trail along the gravel of Highway 603 for three miles, then continue for another eleven miles on the equally gravel York Ranch Road. It's a long, straight hike with acres of ranch land stretching out on either side.

When night falls, we stealth-camp several yards off the road, nestled among juniper trees. The "yip-yip-howl" of coyotes echoes just beyond a nearby ridge. I'm amused by the sound of these wild canines, partly because their distant calls reassure me that they're not about to encircle our tents, but mostly because their howls resemble a baby's cry. To me, it's more akin to the collective whimper of a litter of pups, which is a much more soothing image than a pack of wild coyotes up to no good.

Over the next two days, we continue road walking, covering twenty miles each day. Rumors circulate about possible trail closures due to forest fires north of Grants. To hike through these areas before they potentially close, we take the Cebolla Alternate into the Cebolla Wilderness, shaving off over forty miles. After eleven miles, we reconnect on the CDT on Highway 117. The road walk is brutally hot, with temperatures in the high nineties by midmorning and zero tree coverage. With no streams nearby, we scoop water from stock tanks. As you can imagine, stock tanks can be a breeding ground for nastiness like algae growth, stagnant water, cow-feed particles, and feces. I've seen a cow standing inside a tank, splashing around like it was her personal kiddie pool.

My concerns about water filtration resurface. The warm, turbid green water I just scooped is sure to be contaminated with bacteria. I filter a liter as a last resort.

By midafternoon, the long desert highway, with not much eye candy to offer except dusty, flat land and cows grazing on what I can barely make out as grass, bends to the right. I see El Malpais—"badlands" in Spanish. It's a volcanic landscape, marked by rugged lava flows, cinder cones, and craters. The area is part of El Malpais National Monument, a dramatic terrain that's home to unique wildlife and ancient Native American petroglyphs.

As I approach, I spot the top edge of a cave opening, possibly one hundred feet high, surrounded by sandstone cliffs and towering mesas. I'm struck by how humbling these ancient rock structures can be, making me feel like a fleeting note in the land's story. Just across the highway, five yards away, thousand-year-old charcoal-colored lava flows push up through dried grass. The land itself is trying to reveal its tortured history.

It's hot today, and imagining the heat emitted from the lava many millennia ago has me reaching for my last full liter of water—the cow trough water I've been resisting for the last infernal hour. Just as I'm about to give in and take a gulp, we reach El Malpais Ranger Station, where an outdoor spigot awaits. I'm relieved not to test my filter's effectiveness after all.

From what I've gathered, around 20–25 percent of a CDT thru-hike is road walking, mostly on forest-service roads but occasionally on highway shoulders like this one as well. This is partly due to the CDT being only about 70 percent complete. I typically don't mind road walking, but the many miles on the hot, dark asphalt have also rendered my left leg, from calf to hip, throbbing with pain. I limp into Grants after a fourteen-mile day.

Nature, Dan, Pirate, Doctor Faust, and I sit at the Denny's in Grants, ready to pay for the meal we just devoured. Well, the rest are ready, but I've confused the server's question about wanting our check with "Would you like another round of veggie burger and fries? Because you look like you're still hungry"—at least that's what my stomach heard.

Road walking has turned me into a ravenous beast, ready to devour anything in sight, especially veggie burgers and fries. I have a "town gut," indulging in as much food as possible during a stop in town. Thru-hikers love the opportunity to replenish calories and nutrients after a long stretch on the trail or, in our case, road.

The Santa Fe National Forest north of us is now closed due to two more larger fires, so we spend a couple of zero days in Grants before deciding to head to Santa Fe to wait it out and see if the trails will reopen. We can stay with Teresa, a staff member of the CDTC whom I met at CDT Trail Days in Silver City. She gave me her card in case I ever needed help like this.

Teresa even arranged our two-hour ride from Grants to the Albuquerque train station, where we could catch a train to Santa Fe.

I'm starting to realize that the best trail magic on the CDT is getting rides into towns and back onto the trail.

Corey, our driver, is a short, gray-haired, brown-skinned man who could pass for a relative of Doctor Faust. With a friendly demeanor, he shares stories of the terrain and points at the mesas and buttes that were—and in some cases, still are—homes to Indigenous people. Doctor Faust mentions that his ancestry research has revealed quite a bit about his Apache grandfather.

I also have Native American ancestors, or at least that's what my mother used to tell me.

"Is Prince my dad?" I once asked her.

"Who?"

"Don't play me, Mom. You know, the musician. He sings 'When Doves Cry' and 'Purple Rain.'"

I began to sing, "Purple ra—"

"Derick," she cut me off. "I know who Prince is."

"Listen, my pretty, green-eyed mother, why are your other two children 'light skinned-ed,' but I'm a caramel, *cioccolatino* tone?" I waved my arm and bobbed my head, mimicking a Latina in a heated discussion. I had no doubt that I'm related to my brother—he's a much lighter version of me—as well as my freckle-faced sister, because I have freckles and our ugly cries are identical.

Did Prince have freckles?

"Look, your grandmother was part Indian."

"It's Indigenous, not Indian," I told her. Like the Cuban singer Celia Cruz, my mom's English "is not very good looking."

"I know what I'm saying—American Indian people or Native American," my mom countered.

I'm not sure her Nuyorican accent would allow her to pronounce *indigenous*.

"You have your grandmother's complexion," she continued.

"Wait, what? Grandma is the white one in the family."

"Your dad's mom, not my mom."

My dad's mom also looks white in the old photos I've seen, yet they're faded, so I dropped it. The mention of my father brought up what few memories I have of him. My parents separated when I was five, so I don't remember what he sounds like. Could he have pronounced *indigenous*? Did he have a Nuyorican accent like my mom? Did he have a deep speaking, yet high singing, voice? Was his favorite color purple?

"He was a chief in this area," Corey says in the car to Albuquerque, snapping me out of my daydream. I have no idea who "he" is until Corey gestures toward a nearby mountain and mentions that the chief's people still live there.

The train ride to Santa Fe, the capital of New Mexico, takes an hour and a half. We arrive in a vibrant city nestled at the foot of the Sangre de Cristo Mountains. Its adobe architecture reflects a rich blend of Native American, Spanish, and Anglo influences. There's a thriving art scene, with galleries and museums amid historic sites and colorful local markets.

Teresa picks the five of us up from the train station. She's our intel about the fire progress, and when we are clear to get back on the trail. The fire started, she says, on May 13, near Middle Mesa, in a remote area of the Gila National Forest. We had just left Pie Town and were ahead of it for a while, but no more. It's Thursday, and it sounds like we'll be here over the weekend.

When she pulls into her driveway, I spot *ristras* (red strings of chili peppers) hanging from the *vigas* (exposed wooden beams) in the front of her house. She tells me that hanging *ristras* is a Mexican tradition here and that I must try the chili in New Mexico.

Teresa is a gracious host, making dinner for us on our first night and giving us a ride the next day to the Santa Fe Railyard Artisan Market. On Saturday, we head over to Meow Wolf, an immersive art experience that defies traditional boundaries. Walking through its doors is like stepping into a dream in which reality blurs with fantasy. The air is thick with ambient sounds—faint murmurs, surreal music, and distant mechanical hums—that draw us deeper into the maze of rooms. We enter *The Forest*, an otherworldly space with towering neon trees and glowing, alien flora pulsing softly in the dim light. Further along is *The House of Eternal Return*, a labyrinthine installation where everyday rooms twist into portals to bizarre worlds. In a drearily plain utility closet, I crawl into a dryer that opens into a light-filled tunnel, transporting me to another room entirely, this one filled with socks. The mystery of lost socks, solved.

I feel like a kid again, back when the mundane was transformed into something extraordinary by my imagination. I glance over at my hiking companions and see the same childlike wonder reflected on their faces. It reminds me of what it feels like to be part of a trail-built family—where every moment, no matter how simple, is shared and made special because we're in it together. Out on the trail, we rediscover that sense of awe we often lose in the rush of everyday life.

I'm thrilled to find out that there's a literary festival this weekend, so on Sunday, we head over to the Santa Fe Community Convention Center to see one of my favorite authors, George R. R. Martin, take center stage.

By Tuesday, there's still no clearance for our hike. The so-named Black Fire has become one of the largest wildfires in New Mexico's history and has closed a section of the CDT—from Grants all the way north to Chama, about two hundred trail miles away—for the entire season. Sparked by an improperly extinguished campfire, it has grown to several thousand acres and beyond, its rapid spread fueled by critical weather conditions.

According to Dysfengshuinal, in arid places like New Mexico, when trails close and people evacuate due to fires, some evacuees want to camp, rather than stay in a motel. To prevent the spread of more fires from campfires, the US Forest Service closes all the forest-service roads.

After a fun weekend of making the best of a bad situation, I realize I need to hike. Dan spots a post on social media about thru-hikers taking a road-walk alternate to bypass the fire closures. Although more road walking is the last thing I want to do, some miles on the road is better than no miles on the trail. We set Thursday as our start day.

CHAPTER 11

Forest Closures (Road Walkin' Continues)

NATURE, PIRATE, DAN, and I bid farewell to Doctor Faust, who is extending his time off the trail to visit a friend in Texas. The rest of us pack our gear into Teresa's car and embark on the two-hour drive to the town of Cuba, where we will resume our trek north. Teresa drops us off at the post office, where our next resupply packages await.

Due to the forest closures, our plan is to road walk from Cuba to Chama—a seventy-seven-mile stretch of pavement pounding that I'm not particularly excited about. I remind myself to take it one step at a time. If I attempt to swallow this entire thru-hike in one gulp, I'll likely choke on its challenges.

We start on Main Street/US Route 550, covering four miles before turning onto New Mexico State Road 96. Vehicles are sparse, and we have approximately nine more miles of street trekking ahead until we get to our next water source, at the Regina Mercantile gas station north of La Jara.

Walking along a deserted highway can be monotonous, so we invent some entertainment. I mention that I've spotted four syringes scattered along the side of the road in the last hour, which sparks a syringe-counting game. By the time we arrive at the Regina Mercantile, we've tallied up twenty-two syringes and even stumbled upon a crack pipe improvised from a plastic soda bottle.

I instinctively duck as a car roars by.

"Fab, what are you doing?" Pirate asks.

"Check it out—these syringes aren't sprouting from the ground. People are flicking them out of their car windows. Every passing car is 'sus,' as the youngsters say."

At Regina Mercantile, the owner greets us without surprise. Thru-hikers have been passing through for days now. The wildfires are a major topic of local discussion, and the mercantile owner generously offers us a grassy area in front of the store to camp. While normally I would hesitate to camp so close to a road, fearing potential late-night troublemakers, we're all too exhausted to trek farther. Besides, this road isn't frequented by many—except for those disposed to discarding syringes.

We take our chances and set up our tents tightly packed against a wooden fence. It feels safer this way, and besides, there's limited space available on the grassy area.

Later that night, a patrol car pulls up to the store.

"Pssst, Nature, don't go out there," I whisper from inside my tent. I jokingly remark that she might get arrested for unlawfully emitting an offensive odor.

Despite my warning, Nature confidently approaches the officer and explains our situation, emphasizing that the store owner gave us permission to camp on his property. She returns to her tent, handcuff-free, and explains that the officer was responding to the store's alarm system, which might have been triggered by an open back door. After calling the owner, the officer finally leaves.

When morning arrives, my brain feels scrambled from last night's sensory overload. The road turned out to be busier than I expected, and the cacophony of cars, trucks, and even motorcycles infiltrated my dreams. Not the most restful night.

"I was having problems with my sleeping bag zipper last night," Dan mentions as we break down our tents.

"You should try this." Pirate demonstrates a smoother zipping technique.

"Thanks for your input, sleeping bag expert, who has spent more time in my sleeping bag than me, apparently," Dan responds.

That's hilarious.

After spending so much time around them on this thru-hike, I can tell Dan is getting frustrated with Pirate. Not from his demeanor or tone—Dan is too soft-spoken and reserved for that. Instead, it's his clever, snarky comebacks. They disarm not only the intended target but also anyone within earshot.

As we head into the Regina Mercantile for last-minute restroom visits, a car pulls up and the driver, giving the impression that he might have some trail magic, begins talking to Dan. I hear him say, "I've got something in my car for you." When I step out of the building a few minutes later, the man is gone, and Dan is holding a small Bible.

Dan looks at me with a shy look, as if to say, "What was I supposed to do?" He tucks it in his backpack. Despite the added weight, it appears Dan now feels too guilty to get rid of the Bible. I'd wager my Oreo stash that he'll carry it with him until the end of his thru-hike.

Off we go, continuing our road walk, with its many obstacles. One is the lack of restrooms, or "VIP privies" as I like to call them when I need to do my number-two duty. But the biggest challenge is the scarcity of water sources. It's the end of May, not even summer yet, and already scorching. After nearly ten miles, we're all running low on water.

We take a break by the roadside as Nature, with her kind demeanor, knocks on the doors of nearby picket-fenced homes to ask permission to use their spigots. With no response from the residents, Nature returns to our resting spot.

Suddenly, a red pickup truck towing a trailer passes us, executes an impressive U-turn on the narrow road, and heads back in our direction. The driver's name is John, and he's a forest worker. Due to the fires, he has opened part of his property, four miles up the highway, for any thru-hiker looking to get water or stop for the night.

"It's the house with the red roof. You'll see it from the road," John directs us.

It turns out to be the right decision.

The following day, we find ourselves hiking back under that blazing sun, putting in a twenty-two-mile day of road walking with no trees to offer shade. This is among the most miserable experiences I've had while thru-hiking. The punishing heat has us all—especially Nature—feeling irritable.

"I can't wait to be far away from this state," she gripes.

Forty-five minutes after a break, we spot a shady cluster of pine trees along the dirt road, but I feel it's too soon to stop again. "Let's go a bit farther. I'm sure there are more trees close by."

Nature isn't pleased, but Pirate and Dan will go along with whatever. Nature and I seem to be the only ones who make decisions, which isn't what I prefer. I'd rather have all four of us talk it through, but no matter how insistent I am about us working it out together, Nature and I seem to be the only ones at the helm.

We move on, and I hope my gamble pays off. Fifteen minutes later, we're still walking on open road. Shade trees are too far off the trail to consider. Another fifteen minutes pass, and I'm regretting the choice to move on. Nature is several hundred feet ahead of me, and I think I see angry steam emanating from her head. Pirate is not far behind me, and Dan is a black speck behind us all.

An hour past that potential pine tree respite, I'm feeling truly guilty. It's one thing to put myself in a bad situation, but making others feel the repercussions of my flawed decision-making doesn't feel fair. It's another reason I'd prefer that everyone contribute their thoughts. If something does go wrong, I can blame others and lighten the load on my backpack-carrying shoulders. Nah, I wouldn't blame anyone, but it would be nice to share the burden.

Just when I think Nature is angry enough to go five more miles, I see her stop under a fortuitous group of trees by the shoulder of the road. I join her, parking myself a bit higher on the shady incline. Pirate and Dan arrive, and we all sit in silence.

It's odd; normally, we chat about something during our breaks. Dan tries to break the tension, mentioning the fortunate shade and how far we've gone. Dan is always a nice guy who wants to make things better. It's a cool trait, unless he overdoes it, like the time he bought a burrito at the Regina Mercantile because he was going in to use their restroom, even though he had more than enough food in his backpack. Or when he covers bar tabs for people he just met.

"Dan, you don't need to buy people's affection. It's not expected, unless you're a baller and can drop rolls of Benjamins," I once told him. I want to shake him into relaxing, but I know that will only make things worse.

I decide it's my turn to lighten the mood. "Dan, if you can have anything in that bottle, what would it be?" I say, pointing at an empty beer bottle that's been tossed in the dirt.

"Money," he says.

"What? No, we're out here in the middle of a sultry day. We're thirsty with heat exhaustion, and you want money? Go again," I say.

He thinks for a few seconds, and then says, "Four sexy genies. Wait, I don't know—that bottle is dirty. I don't want anything from in there."

"Dammit, Dan. Imagine it's a brand-new, empty bottle," I declare.

"OK, then that's my answer. Four sexy genies," he finally says. "How about you?"

I want to be smart and ask for some magic liquid that would keep me hydrated for the rest of this thru-hike, but instead I say, "Four sexy genies."

"I'd want a pirate ship," Pirate announces.

Another wasted bottle wish.

"Smart, Pirate. On dry land with no water in sight. I can't even with you," I say, faux-exasperated.

"How about you, Nature?" asks Dan.

"A llama, to carry my backpack," she declares.

Why not a backpack that's as light as a feather no matter what you put in it?

It's obvious that bottle wishes would be wasted on us.

We eventually reach El Vado Reservoir. My three companions are already across the dam, well out of shouting distance, before I make it there. Once again, I am dehydrated, weak, and battling a headache—and alone. Heat sickness grips me, my stomach churning as waves of nausea pulse through me with each step. The pain in my head turns the road into a blurred haze, my vision closes in, and shadows creep at the edges. I struggle to focus, each breath feeling heavier than the last. My steps falter, veering left and then right, as though dodging oncoming traffic—though this barren road is empty.

Over the past few weeks, I've managed to stave off heat sickness and dehydration with various strategies, some of which I learned from a friend who served twenty years in the Army Reserve and the North Carolina National Guard.

While in Iraq, several of his fellow soldiers suffered heat illness. With daily highs hovering around 120°F and their gear weighing up to forty pounds, it wasn't surprising. He told me that once a person experiences any form of heat illness, whether it's cramps, exhaustion, or stroke, they'll be more susceptible to it in the future. That's me. My previous heat sickness has impacted my body's ability to regulate temperature effectively, leading to a persistent impairment that makes me more prone to overheating and heat-related complications. I might also be "chronically dehydrated" or "dehydration-prone," in medical parlance.

Knowing this, I make a concerted effort to address the issues with tablets, water consumption, salty snacks, and energy bars as soon as my dehydration and electrolyte imbalance become apparent. Yet on some days—like today—and despite my best efforts, I still find myself overcome by the heat.

I finally make it across the dam, where I wait for Nature and the others to locate the campground, which is somewhere up the road. I watch as someone riding a four-wheeler, accompanied by a child I presume is his daughter, approaches my companions. Nature engages in conversation with him for a few minutes before he turns around and speeds back up the hill. Nature comes back to where I am.

"His name is Brandon, and he says that the campground is full, but he's coming back with his pickup truck to give us a ride to an RV campground three miles up the road," she says. I lean back against a guardrail, head bowed, feeling a mix of exhaustion and relief. I don't have to trek more miles.

Ten minutes later, a pickup truck arrives with Brandon, his wife Kris, daughter Leah, and their dog. "Kris and I have an empty cabin where you can stay. Leah will need to climb through the window to open the door, as we can't find the keys. There's no running water, but it's a roof over your head," he says.

"Sounds like five-star accommodations for hiker trash like us," I jest.

The others don't hesitate; they toss their backpacks onto the pickup truck.

"Are you sure you own this place?" I half-heartedly question.

"Yeah, of course, I think. I guess we'll see," he says with a smile.

I must be losing my Brooklynite's suspicion because I hop into the truck bed with the rest of my hiking fam. If I were watching these events in a movie, I would say I'd never climb onto a stranger's pickup and then break into a cabin. However, after hiking for twenty miles, feeling dehydrated and hungry, and then being offered a bed, well, heck yeah, I'll accept a potential victim role in the horror thriller *Thru-Hiker's Murder Cabin.*

The cabin is dated, with 1970s wood paneling, but I see no visible danger. A massive, fifty-inch tube TV, stained drop ceilings, and a woodland-green suede couch contribute to the vintage aesthetic. It will do nicely.

Kris and Leah drop off five gallons of spring water and kindly offer their own cabin a few houses away for showers and dinner. I smile, amazed that on a truly bad day on the trail, someone always seems to come to the rescue.

The doubtful voice in my head quiets, but I can still hear echoes of warning.

Remember Derick, in the movies, just when you least suspect it, the jump scene happens, and the twist reveals that the kind hosts are nothing more than aliens ready to probe us.

Yeah, I know, my inner voice is ridiculous.

We spend Memorial Day weekend at the cabin with Brandon, Kris, Leah, and their dogs, Forest and Heidi. I've been taking photos of every dog I encounter on the CDT. I'm not sure why; maybe it reminds me of Magic, the pup I found, befriended, and hiked with for a few days on the AT. Forest, a tan-and-white hound mix, and Heidi, a brown and gray-faced pit bull terrier, join my growing "pupfolio."

When the busy holiday weekend is behind us, we bid farewell to our gracious hosts. Kris gives us all four-leaf clovers that she found and laminated, to bring us luck on our journey.

A hiker friend once told me that when he thru-hiked the AT in the 1970s, the term "trail magic" was referred to as "trail karma." I think of that as we get back on the CDT. "Karma" seems fitting for that hippie decade; it's interesting to consider that if I'd applied this terminology to my beloved canine companion, Magic, who was great at attracting trail magic—hence my name for him—he would have been named Karma. A less delightfully resonant name, sure, but one that still embodies the giving spirit of families like the Craigs toward us weary hiker trash.

— —

Over the next two days, the heat eases up, but the road walking continues. US Route 64 is a busy highway, but wide shoulders make it tolerable. We stealth-camp one night and the next day arrive in Chama, the last CDT town in New Mexico. We plan to take a well-deserved zero day here. While waiting for our room to be ready at the Y Motel, we encounter a group of thru-hikers just returning after attempting to follow the trail into the southern San Juan Mountains.

"There's no way," one says.

"And we're not chancing it," says another.

Snow from a storm a few days earlier still blankets the southern San Juan range, stubbornly hanging on in true mountain fashion, despite it being the first of June. This section of the CDT is known to be breathtaking but fierce, with rugged terrain, wide alpine meadows, and steep climbs that push even seasoned hikers to the edge. Snow lingers here late into summer, clinging to the north-facing slopes and filling shaded hollows.

The returning group reported that they had not been able to find the trail under all the snow. Even with microspikes, they struggled. One mentions that, despite his extensive experience hiking in the snow, this stretch was too much for him.

Dan reads us a description he finds online of the San Juan Mountain Range: "The conditions are still sketchy—there are plenty of snowfields, steep ice walls, and postholing to deal with. It's recommended to carry microspikes, an ice axe, extra dry clothes, hand warmers, and extra food. The snow-covered passes require time, patience, and caution. Some sections, though only between .1 to .5 miles long, can take up to 1.5 to 2 hours to navigate. For the first 60 miles, the trail is almost nonexistent and in poor condition."

This settles any doubts we have about taking another alternate, called the Great Divide, instead of risking the snow-covered South San Juan Wilderness. We road walked past the forest closures, and now we find ourselves confronting a new peril that is forcing us to continue road walking just below, yet contouring along, the hazardous mountain range.

PART 2

COLORADO

CHAPTER 12

Hazardous Snow (Great, More Road Walkin'!)

I'M OVER IT, and my body's over it, yet the CDT still has some road walking left to dish out. Although I have what thru-hikers call "trail legs"—made strong by and conditioned for long days of slogging—the constant walking on pavement has done a job on my hips. My legs are made for mountain trails, and with every step on the asphalt, either my left knee or left hip chimes in with a sharp "Ouch!" I long to hike under a canopy of trees, on a dirt trail that gives gently underfoot. Even so, I'd rather keep moving on asphalt than spend another week of zero days waiting for the snow to melt out. So onward we go on the CDT's Great Divide Alternate.

The alternate trail follows the Great Divide Mountain Bike Route (GDMBR), one of the longest off-pavement bike paths in the world. The route stretches from New Mexico to Canada, covering over 2,700 miles and closely following the CDT through the Rocky Mountains. Some cyclists tackle sections along the route, while others attempt to thru-bike.

After an eight-mile, uphill road walk away from Chama, we make it to the New Mexico-Colorado border. A large wooden sign by the side of the road reads:

Welcome to
Colorful
Colorado

The sign bears some carved initials and what appear to be bullet holes, which I'm learning are standard issue on road signs in the American Southwest.

Beyond the sign, the landscape transitions abruptly from New Mexico's khaki color to multiple shades of green. It's like watching TV in black and white your entire life and then experiencing color TV for the first time. It's a glorious sight from my roadside vantage point and gives me high hopes for traveling in this new state.

By 5:30 p.m., after covering four more miles, we reach Cumbres Pass Railroad Station. Signs nearby convey that the station was established in 1881 as a stop along the Denver and Rio Grande Western Railroad, built to support the booming mining industry. The station once played a key role in transporting silver, lumber, and other resources across the rugged landscape. Today, the Cumbres & Toltec Scenic Railroad operates historic steam locomotives on this route, preserving the area's rich railroading legacy.

An aged sign situated behind the old yellow train station presents our elevation as 10,015 feet, one of the highest railroad passes in the country and 2,100 feet—almost two Empire State Buildings—above Chama. I consider that none of us got altitude sickness while hiking, likely because our bodies could gradually acclimate to the lower oxygen levels. Much of the Colorado section on the CDT will remain above 10,000 feet, which will be uncharted territory for me (the highest point on the AT was Kuwohi—formerly Clingmans Dome—at 6,644 feet).

We find an area behind the station where we can camp just past an old, covered railroad bridge. I assume it was moved here for historical preservation purposes, because the railroad tracks end not far beyond it.

In the morning, we have a playful photo shoot on the tracks. Nature drapes herself across the tracks like a damsel in distress, evoking scenes from silent movies. Dan assumes the role of the dastardly villain, feigning control over the switch lever by the tracks, ready to direct the train toward the helpless maiden. Dan's best wicked expression ends up resembling more of a strained look, as if he were wrestling with a particularly stubborn pickle-jar lid.

Our next photo is inspired by the Beatles' iconic *Abbey Road* album cover. We emulate a similar walk across the tracks. With the timer ticking down on my camera phone, we strike a pose and snap our version, which I dub the *Thru-Hike Rail* album cover.

After spending way too much time posing, we finally begin walking north, continuing along the GDMBR alternate route. Highway 17 winds below the San Juan Mountains' daunting, snow-covered peaks; up close—and with no prior mountaineering experience in snow—I can see they would clearly have been the less sensible choice. Sure, the call of adventure up there is tempting, but preserving my limbs for less perilous pursuits, such as honing my skills as a coffee connoisseur, makes more sense than going full Bear Grylls and risking life and limb for a mountaintop selfie. I look up and wonder if that really was a person I just saw self-arresting on a snow slope. Chances are I imagined it, but there could be climbers sliding down a slope, frantically digging an axe into the snow or ice to halt their descent. They were certainly postholing, sinking deep into snow with each step, as if creating holes for fence posts.

Down below, we hike an easy thirteen miles on a forest road with no traffic. The dirt is much more forgiving on my joints, and the views are spectacular. The forest suits me just fine. I'm hiking alone, since Nature and the Brits left camp hours before I got up. It's a mellow day as I follow the Rio Grande, which flows from the Rocky Mountains in Colorado, through New Mexico, and eventually into the Gulf of Mexico, forming part of the border between the United States and Mexico.

Wait, am I hearing voices coming from the river?

There's something equally pleasant and macabre about the way the rushing flow of the river reverberates like distant conversations, an elusive whispering that is teasingly close to coherence. I strain to catch what my mind insists is there, but that my hearing hesitates to confirm.

My thoughts have turned darkly poetic. I'm having either a profound introspective spell or an eerie encounter with the unknown. Whichever it is, it's a very Edgar Allan Poe moment. I'm not sure how I feel about that, so I push on, leaving the voices behind—voices that I might have missed had I not been alone. While hiking with someone adds companionship, shared experiences, and a layer of safety, a solo hike offers solitude, letting me connect deeply with my surroundings, set my own pace, and catch the subtle sounds of nature.

The river guides me into a town called Platoro. Typically, I'm excited about reaching towns along the trail, but for the first time ever on a thru-hike, I'm apprehensive about this town's potential dangers. According to FarOut, it's important to avoid drinking the water in and around Platoro—extending as far as twenty miles north of the town—due to mining contamination.

The town's name, Platoro, comes from the Spanish words *plata* ("silver") and *oro* ("gold"), reflecting the area's rich history of mining for precious metals. It's the tailings from that history that caused the water pollution.

My Long Trail water-purification trauma flashes before me.

Dammit, Fab. Stop being so melodramatic.

I reason that if, as a child, I was fine drinking New York City tap water, which flows unfiltered through rusty pipes and is fluoridated and treated with disinfecting chemicals such as chlorine, phosphoric acid, and sodium hydroxide, this area won't harm me either. In fact, I'd wager that the Hudson River rendered me immune to all metal toxins.

Chill, Fab . . . chill.

As I approach town, I notice the lack of buildings—just one or two cabins hidden among the trees. There are not many people in sight either, and I wonder if it has anything to do with the water. The population here is so low that they could probably all fit in a camper van comfortably.

Still, the residents manage to make the most of this dusty town, with its natural beauty and peaceful ambiance—marked by the absence of highway traffic and accessed only by a dirt road that winds through the surrounding mountains. It's a perfect destination for those seeking a serene retreat.

I find the Fab Fam sitting on the porch of a store. Nature informs me that they rented lodgings in an old Airstream trailer for the night. It sounds cool, until she walks me over to show me where I can lay out my sleeping bag. Inside the trailer, a stench hits me, an unbreathable combination of gas, metal, and farts. I can't imagine sleeping in here. Quickly stepping out, I say that I want to check out another spot I saw on the app.

While the three continue eating their meal, I head over to Gold Nugget Cafe, where I'm able to get a cabin with two bunkbeds and a couch. I tell Nature and the Brits that they can stay with me, but they decline. The next morning at the café where we meet for breakfast, they say they were fine with their accommodations. I suspect their noses will be out of commission for a while.

I had been more than fine at the cabin. The owners, KJ and Nick, really know how to take care of thru-hikers, even serving me a vegan pizza for dinner and fruit bowl and oatmeal for breakfast. I had even, reluctantly, let KJ fill my empty water bottles and reservoir. If they are drinking the tap water and serving it to their customers—and haven't grown extra limbs—then it should be safe, and likely safer than pulling water from a nearby outdoor source.

In the café, Nature brings up a recent story about a CDT thru-hiker who slipped on an icy slope in the South San Juans. Two Platoro residents volunteered to rescue her on horseback. From a safe distance above, they were able to guide her toward a safer trail but had to retreat when the snow became too treacherous for the horses. Yet the hiker was able to continue to safety, where she was then taken to the hospital. I'm relieved for the thru-hiker and thankful that our group chose not to tackle the mountains. For now, the only San Juan I'd care to visit is the sunny, tropical city on my favorite island, Puerto Rico.

Three hours out of Platoro, I encounter a lake that bears the scars of mining. Its waters are tinged with shades of copper, silver, and gold. The surface gleams unnaturally, like spilled oil on asphalt; metallic swirls and patches disrupt the flow, creating an alien scene. Each metallic glint tells a story of industrial exploitation and environmental degradation, and I spend the rest of the day ruminating on human carelessness and destructiveness.

Lost in thought, I cover more miles than I realized and get ahead of my group. I find myself alone, looking for a place to camp. After two months on the CDT, this will be the first time I'm camping on my own. I'm fine with that—my thoughts are many, and they will keep me company this evening.

It takes a good hour to find the right spot to camp. I pass a section near the road that warns of rockslides. A mile farther, I spot a grassy area, but its unevenness pushes me on. I finally find a cluster of pine trees surrounding a beautiful, open field. The long search and wait feel worth it as I unload my pack. I've hiked twenty-two miles today—farther than we'd planned.

I use this solitary time to assess my physical and mental state. I've become more attuned to my body and can easily spot signs of dehydration and act on them. This heightened awareness has been vital in avoiding more potential setbacks.

"So, what you're saying is that you didn't miss us?" asks Dan, when we regroup the next day.

"Did you not hear anything that I just shared about being more self-aware and proactive about my physical and mental health, using past experiences to prevent issues and stay balanced on my current journey?"

"Oh no, I missed that part," he says with wide eyes.

I laugh. Dan's faked sincerity seems absolutely real, though I know he's kidding.

Good one, Dan.

We pass through Creede, another once-booming mining town that's as small as a neighborhood in Manhattan, like the Bowery or Hell's Kitchen. The only things keeping towns like this alive are tourism and outdoor recreation. And yet there's something special about Creede. Maybe it's banner signs like this one I see on a lawn, framed in metal and standing by the sidewalk:

Love your neighbor
who doesn't
look like you,
think like you,
love like you,
speak like you,
pray like you,
vote like you.
Love your neighbor.
No exceptions.

I visit several shops, and everyone greets me with an extra-big smile and the kindest words. If it weren't for the harsh Colorado winters, I could see myself settling in a mountain town like this. Every day would be filled with kindness and hospitality. I'd like to think I could leave my door unlocked out here—well, maybe not, but it would be a welcoming place to call home.

Yet, I move on with my fellow hikers. Such is the life of a thru-hiker, passing through towns in the blink of an eye.

We continue along the Creede Cutoff Alternate, which will reconnect us to the CDT in ten miles, on a dirt road that climbs steeply. Although Nature is a half mile behind me, I can almost hear her expletive-laden diatribe soaring past me into the swear jar of heaven. I'm sure someone up there is keeping track.

I pass old houses barely hanging on to the steep mountain walls and wonder how they built such structures back in the 1800s. It's impressive.

When the terrain levels off, I wait for the Fab Fam, and together we approach a commemorative rock the size and shape of a football, painted with a blue sea, green mountains, and fiery sunset colors. Light-green vines with pink blooms spell out *Karen's Spring*. Below, in black print, reads *Karen Robinson, January 6, 1955–June 1, 2020*. There are a couple of printed quotes, including one by Thomas Aquinas: "There is nothing on this earth more to be prized than true friendship."

The memorial rock is next to a black pipe sticking out of a cliff, which marks what many call the cleanest water on the CDT. I'm not sure about that. If it ain't obvious by now, I err on the side of caution when it comes to water sources. Yet, it's hard to resist, especially when I once drank straight from "the cleanest spring on the AT" on top of Glastenbury Mountain in Vermont—and survived. We're over sixty miles north of Platoro, way beyond the contamination zone. I balance the pros and cons, my fear versus my adventurous nature.

Uhhh, excuse me, but have we forgotten?

As usual, I disregard my inner voice and fill a water container from Karen's Spring. "If anything, he went down with a sense of curiosity and an adventurous spirit" is how I'd like to be eulogized if things go awry.

It will likely be the only spring I drink from unfiltered out here. I'm not sure what will come, but after a sip of the crisp, refreshing, pure water, I can die saying I've had the best-tasting water ever.

Hours later, I feel better physically than I ever have. I'm not sure if it's that natural spring water or the fact that we're at San Luis Pass, which marks the north end of the Creede Cutoff Alternate and where the trail merges back onto the actual CDT. Our road walking is over, at least for now.

CHAPTER 13

Why the CDT?

WHILE WE CONTINUE along the CDT, Pirate and Dan effortlessly weave British words such as "malarkey," "wiz," and "bollocks" into their conversations, and I try using them as well. In contrast, Nature leans toward good, old-fashioned, expletive-laced rants, starting with a hearty, "Are you f*cking kidding me?" followed by a litany of "assh*le rocks," "sh*t trails," and "bullsh*t inclines." Meanwhile, I find solace in opting for colorful colloquialisms like "flutternfunk," "balderdash," and "gobbledygook" to vent my frustrations.

One of my favorite British phrases is "Are you having a laugh?"—something I say today after Pirate makes a Spanish-language joke about a No Trespassing sign. He insists it doesn't apply to us because we're a group of four, not *tres* (meaning "three" in Spanish), as if the sign only bans trios.

Dan and Pirate both exhibit subtle social eccentricities, and their unique perspectives and offbeat outlook on life on the trail create a comfortable atmosphere where I can feel at ease, especially during the hike's many challenges. However, despite our camaraderie, our different approaches to thru-hiking can hinder forward progress.

Pirate and Dan were mates back in the UK when Dan initially conceived the idea for this journey with the intention of bolstering his self-confidence, and Pirate seamlessly adapted. Now, though, it seems that any preexisting cracks in Dan's self-esteem and assurance may have deepened, leaving him emotionally uncertain, perhaps worsened by just how physically and emotionally demanding the CDT is. At times, due to his fatigue and missteps, we don't see him at camp, but somehow, he always finds his way back to the group.

"What led you to choose the CDT over the AT or the PCT?" I ask Dan one day.

"The easy answer is because I'm stupid. Umm, but for me, I mean, I found the idea of doing the CDT very appealing. Largely because of the different terrains and because I didn't know that I was ever going to get a chance to do any of the other ones. I really wanted to do the one that spoke to me the most," Dan says. He explains that while he knew about the AT, "there wasn't quite enough there to spur me into action," and he only learned about the PCT—a shorter 2,650 miles and overall less rugged—long after he'd decided to do the CDT.

It's a fair answer, and honestly, if he'd said he had no specific reason for choosing this trail, I would have understood. After all, I don't have a clear reason myself for choosing the CDT over the PCT, aside from knowing a few people. But that's part of the thru-hiking mystique; some of us embark on these journeys without fully knowing why or what will come of them.

Dan's intention on the CDT was to discover a stronger side of himself while thru-hiking. However, he was confronted with a trail that doesn't dole out its challenges gradually, but instead smacks you right across the face with hardship.

At one point, Dan believed he could outsmart the CDT by veering onto a dirt side road just before the trail started to climb up a steep mountain. He hoped the road would bypass the mountain, but his improvised route dead-ended, leaving him to scale the mountain anyway on a precarious, non-trail side. What he thought would be a shortcut turned into unexpected, difficult mileage.

It's hard to tell what Dan is thinking after such a flub; he's definitely not thrilled with his actions, but he doesn't embody pessimism. With his melancholic disposition, mopey posture, and emotional distancing, Dan reminds me of Eeyore, the donkey from *Winnie-the-Pooh*. I try to find the words to encourage him, but they never seem to stick. Yet, he's out here trying his best, the only way he knows how, and that alone is commendable.

Dan has hinted that he gladly adopted the trail name Buck Wild in order to cultivate a confident alter ego. Buck Wild is the celebrity everyone wants to meet and be around. When Dan channels his Buck Wild persona, everything seems to fall into place.

"You see, Buck Wild smells like Old Spice, whereas Dan smells like old mothballs," he jokes.

When he finally catches up to us after being gone for hours or days, he says, "Buck Wild is never late. Nor is he early. He arrives precisely when he means to."

It's a shameless *Lord of the Rings* reference yet fitting. And it doesn't get better than this classic one: "The name's Wild. Buck Wild. Men want to be him. Women want to be with him."

"Alright, guys, have a good night," Pirate says one night as he retreats toward his tent.

"Love you, Pirate."

"Love you too, Fab," Pirate responds.

"That's one," I whisper to Nature from inside my tent.

I can hear her laughing. She remembers my challenge: "I'll bet you an Alpine Start coffee packet that I can get both Pirate and Dan to say 'love you.'"

"No way, Fab. I don't see that happening."

Just the statement I needed to get me revved up.

She done did it—it's on!

It did not take long for Pirate to respond with the correct answer. Eeyore, however, has been more of a challenge. "Where's the nearest water source?" I ask Dan the next day, as he's going over our hike for tomorrow on the app.

"It's 4.7 miles away."

After hitting him with a few more frivolous inquiries, I thank him and say, "Love you."

"You're quite welcome, Fab."

"Hogwash," I whisper to myself. Dan is as courteous as a cab driver in London, but I can't get him to play along. I understand, and dig that British folks often have a unique, more muted, and sometimes sarcastic way of conveying affection that might not always involve the word "love." Which I really dig, but balderdash to it all if I can't win this "love you" challenge.

In the morning, as we break down our tents and pack our stuff, I walk over to Dan and wrap my arm around his shoulder.

"Good morning, Dan. It's going to be a great day. Love you, man," I say with such positive energy that I know I've got him.

"Good morning to you, Fab. Yes, I hope so," he says, nodding.

Dammit, that would have worked on a tollbooth operator. I'm losing faith in my gregariousness.

"It will be, Dan. It will be," I say as I walk toward Nature.

I roll my eyes at her big grin.

"Morning, Nature," I say, unamused.

"Morning, Fab," she says through a grin that has gotten even bigger.

"He's a tough biscuit to crumble." I look away from her atom-splitting grin.

"I see that," she says, adding a laugh.

I walk away. While I may have lost this particular round, there's still time for me to emerge victorious.

CHAPTER 14

Nuyorican State of Mind

"WHAT'S A NUYORICAN?" many people ask when I say I'm "Nuyorican."

My Puertopedia explanation is this: "Nuyorican" describes a person of Puerto Rican descent or heritage who was born or raised in New York City. It specifically refers to individuals who identify strongly with both their Puerto Rican heritage and their New York City upbringing or culture.

It's a unique blend of two cultures, rooted in the vibrant, rich traditions of Puerto Rico and also the fast-paced, diverse energy of New York City. Growing up as a Nuyorican means navigating both worlds, carrying the warmth of Puerto Rican family values while embracing the hustle, creativity, and resilience of the city. It's an identity that feels both expansive and grounded, bridging two places that have shaped me in distinct but powerful ways.

"Come on, you weren't a bad kid—a little itchy maybe," Mrs. Sharp expresses via Facebook Messenger.

Mrs. Sharp was sometimes my substitute teacher during my elementary school years. She's the only teacher who remains vivid in my childhood memories, perhaps because, at the tender age of nine, I harbored a quiet crush on her. She had a youthful warmth that set her apart from the other teachers, an undeniable beauty reminiscent of a young Michelle Pfeiffer. Her radiant smile lit up the room, and her eyes sparkled with a kindness that made me feel special. Her dirty-blond hair cascaded in soft waves, always styled to perfection. I thought for sure she would wait for me to grow up so we could get married.

A few years ago, we reconnected. I'd outgrown my childhood dreams of marrying her, and of course she hadn't waited for me. Now retired, she'd reached out to her once-energetic student with some words of life encouragement. We reminisced about little Derick and discussed my perception of my past behavior and how I believed others viewed me.

"You were a child with ADHD," she said.

I was never one to label myself or use diagnoses to justify behavior others saw as problematic. But when Mrs. Sharp said it, everything clicked for me—my constant inattention, hyperactivity, and impulsiveness. How I craved attention and approval from my teachers, my friends, and my family. If clowning around didn't work, I'd turn to sarcasm, often at someone's expense. I wasn't trying to be mean—at least, I didn't think I was—I just wanted a reaction, any reaction, that brought eyes on me. Attention deficit hyperactivity disorder is the neurodevelopmental disorder defined by these very traits.

I was never officially diagnosed, but Mrs. Sharp recognized the signs. Her experience with and understanding of children facing such challenges was evident—she knew just what to say, using the right tone and expression. She'd pronounce my name in a calm, soothing way, not in the angry tone I often heard from other adults. She'd gently ask, not aggressively tell, me what to do. While others shushed me, Mrs. Sharp listened. In a world filled with people who made me feel useless, less than, and lonely, she understood me. It was reason enough to ask for her hand in marriage.

When the acronym "ADHD" popped up in her message, it felt as though a light switch flicked on, illuminating the answers I'd long sought. I wasn't a bad kid—just a little itchy, as Mrs. Sharp put it. This revelation lingered in my thoughts. Throughout my entire adulthood, I'd imagined that my distractedness, restlessness, and precipitateness came from living in manic New York City and from being a Nuyorican, perpetually moving forward without a set destination. The little Derick was a "bad boy," but the adult became someone searching for adventure, trying to fill a void I didn't even know I had. In New York City, I found myself going in circles, never reaching a place of ease. Everything shifted when I discovered the outdoors on that fateful spring day on the AT. Slipping on a backpack and venturing into the unknown ultimately redefined my life.

While Mrs. Sharp may have provided me with an "Aha!" moment regarding my identity and perhaps shed light on my tendency toward impulsivity, there may have been additional factors to consider.

When I informed my mom, in 2012, about my plans to live on a trail for months, her first question was about my diet.

"What are you going to eat? Berries?"

"Yes, Mom. Berries and sticks," I replied with a straight face.

"Ah, I see. So, what you normally eat?" she teased.

Before I could respond, she erupted into laughter, rising from her seat and clapping as if possessed by the Holy Spirit. My mother often has these outbursts when she finds her jokes particularly amusing. During my teenage years, it used to annoy me, but now, as an adult, I catch myself smiling and laughing along.

"Nah, Mom. Definitely no sticks. I'm a survivor, and though I'm a vegetarian—for now—my fellow hikers know that if they perish before me, I won't let myself go hungry. Catch my drift?"

There was a pregnant pause. It took my mom a minute to process my statement.

"Derick, don't say that," she said, her eyes wide open with a smile, an expression that reminded me of how she used to look at me when I was her *niño Travieso*—her "silly little boy."

"What? It's going to be easy for me. I don't remember what meat tastes like, so I'll close my eyes and pretend it's chicken."

"You're ridiculous. You get that from your father," she said, falling back on her go-to response whenever I say or do something she deems offensive, comparing me to a man I hardly knew.

Both of my parents were born in Puerto Rico—my mother, Carmen, in a mountain town called Lares; my father, Jose, in the nearby coastal town of Mayagüez—but both were raised in New York City: Nuyoricans. I didn't know much about my father after his separation from my mother when I was five, but following his passing from cancer later in my life, a cousin on his side of the family revealed that he was quite the storyteller, full of humor. Perhaps it was this shared sense of humor that initially drew my parents together—Mom with her witty one-liners and Dad with his captivating stories. Whatever it was, I wish it had been enough to maintain their bond, to ensure he remained a part of our lives. Unfortunately, there wasn't sufficient laughter or storytelling to hold our family together.

Is that why I share my stories and employ humor? Is it to forge connections with others, or simply to conceal my own pain? I recall reading somewhere that comedians are often the saddest individuals. When I bartended at Gotham Comedy Club in New York, I encountered a spectrum of comedians—some deeply troubled and struggling, others more composed and put together.

What resulted from the humor between my Nuyorican parents? At first glance, one might say nothing but heartache, yet that wouldn't be entirely accurate. My sister and I emerged from their union. Despite the challenges, Mom still retains her sense of humor, and my father, as I've been told, maintained his until the end.

As for me, I suppose, sharing stories or cracking jokes is the easiest way to communicate with others. It seems to be a potent family trait that I carry with me, one I can't relinquish even if I tried.

CHAPTER 15

Vertigo

WHEN I LOOK UP at the towering, jagged San Juan Mountains, a profound sense of insignificance washes over me, and a powerful jolt of fear grips me, as though the mountains themselves are colossal waves poised to crash upon me. I've never been surrounded by such immense landforms, and that alone wraps me in a cloak of intimidation.

Two miles north of San Luis Pass and an hour back on the CDT, I make it to camp just before dark. Pussy willows line the trail, and every few yards the trail opens to small camp areas, like cubicles in an office, giving hikers their own personal space. Up on this mountain saddle, the air feels thinner, and the wind carries a chill that hints at the higher elevations above.

Pirate and Nature arrive minutes later. Dan, I suspect, will make his usual late arrival in about an hour. I sense a distinct kind of cold due to our high elevation. We're over twelve thousand feet up, above tree line, and camping this high means enduring biting winds and bone-penetrating chill.

When my feet grow colder than usual, it's my signal to brace for inclement weather. I nestle in my multilayered sleeping bag with my water filter (to prevent it from freezing), my phone, and a portable power bank. My prophetic feet never fail me. I could start a lucrative business predicting weather patterns with my foot-based forecasting system—something to explore after my outdoor adventuring.

"You're absurd, Derick. You must be tired," I mutter to myself as I pull my sleeping bag over my head and drift into my whimsical dreamland.

To my surprise, I sleep straight through the night, which I am grateful for. I have resolved to make a significant change: I need to wake up and start hiking much earlier. On the AT, I could afford to leave camp midmorning, but the CDT, particularly in Colorado with its elevation gain and severe weather, is not as forgiving. I must ascend, traverse, and descend these Colorado mountains before the midafternoon thunderstorms roll in like clockwork, leaving me scrambling for my life. I'd prefer to jump-start an early morning with coffee in hand rather than some dark, ominous storm nipping at my heels later.

Nonetheless, I'm not at my sharpest in the morning. I often find myself disoriented, unsure of my surroundings. Sleep clings to me longer than I'd like. Theodore Roethke's quote beautifully captures my morning brain fog: "I wake to sleep, and take my waking slow."

Coffee helps, but I'd avoided it during my first days on the CDT due to the desert heat and my fear of getting dehydrated. On those mornings, I found it especially hard to think straight. There were times I couldn't even remember if I'd put on underwear. A few hours into a hike, I'd check and, sure enough, no drawers.

This morning, my watch's gentle beeping wakes me at 5:30 a.m. People who need a moment to work through the morning haze shouldn't be startled by a loud alarm, and I use a watch instead of my phone to conserve the phone's battery life. No matter how hard I try, it constantly takes me two hours to get ready on the trail; I'm always the last one to leave, and sometimes my hiking companions are hiking an hour before me. On cold mornings like today, it's extra hard. I linger in my sleeping bag, attempting to gather myself and my scattered belongings while still staying wrapped up snugly.

By 7:30 a.m., though, I'm ready to go. Nature, who always breaks down her tent first and stands around, watching the rest of us lagging, is surprised to find me hovering over her, eager to get going.

"Who are you? What did you do with Fab?" she says.

"I'm not messing around. It's too cold to start late," I explain. I want to add that she can close her mouth now.

"Just when you thought you knew me," I add.

"You're full of surprises . . . among other things," she jests.

"Thank you—heeeyy," I say with a laugh.

"Since we're getting going so early, we could hike up San Luis Peak—it's a Fourteener," Pirate chimes in.

The first time I heard the term "Fourteener" was here on the CDT. It refers to the mountains standing at least fourteen thousand feet above sea level, of which, famously, there are fifty-plus in Colorado; their completion is eagerly sought-after by peak baggers. Colorado's Fourteeners range from casual hikes through alpine tundra to steep, loose, exposed scrambling, and there are deaths from falls, exposure, and storms every year.

The highest mountain I'd ever climbed before the CDT was Kuwohi—formerly called Clingmans Dome—in Great Smoky Mountains National Park, standing less than half the elevation we're currently at. I'm normally not interested in bonus miles, but I want my first Fourteener. Plus, San Luis Peak is close to the CDT, maybe two miles off the trail.

There's a rub, though: I'm prone to vertigo—the false sensation of movement or spinning, even when motionless—when I'm in high places, especially when there are steep drops all around me.

Yeah, I know, not so Fabulous.

I became fully aware of my vertigo while thru-hiking the AT. The sky spun out of sight while I was climbing the tiny sandstone spire of the Dragon's Tooth in Virginia, and then again weeks later, on a steep gap coming out of a town in Pennsylvania. However, looking back, I realize I experienced it to a lesser degree as a child and teenager. Heights have always been a challenge for me, whether it's flying in a plane or looking down from the Top of the Rock—the Rockefeller Center's observation deck, seventy floors up. My stomach wants me to always keep both feet on solid ground.

Vertigo is disorienting and makes even simple movements feel Herculean. The fear of losing my balance and falling is very real and creates a mentally taxing sense of vulnerability and anxiety. Over the years, I've learned some coping mechanisms to manage it. Taking slow, deliberate steps and using hiking poles for support helps me maintain stability. I also try to focus on the ground in front of me, ensuring myself that I'm not going to trip over any uneven terrain.

A Fourteener brings the possibility that reduced oxygen could make my vertigo worse, though I haven't experienced any altitude sickness on the CDT thus far. Overcoming that will demand mental resilience and determination. It's also crucial to acknowledge my limits and heed my body's signals, as well as that nagging voice in my head. If the vertigo becomes too severe or poses a significant safety risk, I know I must be willing to turn back.

You're as stubborn as they come. Turning back around? That's like trying to unring a bell.

When we reach the cutoff to the San Luis Peak Trail, my doubts run through my mind. Is it foolhardy to tempt fate, or am I just being overly sensitive? Sometimes, the fear of vertigo is worse than the vertigo itself. This makes me wonder: What came first, the phobia or the symptom?

In his book *Man's Search for Meaning*, the psychiatrist Viktor E. Frankl explains that "a given symptom is responded to by a phobia, the phobia triggers the symptom, and the symptom, in turn, reinforces the phobia." Am I stuck in this cycle? If so, that's all the more reason to march forward and confront this fear head-on. I'd rather face defeat in battle than succumb to it by giving up. It's not so much about bravery—in fact, I'm as freaked out as a squirrel in a dog park—but more about taking control, steering my life rather than drifting aimlessly and hoping for the best.

Nature volunteers to stay with our packs, and those of two other thru-hikers, Sedge and Chanin, who happen by and also want to climb the peak. She's not interested in doing any extra climbing.

"At such a high elevation, someone's going to run off with our heavy backpacks," said no thru-hiker ever.

Yet, I acknowledge the New Yorker in me locks the door at night even when I'm in the safest towns in America. Having Nature guard my belongings is a welcome precaution.

"We'll be back before you know it," I say with a twirl of my trekking poles—which I promptly drop and then pick back up; they are coming with me. I don't show my doubt, but I mention to Pirate and Dan that I might have a vertigo situation. I make light of it because it helps me feel more able to face whatever comes.

I start ahead—no sense in procrastinating.

I'm diving in, no holding back.

At least that's what my actions convey. My racing mind and pounding heart say something else entirely. It's like that feeling at the start of a roller-coaster ride, when each click-clack of the chain lift pulling the coaster up leaves a ball of fear lodged deeper in my throat.

I keep my head down, focusing on the scree before me and the larger talus blocks hugging the trail. It's a gradual climb, easy enough for me to use only one trekking pole without feeling out of breath or strained. We're above tree line, and in my peripheral vision, I catch glimpses of blue skies. The sky dominates the scenery, lording over the land and the mountains. If I keep my eyes on the trail and nowhere else, I'll make it through.

"Eyes on the trail. Eyes on the trail," I whisper to myself. Then, for no apparent reason other than that I have a death wish, I glance to my left. It's like being a child forbidden to press a button and yet unable to resist the temptation.

"Yup, we're high up," I mutter.

I turn around to see how far I've come. Dan is several hundred yards behind me, and Pirate is several hundred yards behind him. I can't discern their features; they're just dark, shadowy figures slowly ascending the long, exposed ridge. I am so focused on staying in motion to keep my brain from realizing I'm not on flat terrain that I have quickened my pace.

After another forty-five minutes, I make it to the summit. Sledge and Chanin are lounging at the top, leaning against piled rocks that form the shape of a sofa's back and armrest. With them is a hiker named Onion, who mentions she's been alone up here for over an hour.

"You mean, you had all this to yourself?" I say, waving my arms like a magician revealing an extravagant trick.

OK, that's enough. Stop showing off before you topple over.

Minutes later, Dan joins us, followed by Pirate.

"Someone tricked me; they said there was a bar" are Pirate's first words when he reaches us at 14,022 feet.

"Drink from the loins of Mother Nature," I say, once again waving my arms, though this time my bum is on the ground.

"What does that even mean, Fab?" says a confused Pirate.

"I don't know. It sounded right in my head," I confess. "I meant the view is enough to get you drunk. Does that make more sense?"

"Yeah, that's better. I guess."

I notice he's holding a trekking pole with a blue bandanna tied to the end. "Does that help you determine the direction of the wind?" I inquire.

"It's our thru-hiker flag," he says proudly, a modern-day Betsy Ross.

I settle in, collect myself, and take in the view. Different shades of brown dominate the rolling mountains below, stippled with patches of dark green and small spots of white snow. Peaks in the distance look like egg-crate Styrofoam, creating a fake movie-set backdrop. The blue sky with painted white clouds adds to the surreal and splendid setting.

If this isn't proof of a superior hand in the making of this planet, then I don't know what is.

Dan suggests that I hike down between him and Pirate. The chances of feeling like there's no safe place to land are lessened with other bodies around.

"Great idea, Dan. If I trip, I have someone to grab and take down with me," I say, half in jest.

"I'm game. Dan may be frightened, but Buck Wild is fearless," he says.

Dan and his alter ego take the lead, I follow close behind, and Pirate follows me. This does feel much more comfortable; still, I focus on the purple wildflowers and the yellow wildflowers and the backs of Dan's shoes. We follow the endless scree. Dan occasionally looks back, checking to see if I'm close, and asking if all is fabulous. I tell him it is, which is what I'd say even if it wasn't. No sense in worrying anyone. This is my fear, and I'm not one to pass it on to others.

As the rocky trail transitions into a smooth dirt path, crossing seemingly safer terrain, I break into a jog, passing Dan, who is not about to scurry down for no apparent reason. The gentle incline of the trail beckons me on, creating a sensation akin to gliding along one of those moving walkways in airports. I ponder if the disorientation—or the fear thereof—that I experienced in the vertigo danger zone somehow recalibrated my equilibrium, allowing me to now feel as agile as an Olympic athlete on stable ground. It's a curious thought, albeit laden with psychological jibber-jabber speculation. Perhaps I should consider adopting the trail name Dr. Fab, MD.

I'm still buzzing from the experience when I reach Nature. The fear of vertigo is real, yet the disorientation was sidelined because I was careful not to make quick, careless moves. I learned to push past my vertigo and just soak in the moment. There's an extra sense of gratification in achieving what once seemed out of reach.

Mount Everest, here I come.

Nah, not even. I'm getting vertigo just thinking about it.

CHAPTER 16

Becoming Fab

"WHAT'S YOUR TRAIL NAME?" a hiker inquires.

"Fab," I respond.

I've noticed that along the CDT, hikers frequently exchange trail names, but they rarely delve into the origin stories. Maybe by the time thru-hikers reach the CDT, the novelty has faded. Or perhaps, unlike on the AT, where trail names are a new and curious tradition for many, here they're simply accepted.

I'm not implying that the question isn't ever posed; rather, on the CDT, there's a prevailing attitude of "let's just keep moving" when encountering someone you may not hike with for an extended period. Again, this is different from the AT—perhaps because CDT hikers are generally more seasoned, or maybe because of the harsher terrain that keeps everyone moving or the varying routes and lack of centralized campsites. I've had hikers zip past with a quick hello, and then they're gone. But hey, it's still more interaction than I'd typically get on the bustling streets of New York.

However, today is different. After sharing my trail name with two hikers, I notice their confused expressions. My mind-reading ability kicks in, and I sense that they are thinking, "What's a Fab? Did he say Flab or Fob? Maybe Fa—the fourth note of a major scale?"

I answer their unvoiced thoughts. "It's short for Mr. Fabulous, but there's no need for us to be formal out here."

That garners the desired laughter. My Fab Fam has been exposed to this routine on numerous occasions, and I'm sure they'll hear it many more times. "Hey, if it ain't broke, wear it out until it does break," I send the thought to my trail fam, trusting they'll pick it up telepathically.

Beyond the world of thru-hiking, my friends now commonly refer to me as Fabulous, or simply Fab. Hence, it seems fitting to embrace the nickname of the nickname for official use on this thru-hike.

"Hey, you're only a mile and a half from the road. Need a ride into town?" a runner with her dog offers as she jogs past me in the Sawatch Range in central Colorado.

"Yeah, that would be great. I really appreciate it," I say.

"What's your trail name?" she asks.

"Fab."

"I'm Jackrabbit. I'll be stretching by the black SUV."

I dig it when someone introduces themselves with a trail name instead of their real one. It immediately creates a connection, a nod to being part of the same hiking community. Plus, trail names are way easier for me to remember than real ones—they're unique, tied to personality or a story, and stick in my mind like the trails we hike.

"Great, thank you," I say with a wave as she runs ahead.

Wow, that was the easiest hitch ever.

I have been dreading the idea of hitchhiking, even though I'll do it because hiking twenty-three miles along the highway to the town of Salida for a restock isn't ideal. I doubt I'll ever feel at ease thumbing a ride—it's a bit like panhandling—though I'm comfortable hopping into a stranger's car and have no trouble socializing with someone I've just met.

I reach a sizable parking lot half an hour later and spot a black SUV just beyond a restaurant. Jackrabbit is stretching nearby, so I join in, wishing I could remember to stretch after every hike.

As we roll into Salida, I'm amused by a hotel sign:

PET FRIENDLY! EXCEPT FOR BEARS.
NEVER DOING THAT AGAIN.

Jackrabbit drops me off at the Riverside Lodge Motel & Family Campground, promising to join us for a drink later. I reunite with Nature, who has secured a small cabin for the four of us. Pirate and Dan are a few miles behind me, and I expect they won't have a problem getting a ride. The trailhead parking lot was bustling with cars, presumably some belonging to patrons of the restaurant.

Our stay in Salida will be an extended one—today is technically a "nero" (nearly zero), which means we put in a few miles before stopping to rest and resupply. There's no hard-and-fast rule about what counts as a "few miles" for a nero. When I first started the CDT, a fourteen-mile day was a full day of hiking. Today, even though we hiked fourteen miles, I consider it a nero because we finished by midday and still had daylight left to keep going.

We're also taking a zero tomorrow and the day after. Sidetrack, whom I haven't seen in weeks, will join us tomorrow for some much-needed catching up. He went above and beyond, booking a large room for the Fab Fam for our next two nights in town—the ultimate trail magic.

The next day finds us all at Elevation Beer Company in nearby Poncha Springs. Sidetrack is there, along with Jackrabbit and a hiker named Fireball. Fireball had been thru-hiking the CDT this season but had to get off due to an injury. Now he's driving up and down the trail, giving rides to thru-hikers. He kindly gave Pirate and Dan a lift into town.

As we exchange stories, Fireball says that Cutie was found lifeless in his tent. I do a quick blink, as if hoping to increase the volume and clarity of my surroundings with a mere flicker of my eyelids.

I must have misheard.

"What? Why? I mean . . . how?"

The first time I met Cutie, with his unique hiking attire and long, braided pigtails, was during a night hike with Tie and Salgado in New Mexico. Dysfengshuinal and Lowrider were there too. The last time I saw Cutie was at Trail Days in Silver City.

"They don't know. He went missing for several days, and didn't check in at Lake City. They think he passed in his sleep and was in there for about five days before anyone thought to check the tent," explains Fireball.

Our conversation takes on a subdued tone. Despite only meeting him a couple of times and our interactions having been brief, the always-friendly Cutie left a positive and uplifting impression. He was soft-spoken and reserved, but not in an unapproachable way. His manner was thoughtful and wise, making me want to learn more about him.

The news about Cutie continues to weigh on my mind through our two zero days, and as we resume our journey. I'm unsure of Cutie's age, but he seemed way too young to pass suddenly, and this leaves me feeling melancholic. With no other choice, I press on, letting the trail guide both my steps and my thoughts.

Just when it seems like my brooding thoughts might consume me, I slip on a patch of small, shortleaf pine cones. Instinctively, I extend my arms out to my sides and frantically spin them in circles, as if trying to balance on a tightrope. But it's all in vain, and I end up landing on my bum, as the Brits would say. It's my first fall of this thru-hike. I've stumbled before but managed to stay on my feet every time. I had hoped to complete the entire CDT without a single fall, but I guess it's time to let go of that unrealistic ambition.

I stand up, brush off the back of my pants, and shift my focus to my surroundings. A nearby stream immediately captivates me with the remarkable clarity of its water. I can see the rocks resting on the bottom, a striking contrast to the murky depths of the Hudson River at home, where the water is usually an opaque, dull brown. There, my gaze is often met with the disheartening sight of empty Styrofoam containers, plastic shopping bags, and various other debris. This stark contrast makes what I'm seeing here all the more special.

Nature, Pirate, and I camp that night by a fast-moving stream, its waters crashing over rocks with a wild rush that mirrors the storm brewing above. We haven't seen Dan, who, once again moving at his slow pace, is likely to get caught in the rain. The downpour subsides long enough for us to prepare our dinner. Dan hikes into camp, soaked, wearing an expression that says, "Hey, it's what I do."

Over the next few days, the rain subsides, but the sky remains cloudy, a reminder that it could shower on us if we misbehave. I'm not entirely sure what counts as misbehavior, but I nonetheless offer a silent plea to the trail gods.

We HIHO it into Twin Lakes, Colorado, on the east side of Independence Pass. A HIHO is a "hike in" and "hike out"—going to town to sort out all your necessities before hiking out again that same day. This marks my first CDT mail drop, which my friend Corey has arranged. Corey, also known as Baggins, is a Triple Crowner and works as a product testing and sample coordinator at Oboz. He's been my CDT strategist, offering hiking and trail suggestions via text, patiently answering my myriad mundane questions. Having him in my corner has been invaluable. Plus, I discover, he added beer to my resupply.

"Fab, is that a six-pack?" Pirate asks.

There are two things that thru-hikers can spot from afar: food and beer.

"Yes, to celebrate my new pair of hiking shoes." Baggins has also included a much-needed new pair of hiking shoes. I toss a can of beer to each person present.

"A toast to my worn, torn, and forlorn first pair of shoes. You served me well. And to my second pair, here's to smooth trails ahead," I say, raising my can for a ceremonial clink with my trail mates.

I've been wearing the same pair of socks since day one on the CDT. Are they stinky, crusty, or walking off on their own? Surprisingly, no. After over two months, they're still holding up well. However, I do have a brand-new pair, and I'm not keen on putting fresh shoes on top of socks I haven't washed in a week.

As I slide on both new socks and shoes, the sensation of something clean and fresh-smelling brings a smile to my face.

"Man, this feels good, and my feet are lookin' fly as fudge," I say.

"Let's see how long they stay that way," Pirate remarks.

"I'll be carefully hiking around mud and puddles, like a teen trying to keep his new kicks away from anyone trying to scuff them," I joke.

"Good luck with that out here," Nature says.

"Yeah, I know. At least they'll have a glamorous five-minute debut," I reply with a grin.

After five more days on the CDT, we intersect with Highway 9. Instead of crossing it, we catch a free bus for a five-mile ride to the ski town of Breckenridge. There, an old hiker friend from my AT days, Chiba, picks us up and drives us two hours to Denver, where we plan to take a zero day. Pirate and Dan will be staying nearby, while I'll be at Chiba and his wife's house.

Chiba, his Bordoodle, and I stay up well past "hiker midnight"—the thru-hikers' typical bedtime of 9:00 p.m. or earlier—reminiscing about our AT days. We sit on his back porch, gazing up at the stars and reliving our journey. The more we talk, the more I find myself missing my naïveté and inexperience during those early days on the trail. I was so ignorant about the challenges ahead, especially the tough times. If I had known then what I know now, I tell him, I might not have had the courage to attempt a long-distance hike, and would never know how the experience would profoundly come to shape me.

The next day, after we tour downtown Denver and enjoy some delicious vegan food, Chiba and I meet up with the Fab Fam. Nature's son, Kyle, who also lives here, joins us, along with some friends of mine from Chicago who are visiting Denver. It's a perfect evening of catching up with old and new friends. Even though I could do this all night, we decide to call it early, knowing that Chiba has a four-hour roundtrip drive ahead of him the next day to drop us off back in the mountains.

As much as I'm happy to have stayed with my homie Chiba, I'm glad to be leaving his dog, who has been putting his nose far up my rear every chance he gets, even after I showered several times. I get that anal sniffing is how dogs greet each other, but it's clear that I'm a human. And even if it was just to say hello, how many times does the dog have to tell me?

I heard—well, felt—you the first time, dog.

I'd take a slobbery face lick over a full-on cavity search any day. Is this what an alien probe feels like? Because if it is, I'm not even a little bit curious.

Either way, I walk out of Chiba's house backward, as discreetly as possible. I don't want my trail friend to know that his dog was inappropriately touching me. Regardless, I'll never be able to see a Bordoodle again without clinching my sphincter and covering my butt with my hands.

CHAPTER 17

Is This Type III Fun . . . or Am I Going to Die?

If you find yourself caught in a thunderstorm, get as low to the ground as you can, and steer clear of caves, rocks, and stand-alone trees. When lightning is around, make yourself as small as possible—squat down with as little of your body touching the ground as you can. If you have an Ensolite pad or something similar, stand on it for extra safety. But if it's just raining, you don't need to worry about any of this.

THAT WAS NATURE'S advice about being caught in a storm. It's sound advice. However, as I find myself hiking alone—Nature somewhere ahead, unseen for two days, and the Brits several miles behind—I'm struggling to wrap my mind around just squatting out in the open in a storm. As the sky dips low and the threatening specter of dark clouds descends, I'm not sure I can stay stationary; I'm driven to move toward safety. I might be wrong, but I'm hoping I won't have to find out.

I'm closing in on my first summit of a series of above-tree-line ridges that lead to Grays Peak, a Front Range Fourteener that I'll ascend tomorrow. The downpour is getting intense, and I still have several peaks to climb. Turning back would be the sensible choice, yet I convince myself that I'm too deep into this Thirteener—above tree line, completely exposed, with nowhere to find cover—to easily backtrack. As I navigate a rock scramble, I spot a hiker crouched under an overhanging boulder that offers scant protection from the rain. He seems intent on waiting it out. I briefly consider joining him but decide to push on over and down the scramble, hoping the weather won't worsen.

Instead, when I reach level terrain, I find myself enveloped in thick fog. I'm now inside the clouds.

Damn.

I'm trapped in the storm I promised to avoid. What should I do? Stop, drop, and roll? No, that's not right. I'll keep moving and hope it doesn't worsen beyond the tempest mist closing in from all directions.

The wind intensifies, and I lose the ability to see more than a few feet in front of me. A powerful gust forces me several steps to the right. I crouch down to steady myself as hail the size of quarters pelts my face. Nature didn't mention a safety technique for hail, so I open my sunbrella, relieving me of the hail smackdown but leaving my fingers to go steadily numb in the cold.

The pain sears through to my bones; it feels like I'm maneuvering prosthetic digits, which scares me. I'm reminded of Jack London's short story "To Build a Fire" and how the protagonist lost all use of his hands. Like him, the connection between my fingers and my brain is broken.

I decide to move on, even without a trail to follow. I begin the steep descent and wonder if I'm going in the right direction. I stop, stick my head in my jacket, and check FarOut. Sure enough, I'm far off the red line. The wind pushed me off to the side of the mountain.

I know I should hunker down like a turtle, using my backpack as a shield, and wait it out, but being stubborn, I walk back up toward what I'm guessing is the correct course. For every few steps I take, the wind either pushes me back a step or forces me to stop and wait a few seconds. I finally stumble into a dirt gully descending toward a pass. The freezing rain and wind continue to pound me.

At the pass I lean against a sign supported by two posts. The sign shields my torso from the wind, and my rain jacket offers some protection. My legs, however, take the full brunt of the rain and wind, leaving my pants completely soaked.

I rest my head on the sign, grateful for the pause. I can't believe I'm out here in this Armageddon and the only cover I have is a trail sign that is liable to fly off the mountain at any moment. With chattering teeth, I try to grab my phone, but my fingers won't bend, so I leave it in the plastic bag inside my rain jacket.

Oh, what did I get myself into? Am I going to die?

I peer ahead into the gloom, struggling to see where the trail continues, realizing that this is the kind of situation where hikers need to be rescued by helicopter—or, worse, simply vanish. I want to sleep, but if I stay here much longer, hypothermia will set in. I can't stop shaking,

I'm getting drowsy and increasingly more confused, and my fingers are useless. I know what I must do: keep moving, no matter how cold or desperate I become.

Otherwise, I'll die.

"Let's go, Fab. You can't get any colder or any wetter," I say to myself.

But you can be swept off this mountain.

Troubling scenarios race through my mind, and I decide that if this is my time, I'd rather face my fate while moving, keeping my circulation going, than simply standing here and giving up.

Wasn't that the same rationale the protagonist in "To Build a Fire" had? And how did that end for him?

I squeeze my eyes tight, trying to choke the life out of that pessimistic inner voice.

"I'm making it to camp today," I whisper, amid wind and lashing precipitation so loud that even a shout would be muffled.

"OK, it's now or never." I muster the tiniest bit of courage, but it's enough.

Another quote from Viktor Frankl's *Man's Search for Meaning* comes to mind: "Suffer proudly . . . not miserably." I proudly step away from the sign, but then quickly stumble back to its protection.

"That's . . . too . . . miserable," I say with a trembling voice.

The wind and rain hit me hard. A smack from Poseidon himself.

I need to compose myself, which is nearly impossible with my entire body trembling, and it's only getting worse the longer I stay here. I finally stagger forward again, resolving to continue until either the storm stops or I do.

I turn my thoughts inward. Whatever is happening to my body feels distant, like watching a storm from inside a well-sealed house. I think of how I'll come out of this wetter than, well, a rain-soaked hiker, but at least I'll have made it through.

What was supposed to be a wondrous day of mountain climbing has quickly turned into a major snafu. I'm on the rocky side of the mountain, with a steep drop to my left, hidden in the storm's fury. A powerful gust slams into my back, and I instantly collapse to my right, landing against a wall of jagged rocks as the wind continues to pummel my curled-up body.

I'll endure as long as I'm breathing.

I stand up and press on, and after what feels like an eternity—but is likely only about ten minutes—the wind finally subsides, taking the rain with it. Looking up, I see a welcome sliver of blue through the gray clouds. Within seconds, the gale subsides, and the sun emerges, as if feeling guilty for having left me in such a mess. Thus, the sunshine should dry me off before I reach camp tonight.

"That was not fun," I accuse the withdrawing black-and-gray clouds.

As I continue, I try to make sense of what just happened and how I ended up making all the wrong decisions. I probably should have taken shelter with that hiker beneath the overhanging boulder. I wonder where this experience fits within my other CDT thru-hiking experiences. Overall, I'd say this has been a moment of Type III Fun.

For reference, Type I Fun is immediate and pleasurable, like a leisurely stroll through a beautiful forest. Type II Fun involves challenging activities that push your limits, such as a strenuous hike that rewards you with a stunning view—it's tough in the moment but satisfying in hindsight. And Type III Fun isn't that fun at all, even in retrospect, and is usually just a fight for survival. With Type III Fun, it's time to buckle up and get ready to be pushed to your very limits, both mentally and physically, as I was today.

At an outdoor event that seems like a lifetime ago, an older gentleman offered this quote, which I took the time to write down: "Within the realm of adventures, there exist only two classifications: a good adventure and a great adventure." Today, I'm still not far enough removed from this horrific experience to call it either "good" or "great"—just Type III.

The sun continues to shine as if nothing happened, like a lover's kiss after a heated argument. I remove my rain jacket and drape it over my backpack to dry. Looking ahead, I spot the faint hairline of the trail two miles away.

Within an hour my pants are dry, and the only sign that I was in a life-threatening storm is my damp socks. I'm weary, but the trail doesn't care. Before me is a long, straight climb of about a mile. I slowly walk, picturing myself at certain distances ahead, trying to manifest my progress. When I make it up to a ridge, I look back and study the long stretch of trail I've just traversed. I notice a black speck in the distance, resembling Pirate in his usual dark clothing.

"Woot woot!" I call out.

He waves and responds with a faint "woot" of his own. I smile, relieved that at least one Fab Fam member is safe. I could wait, but judging by his distance—he might be two miles away—I'm not sure I can hold out that long without succumbing to the urge to settle in for the day, and it's only 1:30 p.m. That's *not* going to happen. I give a final wave and turn away, wondering what type of fun Pirate has experienced today.

By 9:00 p.m., the sun is sinking behind the mountains to the west. Night falls quickly. I normally wouldn't hike this late, but I'm determined to get below tree line. Pitching my tent this high doesn't appeal to me, especially if another storm rolls through. I flick on my headlamp as I approach a section of the trail the app labels a "dangerous traverse." The steep descent slopes between 40 and 50 degrees, and the terrain grows increasingly unstable, with loose rocks and scree. The risk of slipping is high. If it were any steeper—like 60 degrees or more—it would be considered hazardous without technical climbing gear. The app advises hikers not to tackle this section if we don't have to.

I'm exhausted and my mind is foggy, yet when I look down the side of the mountain where I need to end up, pack snow clings to the edge like hardened ice, stark against the lightless abyss below.

Do I drop my pack and slide down? Am I sure there's a safe runout?

Shoot, it's too dark to tell if this is even the actual trail. I might not be thinking clearly, but it doesn't need to be explained to me in crayon-eating terms: Taking another step could risk serious injury. I shouldn't tempt fate, even if it means not being with my tramily.

As much as I'd like to reach my intended campground, I'm going to pitch my tent here, crawl in, and pass out. It's been a long day, and I'd like nothing more than to dream it away. In the morning, I'm sure things will look different, and I'll have a fresh start on the right foot . . . literally.

CHAPTER 18

Butt-Puckering Moments

I WAKE WITH my fingertips still tingling from yesterday's storm. Despite finally settling into my tent and drifting off to sleep around 11:30 p.m., I'm awake by 5:30 a.m. Outside, dawn has yet to break through the darkness. Inside, my headlamp casts a red glow as I slowly gather myself and my gear, yesterday's harsh hike still weighing on my mind.

An early start feels like the only solution to avoid another storm. Several big climbs await me today, including the highest point on the CDT, Grays Peak at 14,270 feet. It's still ten miles away, and I'll need roughly four to six hours to cross the several intervening summits and top out Grays before descending, all before the infamous afternoon storms.

Time to outpace those storms—perhaps I'll even challenge them to a race.

"Hush," I quiet my inner voice; it has no bounds, no limits to its hubris. I dare not provoke Mother Nature's wrath.

I must pick up where I left off last night, trying to safely figure out a way down this ridge. There's a dirt road a few yards to the left of the trail. According to the app, if I follow it for three miles, it will wind around to the base of this steep climb. I can see from here where the road connects with the trail down below. However, if I can find a way around the many remnant snowfields and then switchback my way down, I could potentially save an hour. Of course, that's if I survive the precarious descent.

I gaze down at the spot where, last night, I contemplated dropping my pack and sliding after it into the void. I'd been seconds from going for it when something tugged at my common sense, and a good thing it did. There is nothing to slide to—just a thirty-foot plunge off a cliff that would have sent my pack, and then me, careering down the slope. The trail gods were certainly watching over me; now, I hope their favor continues.

I walk along the ridge and spot the snow-free opening I was looking for. It's steep, but if I carefully zigzag, I should be able to navigate the descent unscathed.

OK, here we go.

The initial step proves to be the most challenging. Once I hold a steady stance on the incline, I take a couple of cautious side steps down the exposed scree. It's slow, but the key is to measure my steps, stay upright by leaning back slightly to avoid becoming top heavy, and not roll down the mountain headfirst. As I approach patches of tundra, I find they provide a sturdy foothold; without them, I would undoubtedly slide out of control.

It takes me thirty minutes to descend, requiring my complete concentration. I pause at the bottom and look back up at the starting point. There's no chance I could have done this at night. Once again, I express appreciation to the trail guardians, overseers, or whoever or whatever it is that's watching over me.

In the valley, I follow the dirt road, now integrated into the CDT, alongside a stream that has formed on the trail due to rain and snowmelt. I navigate by stepping on rocks and drier spots touching the side of the trail. Within an hour, I pass a campground with several RVs and campers. I tightrope-walk across a tree bridge over Peru Creek, flush with runoff, and begin to ascend on another dirt road. The app shows that I'll continue climbing for six miles until I summit Mount Edwards at 13,839 feet, almost 3,400 feet above my present elevation. And that's just the beginning of my day. After that, I'll have a couple of short climbs, and then it's a steep nine-hundred-foot climb up Grays Peak—all before the afternoon storm.

I already imagine the Type II Fun (and maybe also Type III) ahead.

After a mile and a half, the trail turns off the road at the Argentine Pass trailhead and crosses Peru Creek once more. The names on this section, I learned, are due to the early miners and explorers who came here from South America during the Colorado gold rush era in the late 1850s and early 1860s.

The creek has a light, milky color to it, like what you might see when whitewater rafting. There's nothing that suggests it's unsafe to drink, but since I've never encountered such a hue in a running stream, I hesitate.

Still, I have no choice but to filter water here. The next water source is on the other side of Grays Peak, six and a half miles away. I fill my 3-liter reservoir and my two 1.5-liter bottles. Seems like a lot, but, as you'll recall, I tend to drink more than your average thru-hiker.

I swing on my backpack and check the time; it's almost 11:00 a.m. Not a horrible time to climb, but not the best either. As I hike uphill, day hikers returning from their summit begin to pass me. One couple mentions how they want to be down before the rain hits. "Me too," I say as I continue hiking up toward the potential rain. The trail begins to switchback in a long, steady climb. The higher I go, the steeper the drop-off to my right becomes. I focus on the path ahead, occasionally stopping to lean against the large rocks. I knew this section could be a vertigo threat—in fact, all of Colorado can be. Still, I try not to linger on the potential peril ahead, instead pushing along at a rapid pace.

It feels like an eternity, but I finally make it to the summit of Mount Edwards, and to my surprise there's an SUV parked there.

What in the lazy-rugged-drivin'-to-a-summit is goin' on here?

I'm not particularly keen on seeing a vehicle on a summit I just struggled for two hours to climb. I'm confused about how it got up here until I cross the ridge and see a dirt road snaking up from a valley below. I can imagine the driver, draped in a sweater and looking like Carlton from *The Fresh Prince of Bel-Air*, asking me, "Why work so hard for hours when you can be up here in ten minutes?"

Needing some peace, I walk several yards up a sloping mass of boulder fragments, which seems to be what the next section of the CDT will look like: rocks upon rocks upon rocks. As if I needed more obstacles between me and Grays Peak.

I take off my pack, sit on a rock, and munch on an energy bar.

Shortly thereafter, a shaggy, white-furred creature breaks my reverie.

Whah, is that . . . that's a mountain goat. Nice . . . what's it doing?

It's poking its head under the SUV, appearing to lick the tailpipe.

"Whatever you're doing, it seems to be a treat for you, buddy. At least one of us is thrilled to see this car up here," I say.

Such an odd place to park.

Then again, I'd drive up here for this view any day of the week. The endless mountain flanks with snow streaking down them look like volcanoes dripping with white lava. I turn to the mountain goat and watch it licking away at the car. I then remember that I'm not driving up Grays Peak, so I should probably get going.

"Is there a way to drive up to Grays Peak? I'm asking for a friend," I ask an older couple on the trail. They're headed back toward Mount Edwards, clearly the owners of the SUV.

"I don't think so, but there is a parking area at the base on the other side of Grays Peak," says the husband.

I tell them about the mountain goat licking their car.

"Oh yeah, we saw it. It must be licking the salt," says the wife.

Nice couple. I wouldn't have minded chatting more with them, but they mention rain in the forecast.

"That's my cue. I've got to go. Enjoy the rest of your hike and drive down the mountain," I say as I scurry past them, racing against the dreaded afternoon showers.

There's no trail to follow, just a direction through the littered boulders, making it a slow hike. I jump from rock to rock like the main character in an old platformer arcade game. I keep moving, but deep down, a sense of fear lingers—this time, I've pushed my luck too far. The distant clouds are a heavy gray, but are they far enough away for me to make it over the exposed mountaintop before the storm wraps its claws around me? The thought shifts me into a higher gear. It's not over, even if I get caught in a storm. As long as I can move, I'm moving.

I'm scrambling on the side of the mountain, with the top of the ridge—where most hikers go but that's too dizzying for me—several feet above me. I must look like those mountain goats when they stand on tiny rock ledges. Except they're agile and graceful, while I, by contrast, am clumsy, slow, and constantly leaning against the rock, shying away from the drop.

I sit down. I know I'm doing this wrong, but I am going in the right direction—at least that's what the app tells me. I lean my head back, looking up at the sky. There are many white clouds, beautiful, yet there are also gray ones. I must move. Suddenly . . .

Wait, that's not a cloud.

I see a mountain goat staring down at me, studying me intently, as if deciding to speak, though I know it won't because of the oath all animals take to never talk to humans. (Well, that's what little Derick used to believe.)

I stare back at the shaggy-coated creature. It lowers its head and then swings away in the direction I'm headed. I follow, reasoning that although I'm not as sure-footed, the goat must be on an easier path. Sure enough, there's a path on the top of the ridge, though it's narrow and exposed. The goat stands several yards away, looking my way, as if waiting. As I walk toward it, the goat turns, jumps, and disappears over a cliff.

I follow flat rocks that I believe might be the trail until I reach a large gap, about two feet across. I've reverted to traversing the slope below the ridge again, but this time on the east side, with a rock wall to my left and a steep drop to my right.

This doesn't seem . . .

Before I even finish the thought, I jump over the gap. Why hesitate? Before I land, however, my backpack hits a protruding boulder and swings me toward the steep drop. I grab onto the wall. My violently pounding heart drops to my nether regions. I pull myself up the rock, and as I lift my head, I see the trail clear as day. I should have realized the trail would never cut across such a wide opening.

I blurt out, "What was I thinking? Was I attempting to un-alive myself?"

Clearly, I had ignored my own inner voice. I lie on my backpack, covering my face with my hands. I need to calm down after this butt-puckering moment, this nearly final instance of Type III Fun.

"OK, I didn't die, so let's go," I whisper to myself as I look at the gray clouds replacing the white ones.

Another hour passes, a few more miles along the ridge, and I find myself back on the side of the mountain. As I sit down to rest, I spot the mountain goat once more.

"Keep showing up, and I'm going to have to give you a name," I say playfully.

Fab, don't go there again.

Thoughts of Magic return. I miss that dog more than ever. I want to cry it out, but then I see another goat, with two younger ones, approaching me on the south side of the ridge.

"Aww, are you introducing me to your family?" I say to my snowy-white mountain guide.

The original goat, the father, responds by getting closer to me. He moves only a few feet, but I realize that a quick charge toward me could knock me right off this mountain.

"OK, stay right there. Thank you for your help, but I don't know you like that. How do I know you won't bite me or hit me with your pointy horns? Git, git!" I sternly say.

I wave my hands, and the goat retreats toward his family. I hate to have done that to my guide, who always seemed to show up to help just as I was going off course, but I'm not taking any chances. I'd rather risk offending than end up injured—or dead.

With the clouds still building to a dark, ominous density, I get moving. I still need to outrun the afternoon storms.

Damn, would it defy the will of the cosmos if I were ever to reach a mountaintop without the threat of a storm, or am I eternally bound to race the elements?

After hours of climbing, I'm beyond exhausted, but I'm finally at the base of my steep and rocky final ascent—Grays Peak. The sky is covered in clouds as dark as the dirty snow, laden with car exhaust and grime.. More clouds rush to join the growing cluster, hurtling toward Grays Peak. The cover is now thick and heavy, as though the sky itself is preparing to collapse.

I don't waste time dwelling on my fatigue; I use my trekking poles to pull myself up and focus on taking controlled breaths. I watch each rocky step to avoid tripping or twisting an ankle. When I do look up, it's usually to behold a false summit. Initially, I don't fall for the mountain's tricks, but as time passes, I find myself hoping that each new high point will be the one that ends this taxing day.

I reach a level area, with a stone on the ground that I would have missed if it wasn't for the writing:

Grays
14,270 ft

"Shazam, I made it," I say, breathlessly.

It's 4:30 p.m., and no one else is here. Filled with elation, I look at the snow-covered mountains beyond and the vastness below me. I want to sit here and soak in this monumental achievement. It took hours (well, really, months) to get to this spot, so I figure I deserve a moment to let the view reward me for it. Yet, there's no time: A menacing cloud—like a hidden prankster ready to jump out and shout "BOO!"—is creeping up behind me. It's a few feet away, covering the trail I just climbed. If I stand here a moment longer, I'll be marooned in a disorienting whiteout.

"Flying fudge freckles!" I shout.

I turn to begin my descent, but decide to stretch my luck first, grabbing my phone to take a 360-degree video of my situation. No one's going to believe me. I need proof.

"OK, got it. Let's go," I say, pocketing my phone and jumping, leaping, and skipping down the peak like a drunken stuntman. I'm far from graceful. Fear-running down a mountain will do that to you. I thought the rock steps on the more popular side of the mountain would help, but my landings are hard, and I sense I'll pay for such abandonment. When I look back, dark clouds cloak the spot where I just stood.

Four miles and three thousand vertical feet of agonizing stampeding later, I'm down off the mountain.

I find a campsite hidden just off the dirt road leading to the Grays trailhead. A few feet from my tent is Quayle Creek, whose rushing sounds will be my tranquil melody for the night.

I rip off my shoes. My feet are in excruciating pain, unrecognizable with wrinkles from being in shoes still wet from yesterday's rainstorm. Agony courses through every tendon, ligament, and muscle. Ibuprofen is good for swelling, but I don't have any, so I acknowledge the pain, nursing it to prevent it from worsening, perhaps even avoiding shin splints.

In the morning, the pain has lessened, though my feet still tingle as if I were wearing vibrating socks. I limp down the dirt road away from the trail up Grays Peak. Cars line the shoulders, since the parking lot is already full of day hikers eager to say they climbed a Fourteener.

But did they?

I suppose so, though thru-hikers *truly* climb it, having come all the way up from 4,900 feet at the Mexican border. Still, the distinction doesn't matter—well, maybe only to this thru-hiker hobbling down the mountain.

I stop moving awkwardly after an hour. Despite the trail's ongoing, short ups and downs, this stretch of the CDT feels so much easier. Near the end of my day's hike, I come upon a group of thru-hikers with big backpacks, taking a break—the first thru-hikers I've seen in three days. Where were they when I could have used some moral support, distraction, or a warning about possible butt-puckering moments? It's like that friend who always shows up offering to help you move once your stuff is already off the truck and inside your new place.

I don't recognize any of them except for the one sitting on a fallen tree.

"Nature, you're alive!" I reach in to give her a fist bump.

"You better come here and give me a hug," she says.

Turns out Nature had her own Type III Fun on the high peaks, though she also had three hikers from the Czech Republic helping her through it. She introduces a married couple named Fuego and Master Chef, and a hiker I recall seeing along the trail earlier, named Jingle Bell.

Although rain is nearing, the three plan to hike toward a road and hitch a ride into town. Nature's not having any of that. The hike is too long, she says, and it will be dark soon. I concur, and we agree to find a spot soon to camp. We bid the Czech hikers farewell and good luck.

Nature and I swap stories of our respective "bad day" as we cover a few more miles.

"That was the f'ing worst!" she insists. During the storm, she stayed close to the three Czechs. Like me, they kept moving, with no shelter from the relentless wind and rain. She also camped just below the "Dangerous Traverse" section the night I chose to camp above it.

I was right about Pirate and Dan not being together anymore. Nature and I both receive messages from Pirate telling us about the separation. They usually hike at different paces, but the storm widened the gap between them. Text messages confirm that everyone is safe, though we're now several miles apart.

Thunder rumbles ominously in the distance as Nature and I scramble to find shelter. We duck off the trail and set up camp beneath towering pine trees with thick, drooping branches, offering the only refuge from the storm. We manage to pitch our tents just in time; the first drops of rain fall as we drive the last stakes into the ground.

Finally, a break.

CHAPTER 19

Dear Mr. Moose II

NATURE QUIETS HER STEPS through the evergreen woods, hoping for an unexpected moose sighting that we can record. Over the last few weeks, she's been more determined—and even a bit more anxious—than I am about spotting one of these animals. This marks her third and final thru-hike, and she's both desperate and somewhat surprised not to have seen a moose yet. This denial feels like an act of the gods.

Several days ago, she even became indignant at the birds disrupting our attempt to maintain silence for a moose sighting.

"Stupid birds," she grumbled, then mimicked an alert she imagined the birds were relaying to the entire animal kingdom. "It's humans—BEWARE!"

On this early morning, Nature and I have been hiking for over an hour, nearing Colorado's largest natural body of water, the five-hundred-acre Grand Lake that sits at the west entrance of Rocky Mountain National Park. The morning has us navigating ups and downs, circling the lake.

"I told you. The trail, for some stupid reason, insists on ascending and then descending around lakes. Why can't there be a level path along the water's edge? How difficult could it be? In fact, it should be simpler than building it uphill. Stupid trail creators," Nature grumbles.

"Stupid" is Nature's description for anything that doesn't make sense to her or she thinks shouldn't exist. It took me a while to understand why she would grumble whenever a lake was slated to be part of our hike. I envisioned lakes as treats, but after encountering many along this trail, I finally grasp her perspective—you rarely get a chill, flat stroll along the shore.

During one of our climbing moments, I notice a ballet of swans.

Nature corrects my bird identification. "That's actually a squadron of pelicans," she says.

"Pelicans? OK, I see that now. But a squadron? You made that up. Oh wait, I see that too. The way they swim in a triangle formation, like aircraft. How clever."

I really dig the various terms used to describe groups of birds, such as a "raft" of ducks or a "colony" of penguins. A personal favorite is a "charm" of hummingbirds. Yet, the one that consistently surprises others is a "murder" of crows; whenever I share this term, no one believes it's real.

"Murder? Who's making up words now?" Nature says.

See, I told you.

It's such a cruel description. Is that why crows get a bad rap? I know some cultures see them as harbingers of death or as bad omens; crows are also often mythologized as tricksters and messengers between realms. My Hispanic family believes seeing a crow foretells a death or tragedy. The bizarre death of the actor Brandon Lee during the filming of *The Crow*—being accidentally shot by a fragment of a dummy bullet lodged in a prop gun—only adds to the lore. Some myths also depict crows as shape-shifters with mystical qualities. They are the antagonists of the avian realm.

Despite all that, I'm personally intrigued by crows—they captivate me with their intelligence, mythological symbolism, and diverse roles in cultures worldwide. The term "a murder of crows" holds a certain resonance, like some line of dark and mysterious poetry.

"I think it's Old English. I had a neighbor who—"

"Stop," Nature interjects in a whisper. "It's a moose."

I freeze. Everything is still except my racing heart and my hand reaching for my phone in my back pocket. I don't look for the moose, fearing it will flee if I do, which has been my experience in the past. Setting my phone's camera to video, I wait for Nature to guide me toward the moose's location. This moment won't be jeopardized by any stupid and sudden moves; my next action will be like Ethan Hunt in *Mission: Impossible*, meticulously strategized.

"At your ten o'clock," she murmurs.

Nice. That was very field agent of her. Glad we're on the same mission page.

I turn my head left, but the trees obstruct my view of the field that lies just ahead and below us. As I navigate as swiftly and silently as a ninja, anticipation builds. "We're finally going to see a moose. We're finally going to see a moose," I repeat, attempting to manifest it into reality.

The trees whip by as if glimpsed from a train window, until a root challenges my balance. I avoid a fall with drunken ninja-like agility.

"There it is." I halt as the moose stops and gazes our way, about one hundred yards off the trail. It starts to walk, hinting that it might cross just ahead. I synchronize my movements with its pauses, a silent dance of observation. Time stands still as the creature and I share an unspoken primal understanding.

"There you are, Mr. Moose," I say under my breath.

"Maintain your distance" seems to be our shared sentiment.

Then my ninja skills falter again when I inadvertently step on a twig, and the moose, with deliberate and commanding grace, crosses the trail some fifty yards ahead of us, ensuring a safe distance for both parties. I observe its rippling muscles and heavy steps, the creature radiating strength and confidence in its natural domain as it disappears into the dense trees to our right.

A decade after completing the AT and writing a blog entry titled "Dear Mr. Moose," I now reflect on the long-awaited answer to my plea. It seems fitting, this day, to respond with a social media thank-you post containing a clip of the moose and the following message:

Dear Mr. Moose, better late than never.
Peace, Love & All That Good Stuff!
—Fab a.k.a. Mr. Fabulous
PS. Thanks for not giving chase.

CHAPTER 20

Altitoots

I WAS AWARE that our high-altitude adventure could potentially lead to altitude sickness. However, I didn't realize that upon reaching a certain elevation, individuals may also experience a phenomenon known as High Altitude Flatus Expulsion, or as thru-hikers humorously refer to it, "altitoots."

Choosing between the two terms is a dilemma for me. On one hand, High Altitude Flatus Expulsion is hilariously descriptive, but it might be too lengthy for a spontaneous joke following a fart. "Altitoots" flows more smoothly and is easier to deliver in a pinch.

I must admit, much like an elementary school kid, the sound of farts never fails to make me laugh. I find myself unable to suppress a giggle when a symphony of altitoots emanates from different tents, reverberating through the campsite.

Doctor Faust was a true champion of altitoots in the early days, even if the elevation in New Mexico was mild. In the evenings, after dinner, I would hear rear-end rumbles coming from his tent.

"Oops! Did you hear that thunderous applause?" he'd say.

When I'd hear another altitoot, I wondered if his evening coffee digestif was to blame. Altitude alone may not be solely responsible for thru-hiker flatulence.

The fact is that hikers who embark on long-distance hikes often find themselves experiencing increased flatulence. This can be attributed to various factors.

First, our diet tends to consist of high-calorie foods packed with fiber and carbohydrates to sustain our energy levels. Such fiber-rich foods, consumed in large quantities, can lead to elevated gas production.

Second, the abrupt change in eating habits on a thru-hike can disrupt the gut microbiome, also resulting in increased gas production. Rigorous physical activity also accelerates digestion, which can cause an incomplete breakdown of food and thus increased gas.

Moreover, traversing high-altitude regions during a hike can subject the body to reduced atmospheric pressure, leading to bloating and increased flatulence.

Last, our on-the-go eating style, often involving quick consumption, inadequate chewing, and swallowing air, can contribute to higher gas levels.

This was all a surprise to me on the AT. I'd be peacefully hiking, only to be suddenly startled by a fart.

"Who's there?" I'd shout, spinning around with flailing arms, as if swarmed by bees, only to realize that I'd been hiking alone for three miles.

These aren't your average, respectful farts, politely giving a warning before making an appearance. No, these thru-hiker farts are a law unto themselves, devoid of any semblance of courtesy, erupting violently like a prison break.

A couple of weeks ago, on John the fire worker's property, we decided to declare a Mac 'n' Cheese Extravaganza Night because, of course, we were fully stocked up. (As the resident vegan, my mac and cheese is, naturally, of the plant-based variety.) After feasting on our gooey goodness, we retired to our respective tents. As I lay there pondering why we'd set up camp so far apart, a telltale sound pierced the night air, suddenly making me glad we'd done so. The noises escaping from our tents carried throughout the campground, much like sound through the thin walls of a New York City apartment.

I make a conscious effort to keep my altitoots to myself, but unfortunately, on a different day, a misstep on the trail led to an unavoidable emission. To my dismay, Pirate was right behind me and, true to form, couldn't resist making a quip.

"Was that Dan? That sounded like Dan," he joked, though Dan was miles behind us.

"Yeah, his farts echo for miles," I said, knowing full well I wasn't fooling anyone.

The last thing you want to do is strain while lifting your pack and accidentally let one slip. But we don't even need to exert ourselves—just a quick glance at FarOut can trigger a fart. Nature let one out one day while checking the distance to our next campsite. We pretended it didn't happen until a further chorus of farts ensued. She quickly stashed the phone in her pocket and set off hiking, leaving me to deal with the aftermath. I was torn. I didn't want to follow the source of more potential altitoots, but I also didn't want to linger where the gas had landed. Opting for a compromise, I bushwhacked around the trail, keeping a safe distance for a few minutes.

One evening, while enjoying dinner at camp, Dan decided it was the perfect moment to regale us with what he affectionately termed his "I dropped my guts" story.

"Go on, Dan," I encouraged.

"Well, a while back, I'd arranged to meet up with one of my friends to watch a football game at a local pub. I got there first, and this pub has a bit of a reputation. As you know, I've always struggled to make friends—I get a bit anxious in social situations. So, I was standing there looking awkward, holding my beer, and there was a group of people playing on a quiz machine. I thought maybe I could help with the odd question. So, I slowly walked over and joined the back of that group. Then, without any warning at all, I dropped my guts, but it was silent. You know, sometimes, you do that, and though you don't have a nose down there, mercifully, you know it's going to be bad when it hits. It was like that, and so I started backing away. I figured I had a couple of seconds before everyone noticed.

"When the smell hit the group, they all backed away, and the time ran out on the quiz question. They lost their money, they lost their game, and they all knew it was me. From their perspective, it looked as though I'd walked over there just to do that. So, no, I didn't make any friends that evening."

It took me so long to contain my laughter that I feared dropping my own guts from the sheer force of my amusement.

"Dan, this goes beyond mere social awkwardness. You must be cursed," I jested, still laughing.

"I believe you're right, Fab. I believe you're right."

There's no stopping altitoots sometimes, and that's OK. When you hike with a group for an extended period, you're bound to encounter everyone's rear-end announcements. It's just part of our experience—the melodic sounds of thru-hiking, if you will.

"The hills are alive with the sound of farting," I imagine Julie Andrews singing our unofficial theme song.

While nestled in my tent post-Dan's story, I serendipitously stumbled upon enough cell service to delve into some entertaining fart facts. Because, really, why pass up such an opportunity? Here's what I uncovered.

Fun Fart Facts:

Frequency: On average, healthy adults pass gas around thirteen to twenty-one times a day.

Gender: Men tend to fart more often than women, but women's farts have a higher concentration of gases, making them smellier.

Silent vs. Loud: The noise of a fart is determined by the speed at which it is expelled from the body and the tightness of the sphincter muscles.

Speed of Expulsion: Farts can reach speeds of up to ten feet per second (seven miles per hour).

Fart Myths: The idea that suppressing farts can lead to severe health issues or explode the body is a myth. While holding in gas for extended periods might be uncomfortable, it won't cause significant harm.

I also researched the names for different kinds of farts:

The Misfire
The Thunderclap
The Squeaker
Stealth or Ninja Farts—the famous silent-but-deadly farts
The Shart—a fart with an accident

The list went on and on. But one point I'd like to conclude with, and which I think all thru-hikers should adhere to, is never trust a fart after mile five.

CHAPTER 21

Jam Boy

I WAVE AT a passing car, and the driver waves back.

"That's six," I say to Pirate, who is trekking along the highway behind me, with Nature behind him. We're cruising down the flat, straight stretch of Highway 14, heading to our pickup spot for a ride into Steamboat Springs. For amusement, I attempt to get passersby to wave back at me. We cheer when we finally get a response after a dozen cars pass without even a nod. I count the nods as a salute too, reminiscent of what I nostalgically call a stranger's New York greeting.

Eighteen reactions in six miles is our final count when we reach Highway 40, the road into Steamboat over Rabbit Ears Pass.

Kate, our ride, pulls up in a Big Agnes–branded SUV. The company, based in Steamboat, has been my go-to brand for backpacking gear on this thru-hike. They've been a supporter of mine for a while, but picking up four smelly and tired thru-hikers is going above and beyond.

Steamboat Springs is a mountain/ski/ranching town nestled in the picturesque Yampa Valley, with green hillsides and massive aspen groves. It's a bustling tourist destination, and I can see why. The town offers a plethora of outdoor activities, from skiing and rafting to fishing, rock climbing, and backpacking. It boasts a charming downtown area with quaint shops and restaurants. Kate points out the town's hot springs, a popular attraction year-round. With its classic western vibe, Steamboat Springs offers a perfect storm for a thru-hiker's town vortex.

Our two-day break couldn't have come at a better time. My hip is strained from our road walking. My "town walk" is slow, wobbly, and-complete with a limp; I look like Fred Sanford, from the classic TV show *Sanford and Son*. We all have our own "town walks"; Pirate looks like a bowlegged broncobuster, which is perfect for a town where big ranch trucks and cowboy hats and boots are a common sight.

The next day, Kate gives Dan and me a tour of Big Agnes's repair shop. I'm not a gearhead, but the creative process of making and repairing sleeping pads and sleeping bags intrigues me. Plus, I've been having issues with my tent fly's zipper.

The shop is in a warehouse filled with parts, and its upper walls are adorned with various versions of sleeping pads, both past and present. It resembles an evolution chart, showcasing how designs have progressed over the years.

I'm impressed by this place. It has every piece of a tent you can imagine, down to the metal doohickey that goes in the thingamajig. They even have the plastic doodad that goes over the loopy clip. Did I mention that I'm not a gearhead?

I leave my tent fly with them, and they promise to do what they can before I head back onto the trail in a couple of days. When Dan and I meet up with Nature and Pirate, they tell us that they were looking for car wax. Nature concluded that car wax has repelled water off her car for years, so why not try it on a backpack?

This is both the most hilarious and the worst idea I have ever heard, and what makes it even more so is that Nature is as serious as a thru-hiker in search of an all-you-can-eat buffet. Car wax, of course, is not designed for fabric, but I don't mention this. Semantics aren't important right now—what matters is the comic relief that will come from her attempt. Nature boasts that, on other hiking expeditions, she's put her backpack through a car wash, and it came out remarkably clean. I think she's taking this waterproofing obsession to another level.

After our two zero days, it's time to return to the trail. Kate drives us back to the trailhead parking lot, and as soon as we step out of the SUV, mosquitoes converge as if they've been anticipating our arrival. The air is thick with them, and within moments, we're being attacked from all sides, their bites sharp and unrelenting.

"Have you heard of the Jam Boy?" Kate asks as she swats a mosquito dead on her arm.

"Yeah, that was Run DMC's DJ," I respond, "Oh wait, that's Jam Master Jay."

She explains that during the 1800s, when British nobility played golf in places such as Kenya and India—both part of the British Empire—they were accompanied by two individuals: the caddy and the Jam Boy. The primary role of the Jam Boy was to deter mosquitoes from bothering the golfers by coating himself with jam to attract the mosquitoes, diverting them from the players.

I eye the Brits up and down accusingly. “What do you have to say about that?”

“What? We didn’t do that!” Pirate says.

“That’s the problem. Where’s our Jam Boy, guys? You knew about this technique, but I see no Jam Boy. Wait, am I the Jam Boy?” I ask, wide-eyed.

An hour later, we find an open field perfect for four tents and decide to camp. However, as I’m staking down my tent fly, I feel tiny vampire bites all along my arm and neck. I can’t pitch my tent fast enough. Instead of fixing the zipper on my tent fly, the folks at Big Agnes had provided me with a bigger, yet lighter, one.

Bigger yet lighter—how is that even possible? It must be magic.

I’m thrilled with how spacious this new tent is at twenty-eight square feet. From inside, I watch a congregation of several hundred mosquitoes just on the other side of my screen but inside the tent fly. I hear a tiny voice saying, “Excuse me, do you have a moment to talk about our lord and savior, Bloodsuckius Maximus?”

Turns out, even mosquitoes have their recruitment spiel ready for unsuspecting hikers.

When morning comes, the mosquitoes continue their relentless assault. With a bug net over his head, a rain jacket on, and a rain cover on his pack, Pirate looks like a postapocalyptic beekeeper.

“These mosquitoes must be on some super serum or genetically modified somehow, ’cause they’re sipping my blood right through my long-sleeved shirt,” I complain. I don’t know if manufactured mosquitoes are a real thing, but I swear I saw a few of them with big mosquito biceps, arm wrestling.

We take our packs off for a quick break—quick because these malarial minions remain eager to torment us.

“Fab, you have a back full of those buzzers,” says Pirate.

I shake my shirt, and they fly right into my face.

“This is awful. I’m getting going again, to make it harder for them to settle on me,” I announce as I swing my backpack on.

Pirate follows closely behind me as we try to outpace the mosquitoes. “Along with the mosquitoes, the trail today has been steep, muddy, and rocky. It’s Colorado’s last trump card,” he announces.

We begin discussing the hierarchy of discomfort. It's close, but we'd barely take mosquitoes over the ordeal of being atop a Thirteener or Fourteener in a severe storm, enduring frozen and painful fingers followed by weeks of numbness. (I've only just begun to regain feeling in my fingers.)

Pirate's right; we're at the end of this state. With its frigid monsoon storms, Colorado mercilessly made up for the lack of water and rain in New Mexico. I wish both could have shared the precipitation more equally, instead of one being hotter than a jalapeño in a turtleneck and the other wetter than a Super Soaker fight at AT Trail Days.

We're about to enter Wyoming, which will surely have its own unique and forthcoming challenges. Just as I'm anticipating more outdoor adventures, I accidentally step on a butterfly. It fluttered beneath my shoe, its delicate wings meeting the earth unexpectedly.

I'm surprised, but not as surprised as I am when I'm instantly attacked by its family. There's something earthly wrong with being assaulted by butterflies, who are typically seen as embodying gentleness. It's like being targeted by fairies. The attack feels like a million tiny karate chops. It doesn't hurt physically, but my feelings are wounded. I run, only to feel one last roundhouse kick to the back of my earlobe.

Just before my AT journey, I spent a year living in Italy. There was a park in Milan with a butterfly house where you could stroll amid fluttering butterflies. My Italian friend Celeste, however, was petrified of them and adamantly refused to enter. At the time, I found her fear excessive, but now I can empathize.

I know it's silly, but I feel guilty, even though the butterfly dove right under my shoe. I couldn't feel worse if I were a time traveler who accidentally stepped on a butterfly and altered the course of history into some much darker future.

"The butterfly unalived itself, I swear," I say to no one in particular, though hoping it reaches the other butterflies' ears.

Do butterflies have ears?

Still, even with the butterflies' retaliation, I prefer a flutter of them than a swarm of mosquitoes. I'd coat my arm in nectar just to attract and try to befriend those butterflies and turn their spite into love. Then again, like the Jam Boy, I'd probably just end up attracting mosquitoes.

PART 3

WYOMING & IDAHO

CHAPTER 22

Changes—That's Just the Way It Is

PIRATE AND I are taken aback by the sound of a falcon chasing a duck. The falcon's wings slice through the air with incredible speed, generating a roaring, whooshing noise that sounds uncannily like a fighter plane. The sound reverberates through the surrounding trees, contrasting with the rustling of the leaves and the chirping of birds.

"Pirate, I thought a missile was about to land on us," I exclaim, bewildered and filled with wild thoughts.

I'm too young to die. I won't get to finish the CDT. I'll never know the ending of the Game of Thrones.

The sight and sound are both frightening and remarkable. I never imagined such a noise coming from a bird. I'm doubly amazed that the clever duck manages to escape by flying into a thicket of dense trees. It's quite the cunning getaway. Adding insult to injury, I hear the duck assert a victory quack just as the falcon pulls up and abandons its attack.

This day, my ninety-sixth on the trail, we're navigating the trail with the quickness and precision of Fastest Known Time (FKT) athletes, though we're certainly not setting any records. Perhaps the thrill of entering a new state is propelling our pace.

Things get interesting while crossing the Colorado-Wyoming border.

"Alright, there's a lot happening here," I remark.

Amid the dense spruce-fir-pine forest, we're at a relatively low 9,300 feet—modest compared to Colorado. We're nearing the end of the trail's loftiest sections. Perhaps the view before me marks the beginning of a different traverse altogether. Just off the trail to the left, a tree leans precariously at a sharp 70-degree angle, its weight hovering ominously over the trail. Passing it generates an instinctual urge to sprint. Long ago, someone pressed pause while the tree was falling, and it now exists frozen in time, anticipating the touch of the play button.

The half-fallen tree is decorated with a tin sign that reads:

WYOMING
STATE LINE

A foot below it is a plain white license plate that reads:

016 - ZWA
COLORADO

Tacked onto the flip side of the tree is another license plate with a blue sky, grass, and a silhouette of a cowboy on a bucking horse. This one reads:

4 [cowboy and horse] CDT
WYOMING

A small US stick flag is pinned behind it. To the right of the trail, there are white rocks arranged to spell out WYCO.

"What's a WYCO?" I start to ask, but then I notice a gap between the *Y* and *C*. *Ahh, it's the abbreviation for Wyoming and Colorado.* Just below it, spanning the trail, a line of fist-sized rocks marks the border. An upright two-foot log sits nearby, with a variety of colorful rocks scattered atop its flat surface. Two large rocks resemble salt lamps, while the smaller ones, about two dozen in total, resemble crystal gemstones. It's a setup reminiscent of a holistic healer's home.

I glance around, searching.

"Lose something, Fab?" Pirate interrupts.

"Yeah. Looks like someone stole the essential oils that should accompany this setup," I reply, brushing aside grass with my foot. "And what about the incense? This nature-mystic station is lacking. How about a crystal gazer?"

Pirate gives me a "you're speaking rubbish" look.

Perhaps, but imagine the novelty of having a Spanish fortune teller named Estrella del Bosque, Star in the Forest, at this border. Wouldn't that be a delight for thru-hikers? She could predict whether they'll complete the CDT, potentially saving them time, heartache, and money.

Although there's no palm reader in sight, we patiently wait for Dan and Nature, who decided to hike with the perpetually slow-moving Dan today—not to rush him, but to offer encouragement.

Pirate and I have seized the opportunity for a challenging, FKT-style blitz.

However, after an hour of waiting at the border with no sign of them—or a mystical trail prediction from Estrella del Bosque that I'll find love beneath a sycamore tree—we hike on for a few more miles.

After we set up camp, I mark an arrow in the dirt pointing toward our tents, positioned several yards off the trail. I add a neon-orange ribbon that I found earlier, tying it to a long branch that I position to lean halfway across their path.

Another hour later, from the confines of my tent, I hear their arrival. As Nature and Dan settle in, I can't shake the feeling that changes are on the horizon. With one and a half thru-hikes under my belt, I've learned to recognize the early signs of a tramily disbandment. A long-lasting thru-hiking group is a rare gift, requiring shared goals, mutual tolerance, and other factors to strengthen its bond. While difficult, the bond is not impossible to maintain. However, it may have become a challenge we're not equipped to overcome. This is a harsh realization to accept, but that's just the way it is.

The weather in Wyoming has been idyllic these last few July days. The skies are a brilliant shade of blue, with fluffy clouds dotting the horizon. It's a rare day on the CDT when I can comfortably wear a short-sleeved shirt and shorts in the morning. Plus, it's a relief to wake up to dry weather. It appears that once we entered Wyoming, the weather is in our favor.

We're in the Huston Park Wilderness, surrounded by lush green trees and thick grass that gives way to a narrow, impeccably manicured trail. Pirate and I once again find our rhythm. We've hit our stride, making the hike feel effortless, the ground itself propelling us forward.

It's Sunday. Usually I lose track of the days, like most thru-hikers do, except maybe on Sundays when the post office is closed. We try to synchronize our town arrivals with the post office's schedule so we can pick up our mail drop, but today, that won't be possible.

By 4:00 p.m., Pirate and I make it to Highway 70, just ten miles from the twin towns of Encampment and Riverside, where we plan to camp for the night. As I mentioned earlier, I've never been a fan of hitching a lift, not even on the AT. There are several reasons for my discomfort, some justified and others possibly stemming from insecurity. My appearance isn't that of your standard white hiker dude. I know it sounds irrational, but part of me believes it's true.

So, I sit on the brick base of the Battle Pass-Medicine Bow National Forest sign—named after a famous battle between fur trappers and Native Americans (Sioux, Cheyenne, and Arapaho warriors) in 1841—observing as Pirate makes a feeble attempt at hailing a ride. Thirty minutes later, Nature arrives and takes over, relieving Pirate of fruitless thumb-waving. Nature has a knack for stopping cars, especially when she hunches her shoulders and puts on her most sorrowful expression—it's usually a fail-safe act, but not today.

I finally decide to give it a try. It can't be any worse than their attempts.

"Let me show you guys how it's done," I boast half-heartedly.

I put on my backpack, doing it for show, to let drivers know I'm a hiker, not a serial killer needing a ride to his next murder scene. Strutting to the edge of the highway, I spot a car drawing near and stick my thumb out. A pickup truck approaches, and as it begins to pass, I make the prayer gesture with my hands, as if pleading. To my surprise, the truck slows to a stop. I glance back at my two amazed hiking partners with a look that says, "Now, that's how you do it."

The woman in the passenger seat rolls down her window. I thank them for stopping, explain that we're thru-hiking the CDT, and politely ask if they could give us a ride into town. The driver shakes his head no, but his wife says yes. He looks at her, mentioning they don't have room, as his fishing gear occupies the back seat. Without hesitation, she suggests moving the gear to the cargo bed. Reluctantly, he agrees, and together, he and I make room for the three of us.

Once settled, I apologize for my hiking companions' smell, partly to deflect any notions that it might be me. This sparks a friendly conversation with the truck owners, Mary and Tom. The couple is in their seventies, married longer than I've been alive. Judging by how Mary convinced Tom to stop and give us a ride, she's clearly the one in charge.

As they drop us off, I smile. I wonder how fortunate I would be if, at their distinguished age, I had someone who loved me enough to boss me around.

The following morning, we wake up at Lazy Acres Campground in Riverside and walk half a mile to the nearby town of Encampment to collect our mail drops. On our way, a car slows down, revealing Dan in the passenger seat. He's just arrived in town and appears sleep deprived. He says he'll catch us at the post office after returning from the store.

Dude's looking like the walking dead.

At the post office, thru-hikers line the exterior side wall, eagerly tearing into their resupply packages like it's Christmas in July. I head back inside and begin taping up a box of extra resupply items that Nature and I are sending to the post office at Rawlins, eighty-two miles farther north. Pirate comes over with a mournful expression. If he were a true pirate, I'd say he'd just found out his treasure map was written in invisible ink.

"Dan's staying a few days here. He's weak, tired, not feeling well again," he says, on the verge of tears.

I understand the implication. "Damn, that means you're staying as well."

"I really don't want to. You and I, we've been covering some great miles together," Pirate laments.

A thru-hiker who can maintain my pace and even improve it is hard to come by out here. Even so, Pirate must stay with Dan. No matter what happens on this trail, they came to this country together to accomplish something special. It's only right that they leave together.

"You should stay and look out for him. He's your closest mate," I reassure him.

He nods, looks down. I keep quiet, worried he might become overly emotional. Part of me wants to lighten the mood with a joke, like "Avast ye, we can't have a pirate blubberin' like a landlubber!" But instead, I just stand there—as Nature would point out, it's probably most sensible not to exacerbate Pirate's distress.

I find myself harboring a hint of resentment toward Dan. After all, we've repeatedly urged him to eat more and not skip meals to lose weight, which was one of his goals out here. At this moment, I know Dan needs his friend more than I do. Hopefully he'll confront whatever trail demons haunt him, just as I did on the first few days of hiking in the New Mexico desert.

Getting a ride back to the trail will be surprisingly effortless. A few blocks from the post office, Encampment built a bench at a street corner, resembling a bus stop, specifically for hikers needing a lift back to the trailhead. The locals are aware that if someone is sitting on the bench, they require transportation. I think it's a brilliant idea, one I hope more trail towns will adopt.

After Nature and I load our backpacks with enough resupply to get us to Rawlins, we bid farewell to Pirate and Dan. I grasp Dan's face like a don in a Mafia movie. "You gotta eat or you're not going to make it." He nods.

We leave them at the post office, unsure what their future on the trail looks like. Nature and I are more determined than ever to make it to the finish.

A few days later, Pirate unexpectedly catches up and regales us with an outrageous story. He was hiking along a road ahead of Dan. How far ahead? He couldn't tell because when he looked back, Dan was nowhere in sight. At one point, the driver of an SUV that had passed Pirate twice earlier returned, and the driver told him that, during his second pass, he hadn't seen the hiker Pirate was with, but there was nowhere else for Dan to have gone. Pirate jumped into the SUV to help search for his missing partner.

As they drove slowly, scanning beyond the shoulder, they spotted Dan emerging from behind a bush. He had decided to take a break, feeling exhausted, and ended up falling asleep.

I wonder how many times Dan has napped like this, and if this is merely the first instance of getting caught. It could explain why he often arrived at camp three hours after everyone else, and sometimes not at all.

"This is bonkers. Ask Dan to come see us," I exclaim, eager to assess his condition firsthand.

Minutes later, Dan arrives, and I'm stunned. He's hunched over, resembling Nature's exaggerated weary posture when she's trying to hitch a ride. He shuffles past and sinks into a chair. His movements seem strained, reminiscent of a patient in rehabilitation who's gradually relearning to use his limbs. If hopelessness and demoralization had a face, Dan wears it like a well-fitted mask.

He greets us with a slow nod, his face a mix of sadness, exhaustion, and perhaps hunger; my guess is all three. His gloomy, detached demeanor, combined with his gaunt face, gives him a grandfatherly appearance.

I want to inject some humor, but I doubt it will lighten the mood.

So, Dan, were you with Winnie-the-Pooh in the Hundred Acre Wood? Sleeping in a makeshift dwelling of branches, leaves, and twigs?

Nature expresses her concerns about Dan's health, but I'm weary of repeating those sentiments, as it seems he never really hears what we're saying anyway. Instead, I take a different approach. I tell him that it will be challenging for us to continue hiking together. At this stage of our thru-hike, maintaining a steady pace is crucial; otherwise, we won't finish before the first snowstorm hits, which is usually in September.

I dislike how I sound because Dan is a good guy and a good friend, but it's July 21, and at this point in our journey—over 1,600 miles into the 3,100—certain realities can't be ignored.

Dan doesn't respond. I continue my tough-love approach, explaining that he really can't keep hiking the way he has been in his current condition. He nods. With a motion of his hand as if pushing the words out, he finally says, "Well, I understand, but I'm determined to finish this."

I'm not certain what it is—definitely not his past actions—but these words resonate with me. He could have made excuses or expressed a meager willingness to try, but instead, he's determined. I believe he will manage it. I consider suggesting my friends purchase winter clothes but hesitate, fearing it might sound pessimistic regarding their chances of finishing before snow flies. Besides, I'm rooting for both Dan and Pirate, my Fab Fam, to make it all the way.

As they leave, we part ways with enough memories to fill a book. Although I'm no longer hiking with the Brits, something tells me it won't be the last time our paths will cross. However, until then, I have my own challenge to tackle.

CHAPTER 23

Another Twenty-Four-Hour Challenge

DURING MY AT hike, I attempted a Quad State Challenge—hiking through four states in twenty-four hours, covering approximately forty-three miles. I ticked all four states, but took more than twenty-four hours, and I resolved never again to subject my mind or body to such an ordeal. Yet now I'm contemplating another twenty-four-hour challenge: this time blasting through the Great Divide Basin in Wyoming as quickly as possible.

The CDT runs through the basin for 120 miles, beginning in Rawlins and ending in South Pass City. It's a vast, arid expanse characterized by sagebrush plains, sand dunes, and alkali flats. In other words, it's another flippin' desert. Just thinking about this upcoming stretch of trail takes my mind back to the harrowing first days in New Mexico. I adamantly refuse to revisit those parched, agonizing times, and even Nature balks at the thought of hiking the basin.

"I won't do it. I'll cycle the surrounding roads or, better yet, ride a horse across it, but hiking through that desert is not what I'm doing," she declares.

"So, if conditions are favorable, you might reconsider hiking it?" I sarcastically inquire.

"Absolutely not. I'd sooner bypass the entire stretch."

I nod. I'm also seeking a solution that doesn't entail enduring the relentless sun beating down on me like an MMA fighter's fists.

A couple of days ago, after leaving Encampment, we came across Fuego and Master Chef—the Czech couple who'd helped Nature during the storm in Colorado—taking a break sitting on a log by the trail. Fuego rolled a cigarette, which struck me as incongruous. It seemed akin to a vegan indulging in crack cocaine—an unexpected action in an otherwise goal-oriented and healthy pursuit. But as they say, "different strokes for different folks," or as I like to say, "different tales for different trails."

Master Chef squeezed a tube of what looked like toothpaste onto dried apricots. It turned out to be salted caramel peanut butter.

"Would you like some?" she offered.

"Ah, sure, I'm intrigued," I replied.

She handed me an apricot generously coated in the mixture. I took a bite.

"So, what do you think?" She awaited my critique wide-eyed, as if I were a food critic with the power to award a Michelin star.

"Woo, now I see why they call you Master Chef!" I exclaimed with sincerity. It was delicious.

We discussed the upcoming Great Divide Basin, and they described their plan for a twenty-four-hour nonstop hike to cover as much ground as possible, minimizing their time in the desert during the hottest periods of the day.

The figurative bulb lit over my head, but I could sense Nature's reluctance.

"Mind if I join you?" I asked the Czechs. Maybe this time the twenty-four-hour challenge would be easier, driven more by necessity than pride.

Nature and I hike with the Czechs for the next two days. The first turned into an unexpected thirty-mile trek, the most miles Nature and I had covered in a single day so far. On the second day, we managed the sixteen miles into Rawlins before 2:00 p.m. That gave us the rest of yesterday and most of today to chill before Fuego, Master Chef, and I set off.

There are many hikers in town, and to save money, Nature and I share a motel room, which becomes a hub for our prep work and planning—which is simply to hike, take coffee breaks, and repeat for twenty-four hours. The Czechs and I will cover as many miles as possible this evening, throughout the night, and into tomorrow morning, then take it easy during the peak sun hours, hiking more slowly during the worst of the heat. Meanwhile, Nature will hitch a ride or catch a rideshare to Riverton—the only town with a rental-car outfit—and then pick us up at a designated trailhead to drive us to Lander, the next CDT town, for our well-deserved rest.

I've learned never to underestimate potential challenges, especially ones as strenuous as this. However, if we stick to the plan and stay healthy, much like a championship football team, we should reach our destination with minimal issues and a sense of victory—no trophy, but it will certainly feel like we've won the Super Bowl.

At 5:11 p.m., Fuego, Master Chef, and I stand by a blue, two-by-two-foot CDT logo painted on the sidewalk at the corner of Third Street and West Cedar Street. The CDT passes through Rawlins, following Third Street, which turns into Highway 267 as it leaves town. After three miles, the CDT veers left onto a dirt road in a vast, open field, moving away from the highway and eventually running parallel to it for twelve miles. We can see the trail, worn into the ground by car tracks, weaving through sagebrush for miles ahead of us.

We are all smiles and feeling confident. When I tackled the Quad State Challenge on the AT, my pack weighed over forty pounds and contained five books. Today, my load is light. I left everything except my sleeping bag and a day's worth of food with Nature.

After four hours of hiking, covering a little over twelve miles, we take our first break as a golden hue in the sky follows the sun behind the horizon. We rest next to a wood-fenced pool of water, beside a solar panel. Night slowly swallows us in a grayish gloom. We're in good spirits as we retrieve our headlamps and sip coffee; I'm willing to exceed my daily single cup, knowing caffeine will play a significant role in helping us achieve our goal.

The Czechs have longer strides than I do, covering more ground effortlessly and without stumbling over sagebrush like I do. Someone on social media enlightened me about how big sagebrush boasts at least a nine-foot taproot and nine-foot lateral roots. This explains why the bushes don't budge when I accidentally kick them; instead, I'm the one sent flying. And, when I'm not tripping over the sagebrush, they are pecking at my ankles, as I can't seem to avoid scraping against them.

For the last hour, I've found myself in the middle of our conga line, with Fuego leading and Master Chef behind me. While I don't mind her position at the rear—she'll be the first victim in any potential wolf attack, as they often target a group's trailing member—a part of me prefers her in front of me so I can chivalrously cover the rear. After she declines a few of my offers, she finally admits that it's safer if I stay ahead of her.

"Hmm? Ohhh," I finally grasp her meaning and laugh, finding it amusing to hear a woman openly acknowledge flatulence.

"I started the trail behaving like a nice, young lady, and I'll probably end up acting like an old truck driver," she remarks, prompting another laugh from me.

"It's a reality," she adds.

Fuego chimes in, "I used to be a truck driver, so I know exactly what she means."

"This is a good strategy, MC. It will repel any threats lurking in the dark behind us," I point out.

"Yes. This truck driver will keep blowing her air horn," she jests.

Speaking of trucks, as the trail merges back onto Highway 287, Fuego suggests we continue walking in single file, with the people at the front and rear turning on their headlamps' red night-vision lights, while the person in the middle keeps their regular bright light on. Although we'll only be on this road for less than a mile, it's better to err on the side of caution. This wouldn't be a concern on the well-lit Brooklyn–Queens Expressway, but here in the middle of nowhere, the freeway is pitch black, with only the headlights of approaching cars and semitrucks piercing the darkness.

"It's 11:11. Make a wish," I announce. I'm guessing we harbor the same wish, to complete this challenge unscathed.

We're soon back on the desert dirt, six hours in, with a little over sixteen miles completed. The sky above us is filled with sparkling stars, but no moon yet.

We break at 1:11 a.m., eight hours and 22.2 miles in, to go for our second round of coffee.

Around 2:00 a.m., I glance behind me and finally spot the moon just above the dark horizon. It's not quite the full moon of my first night hike here on the CDT; we missed it by a few days. Nevertheless, the waning gibbous shines brightly, casting a pale light that outlines the darkened mountains just below it.

"Thanks for showing up, moon," I remark.

We lose the trail and find ourselves in a barren expanse of dried, cracked terrain, parched from a lack of water. Unfortunately, it's not devoid of that damn sagebrush, which continues to scrape against my legs and get caught in my socks. We try to navigate around the bushes, but they persistently jab at our legs.

At hour nine, Master Chef mentions that seventy-six miles would be the most she and Fuego have ever hiked in a push. They attempted it on the PCT and fell short, so she would be remiss if she didn't seize this opportunity. I'm game, but with only 24.2 miles completed, I doubt we will reach that goal. Nonetheless, we forge ahead.

Sometime before our 4:00 a.m. coffee break, a coyote scare interrupts us. Fuego and MC need water, so we approach Bull Springs—a fenced-in cistern right by Bulls Creek and the trail. We hear angry barking. We pause as the sound draws closer.

"It sounds like it's coming from over there." I point toward a low rock ridge. "I don't need water, so I'll keep an eye out."

The adventurer in me feels a primal thrill. Having my hiking companions rush to get desperately needed water while potential danger approaches and I'm their defense is like something out of a wilderness thriller. I'm sure trekking poles weren't designed to be weapons, but here I am, holding one across my shoulder like a broadsword.

I strain my ears in the direction of the coyote's sharp, high-pitched bark. The rapid "yip-yip-yip" grows closer. A slight howl follows short, yapping barks that rise and fall in pitch, echoing through the night. It's eerie. Although it sounds like just one coyote, I'm wary, wondering if I can fend it off with my trekking poles and my own sharp, high-pitched screams. The darkness just beyond my headlamp makes the situation even more frightening, and my overactive imagination conjures up a slavering pack of wild animals just waiting to pounce from the shadows.

"Almost done, guys?" I say, keeping my eyes fixed on the direction of the approaching bark.

"Done. Let's go," says Master Chef.

We had planned to take our break by the water source, but the coyote's presence convinces us to hike another mile or two. Although I didn't catch sight of the animal, I'm sure it was just a few yards from us, trying to intimidate us away from its territory, its offspring, or the water source.

"No, I didn't soil my pants. Just in case you were curious, Master Chef," I jest.

"Well, it smells like it," she retorts with a laugh.

"Aww snap. Guess I'll take the rear this time," I say, simultaneously reminding my hiking companions not to leave me behind with their long strides.

"I feel like a robot," Master Chef remarks when I check in on her.

"Yeah, I agree." I feel similarly mechanical, as if guided by some external force. It's 5:11 a.m., and the night sky has begun to give way to pink and orange morning hues—punctuated by the crowing of a rooster. We pause and exchange a look that says, "There's a rooster in the desert?"

We're twelve hours and 31.8 miles into the challenge, and we certainly lack the optimistic energy we had during our first hour. We hike along a rutted dirt road surrounded by a sea of sagebrush. The road stretches endlessly into the distance, disappearing into the horizon like a vanishing point on a canvas.

As Master Chef puts on her pink, oversized sunglasses, she mentions that they help conceal the effects of a night spent partying. I chuckle, noting that hiking all night does make her look like she's been at some wild social gathering.

"I have to look good because everything below the neck just feels numb," she half jokes.

We all feel weary, and Master Chef shows signs of struggle. To alleviate her knee pain, she has improvised by compressing one knee with a tied shirt and the other with her multifunctional headwear.

By 9:11 a.m., sixteen hours into what now feels like an audacious challenge, we're approaching a marked water source. With 42.4 miles covered, it's the most I've hiked in a single day. Despite the looming heat and the risk of dehydration, I indulge in another cup of coffee for the caffeine boost. I assure myself that before leaving the cattle trough, where we're filling our bottles, I'll drink plenty of water to offset the coffee's diuretic effects.

Truth be told, coffee and chocolate have me feeling pretty good. Still, the next two hours yield only 2.4 miles due to the extended coffee break. We regain a better pace by 1:11 p.m., twenty hours in, and we near the fifty-mile mark. Master Chef shares that she's hot, sore, and definitely not feeling sexy. I concur, as any semblance of glamour melted away two hours ago.

"My soles are melting, and I'm tired and hungry," shares Fuego.

By hour twenty-one, I'm utterly exhausted, and my thoughts are starting to blur. I'm pretty sure I just saw a cactus wink at me, and I might have been arguing with a rock about directions for the last five minutes.

As another hour passes under the desert sun, we reach 54.4 miles. The terrain hasn't changed; we're still on a dirt road amid endless sagebrush. With two hours remaining, we are still 21.6 miles short of Master Chef's seventy-six-mile goal. At our current pace, we'll require at least seven more hours to reach mile 76, but it's more likely to take us ten, which isn't feasible in our condition. Before we started this challenge, we agreed that if one of us needed to tap out, we would all tap out. Just before hour twenty-two, I text Nature, who picks us up at Crooks Gap Road near Jeffrey City—sixty miles south of Lander—where the CDT crosses before turning back into open land.

Master Chef later tells me that she has hiker's rash, also known as exercise-induced vasculitis, golfer's rash, and golfer's vasculitis. This skin condition stems from a combination of factors including heat, pressure, and friction during long periods of walking or hiking, perhaps exacerbated by repetitive motion and the compression of blood vessels in the legs. Hiker's rash is generally harmless and tends to resolve on its own within a few days or weeks. Master Chef's symptoms started at mile thirty-five, but she pushed on, hoping that, somehow, we could hike for twenty-four hours. It was wise that she acknowledged her limits instead of risking an injury that may have permanently derailed her thru-hike.

Personally, I am proud of the miles we tackled, shaving off nearly half of a section I dreaded. However, mark my words, this will be the last twenty-four-hour hike I'll ever do . . . on this trail.

Fuego and I hit the trail again at 8:00 p.m. for a short night hike, while Master Chef remains in Lander to recover. Nature dropped us off at Crooks Gap Road at the spot where she picked us up yesterday. We'll see her and Master Chef in Lander in a couple of days.

We hike a few hours, covering another 10.8 miles by 12:30 a.m. After passing a herd of grazing cows—somewhat eerie in the dark—we find a suitable camping spot just off the trail, the only area free from clusters of sagebrush. There are just fifty-five miles remaining of the 120-mile Great Divide Basin.

The next day, we find ourselves once again on a dirt road carved through the sagebrush. Despite the harsh desert surroundings, the sagebrush retains its aesthetic appeal. The sky, chalked with clouds, offers a glimmer of hope that we won't be scorched alive.

I have a love-hate relationship with hiking in such expansive landscapes, where the view stretches for miles in every direction, unobstructed by trees, boulders, or mountains. It's breathtaking, yet when nature calls and I need privacy, there's nowhere to hide. I become a spectacle for any fellow hikers—and fauna—with keen eyesight.

I've had the experience of relieving myself in front of cows. They hardly seem to notice, but I glance nervously from one to the next, half expecting them to nudge me over with their massive heads—karmic retribution for centuries of cow tipping by mischievous human pranksters.

Still, I'm at my breaking point, on the verge of dropping my backpack and pants right here on the trail. That's how desperate I am after holding it in, hoping to find some cover. Just as I assure Fuego I'll catch up and to please keep moving, I spot a car door lying randomly on the desert floor, just yards from the trail. I realize I can use it as a visual barrier to shield me from anyone approaching from behind—a rare eventuality, but it still makes me feel better. I veer toward the door, toss my pack aside, scoop out a cathole, pull my pants down, and squat. I lean against the car door as if I were cruising down the road, arm out the window.

My mind conjures up a car horn blaring behind me and someone shouting, "Hey, the light's green, let's go!"

In response, I holler back, "Hey, I'm poopin' here! I'm poopin' here!" I put on my best New York accent, while pounding the outside of the car door with my hand. I nearly fall backward reenacting the iconic scene from *Midnight Cowboy.*

The desert sun has me acting a fool. I couldn't care less, but I'm grateful that no one wandered up the trail and caught me and my bare bottom arguing with an invisible antagonist. It would be difficult to explain, unless they already knew who Ratso Rizzo was.

By midday, as Fuego and I collect water from a cache right off the trail—the best trail magic for the desert—a hiker joins us. I recognize Chee Mack under a white sun runner cap. Fuego has hiked with him, and I've spotted him in a few towns. He's about five feet eight, of Asian descent, and sports a gray goatee, though he looks to be only in his thirties. He exudes a calm, humble, and serene presence, so much so that I tried giving him the trail name Chi Monk, but he wasn't convinced.

He shares that he unknowingly camped by a cow's corpse the night before, and I realize I saw that cow earlier in the day, but assumed it was just resting. I comment that Chee Mack is fortunate this isn't grizzly country, as it could have been a horrific night—grizzly bears are territorial and aggressive, especially when protecting their food. We talk about the incident of a woman recently attacked by a grizzly on a different trail because she was too close to its food.

The fortuitous thru-hiker accompanies us for the remainder of the day. Fuego and Chee Mack forge ahead; Fuego's long strides carry him effortlessly, while Chee Mack, despite his shorter stature, moves with remarkable speed. It's one thing to hike quickly while appearing to be exerting extra effort, but quite another to resemble Yoda, seemingly moving slowly yet actually swiftly navigating the trail, as if harnessing the Force.

The sky begins to darken, signaling an approaching storm—out here, I welcome the rain over the relentless dry heat. As the dirt road winds down into a valley, I spot Fuego and Chee Mack chatting near a tent pitched close to the trail. Blister, a fellow CDT thru-hiker from the Netherlands, is sitting inside the tent. Lanky, with a scruffy blond beard and an easygoing demeanor, he shares that he covered thirty miles yesterday and another thirty today, leaving him thoroughly exhausted. With the foreboding clouds looming overhead, he's decided to call it a day. Despite his fatigue, he maintains a buoyant demeanor and offers an enthusiastic "Go get it" fist bump in a gesture of camaraderie.

We press on for a few more miles as the crimson sunset sky is overtaken by ominous clouds. After covering 35.5 miles, Fuego and I decide to make camp alongside the dirt road. Chee Mack, undeterred by the approaching storm, continues. He's less than two miles from reaching forty miles in a day. It's a feat he's never accomplished, and it's within his grasp.

"So true. Enjoy it, whether wet or dry, but mostly untouched by lightning" is my parting wish for him.

As Fuego and I set up camp, we're transfixed by the battle unfolding between the fiery rays of the setting sun and the darkness of the encroaching clouds. It's eerie, exhilarating, and breathtaking. As the rain begins, I glimpse drops raising tiny bursts of dust as they strike the parched ground. The rain hammers against my tent in a steady, unyielding rhythm, pelting the sagebrush with sharp cracks.

Just as suddenly as the storm began, it's over, the threat having lasted far longer than the actual assault.

Morning arrives, and Fuego and I are up and ready for the next nineteen miles to South Pass City, a historic mining town and former stop on the Oregon Trail. During the mid-nineteenth-century gold rush, it drew thousands of prospectors. Today, it stands as a well-preserved ghost town/museum, and a popular tourist destination providing a window into the Wild West.

The trail leads directly through town, and we wander down the immaculately preserved streets, feeling as though we've stepped onto the set of a spaghetti western. Some of the original buildings are remarkably well restored, including small log cabins, the Carissa Saloon, the Exchange Bank, the South Pass Hotel, and a general store stocked with replica food props—we've hiked into the distant past instead of just nineteen miles closer to our destination.

I'm thrilled to leave the desert section of the Wind River Range behind us. It's also remarkable to think that I now consider nineteen miles a short day, whereas just a month ago, it would have been a full day's hike. Like anything in life, repetition breeds improvement.

I collect a resupply package at the historic general store. We had hoped to catch a ride from here, but there are no tourists around. Instead, we hike three more miles to Highway 28 and manage to hitch a thirty-five-mile ride back to Lander, where we take a well-deserved day off.

Fuego and I covered 120 miles of desert in a total of three hiking days, much of it at night or under a cloudy sky. Although my feet are currently swollen and protesting every one of those steps, I'd say our boldness paid off, mollifying the prolonged inferno we would have otherwise experienced. I hold on to that reasoning as I rub my feet, which now resemble overstuffed pillows.

CHAPTER 24

Blowdowns and Puddles and Poop . . . Oh My!

NATURE AND I leave Lander earlier than the Czechs and Chee Mack, but 10:00 a.m. is still a late start for us. We stand by a grassy area at Antelope Park right on East Main Street, which turns into Highway 28, leading directly to the trailhead where we left off. A nice nurse pulls over and offers us a ride, but not all the way; she needs to make a turn to Interstate 287. Since we've already been waiting for an hour, we take the offer.

"Hey, it's ten miles closer than we were an hour ago," I say as we position ourselves at our drop-off spot for another expected long wait.

We're at the edge of the Great Divide Basin, and the temperature is already well into the eighties. A gooseneck flatbed trailer parked by a large pull-off offers me partial shade as I rest, watching Nature thumb at passing cars. When one finally pulls up, I step out of the shade, but the driver says he thought only one person needed a ride, and he doesn't have room for two hikers and two backpacks. He's not lying—his back seat is packed with clothes boxes and other junk. This guy might be living in his car.

"Go ahead, Nature. No sense in the both of us being out here all day in this heat," I say with all sincerity, though I'm not thrilled about being out here alone. Again, I truly dislike hitchhiking.

"Are you sure?" Nature says. She doesn't want to leave me, but she doesn't want to be out here begging for a ride either.

"Go," I say, and turn away, not giving her a chance to think it over. I know she'd rather be hiking right now—heck, she would have liked to be on the trail five hours ago. I hear the car door slam; I look back to see the car racing off to what I'm hoping is the CDT trailhead.

Man, I hope she doesn't get abducted.

Surprisingly, it doesn't take me long to hitch a ride after that. As I'm dropped off at the trailhead, I catch sight of Nature walking toward me from farther past the trailhead, as if her driver had missed her stop.

"Hey, what happened?" I ask, confused.

"Damned guy kept going."

"At least he didn't murder you. That's something," I jest.

"Yeah, I was ready. I go with intuition, and that guy had bad vibes. He was in his own world and didn't talk, but there was something off. When he passed the trailhead, I thought, 'Here we go—this is where it's going to happen.'"

"Yeah, I totally thought you were a goner," I coolly exclaim.

"Thanks, Fab."

We acknowledge that successfully and safely hitchhiking our way here sets a positive tone for the day. Despite it being nearly noon, we opt to pace ourselves, ensuring a relaxed day. We reach our campsite by 6:30 p.m., having covered a mellow thirteen miles, mostly all flat terrain.

According to other thru-hikers and the guide app, we're close to entering grizzly country, which makes sense—there are plenty of trees for them to hide behind before pouncing on unsuspecting thru-hikers. With that in mind, we decide it's time to start our first bear bagging of the thru-hike.

Nature, who claims her tossing skills are terrible, finds a sturdy tree with a suitable branch about fifteen feet off the ground. She clips some paracord to a small zipper pouch it was stored in, adds a rock, and with a flick of her wrist, sends the cord sailing over the branch.

"You got it, first try." I'm impressed.

"Sweet. I can't believe that happened." She grabs the pouch, unzips it, and removes the rock.

We attach our bear-resistant food sack—a durable, puncture-proof fabric, often made of high-density polyethylene or Kevlar, designed to withstand a bear's efforts to tear or chew through it—to the carabiner, then hoist our food bags about twelve feet off the ground and a good six feet from the tree trunk. Once the bag is safely suspended, we tie the pulling end of the paracord to another tree, double-checking to ensure it won't come loose.

Although we're confident that this area, so close to the Great Basin Divide, won't have curious bears prowling in the night, it's smart to start the habit of bear bagging now so it becomes routine.

As we settle in, Nature mentions that we'll likely encounter quite a few blowdowns tomorrow on the Cirque of the Towers Alternate, which leads to the cirque itself.

"Of course we will. We don't want to start thinking this trail is getting any easier," I quip.

Everyone has been raving about the Cirque of the Towers, and I must confess, I had no clue what they were talking about. Given that the only "cirque" this Brooklynite was familiar with was the Cirque du Soleil, I immediately conjured images of mesmerizing acrobatics, artistic performances, and theatrical spectacles. However, this cirque refers to a bowl-shaped depression at the head of a glacier, formed by glacial erosion. It's typically surrounded by steep cliffs on three sides and often contains a small lake known as a tarn.

"So, there's no aerial silk performance?" I ask Nature from inside my tent.

"Nope, but it's beautiful. You'll love it," she replies.

The next day, our first fourteen miles unfold as smoothly as we could hope. The trail is far more level than the steep climbs we faced in Colorado.

We reunite with Master Chef, Fuego, and Chee Mack, who manage to catch up with us after leaving Lander yesterday afternoon, and we all hike together. Just before we reach the junction for the Cirque of the Towers Alternate, we climb a ridge and pass through a few pine trees. From here, we can look down at Little Sandy Lake—which is anything but "little"—cradled by the gray mountains that form the Wind River Range.

On the alternate route, we are surrounded by thick pine trees, and as Nature predicted, we begin to encounter an endless array of blowdowns. I can't locate the trail amid the tangle, which resembles a colossal game of pickup sticks.

Navigating under fallen trees isn't a problem—I can limbo with the best contortionists out there. However, going over them is a different story. I often end up scraping my legs or bumping my knees, especially when I'm just about to clear the obstacle with my other leg. I'm not sure if it's because I get lazy, overconfident, or simply forget to lift my trailing leg high enough.

Rain starts to fall just as our Ninja Warrior course gets underway. We take shelter under trees, joined by Princess Ann, a seventy-five-year-old solo hiker. She's section-hiking this area and seems to be relieved to have some company. Once the rain lets up, we resume hiking cautiously, with the fallen trees now wet. The ground is soggy, and the boulders we scramble up are slick.

Despite our slow pace, Princess Ann soon falls behind. I tell Master Chef and Fuego to continue ahead; Chee Mack, with his supernatural speed, has been farther ahead for hours. Nature and I stay with Princess Ann, realizing that reaching camp before dark is unlikely. To our concern, our companion eventually decides that the remaining three miles are too much. Nature and I help find her a suitable spot to camp by a flat stone surface, with a dirt patch that's clear of blowdowns where she can pitch her tent. After sharing some of our water, Nature and I wish her well.

"I'm uneasy about leaving her on her own," I confide in Nature as we reluctantly continue hiking.

"This isn't her first hike," Nature reasons. "She knew what she was getting into. Although, I can't believe her family wouldn't be concerned about her doing this alone at her age. Either way, I'm sure she'll be fine."

"Yeah, I suppose, but still . . . "

The blowdowns gradually lessen. Nature and I navigate around pools of water and find ourselves on a grassy trail with a wide, shallow stream to our right. Across the stream stand beautiful granitic mountains, while a pine-covered rock hill stands tall to our left. The trail hugs closely to the left, with the stream meandering alongside us, at times drawing nearer and then drifting away.

It's a striking view, but with the day wearing on, I steal only a moment to soak it all in. Avoiding hiking in darkness takes precedence—limited visibility in this complex terrain will only compound the difficulty. With less than a mile remaining to our friends, the path veers uphill. There's no defined trail here; instead, we traverse rocky terrain with patches of grass sprouting amid the rocks. Small streams intersect our route, slender like veins. According to the app, our destination lies beyond and to the right of a distant but visible boulder.

I spot Master Chef and Fuego near the summit by the boulder.

"Woot woot!" I cheer.

They glance down and respond with a cheerful call of their own.

Nature is quiet, her head bowed in concentration. I can sense her weariness mingled with fierce determination, her resolute spirit driving her up this final ascent.

Our campsite nestles amid a stunning panorama of rugged peaks. I gaze up at the majestic amphitheater of mountains, adorned with patches of snow. Despite the ground being strewn with rockfalls of various sizes, from small to boulder sized, there is ample space to pitch our tents.

To our surprise, Pirate and Dan are also here.

"Missed you, dude," I say to Pirate as we hug.

"Missed you too, Fab."

I turn to Dan, and go for a hug, "You too, Dan. Love you, brotha."

"Love you too, Fab," he replies.

Got 'em!

I look over at Nature, who has taken off her pack and walked over to lean on a flat boulder. She seems utterly spent, so she must have missed my winning of our love bet. It's unfortunate, because she's not going to believe me. C'est la vie.

We set up camp in a state of weariness. I prepare dinner with Master Chef, Fuego, and Chee Mack. Nature is so depleted that she either doesn't feel hungry or lacks the strength to eat. When I ask if she's joining us for dinner, she replies that she's going straight to sleep. I understand her fatigue; I, too, am eager to rest, but I hesitate to skip a meal, especially after such a strenuous day. I know I'll feel it tomorrow if I do.

The next morning, we all hike out of the glacial valley at different times but agree to meet at Sheep Creek, a lake-view camp area twenty miles from here. Chee Mack sets off by 5:00 a.m. Dan and Pirate camped up higher at a lake, which isn't visible from our campsite, but I overheard them telling Nature that they intended to start late. Nature starts her ascent as I start dismantling my tent. She prefers hiking alone when climbing mountains, since she believes she needs a head start since she's slower on inclines. I attempt to keep track of her against the gray rock of the mountain, but she eludes my sight.

"There she is," says Master Chef, pointing upward at the rocky expanse.

"Oh, yeah, there she is," I gesture in the same direction, though truthfully, I don't see her.

Master Chef, Fuego, and I depart about an hour after Nature, who I figure must be up and over the peak by now. The ascent doesn't take us long. After hiking less than two miles, we descend to Temple Lake, on the northern side of the mountain, and take a break on a flat boulder facing the lake. The Czechs appreciate their breaks, and I don't mind them either; they remind me of my time with Doctor Faust.

After twenty minutes, we continue, and just when I thought we might have a rain-free day, it starts raining. We shelter under a tree. Waiting out the rain is another habit of the Czechs, while I know that Nature hikes through it when she's alone. I don't anticipate catching up to her or Chee Mack anytime soon.

We resume after forty-five minutes. As we continue climbing along the Wind River Range, the sky threatens to open again, with dark clouds hovering over the towering granite spires before us. I glance down at a small lake.

"See that lake over there?" I say to Master Chef.

"Yeah."

"Well, it was just a puddle two days ago, but with all this damn rain, it's bound to keep growing until it fills the valley and spills off the mountains," I joke.

We're drenched from head to toe. I'm not thrilled about hiking in wet socks, but there's no avoiding it, so why not embellish a bit?

"*Bez práce nejsou koláče,*" says Master Chef.

I turn back to face her, and she explains, "It's a Czech saying: 'There are no pies without work, no successes without effort.'"

There's no pie in Pie Town either, I want to add, but don't.

"Ah, like no pain, no gain," I say instead.

Nothing ventured, nothing gained is another equivalent. Either saying is apt, especially here on the CDT. Completing this challenging endeavor demands both effort and a strong will.

Another Czech phrase she keeps saying to Fuego is *Jsi dobrý?*, which means "Are you good?" Or just *Dobrý?*, meaning "Good?"

I start asking them how they're doing about every ten minutes. I've just gained a superpower.

"Fuego, dobrý?" I ask, looking up at Fuego as he continues to climb.

I don't hear his answer, so I look behind to Master Chef and say, "Master Chef, dobrý?"

"Dobrý," she says with a thumbs-up.

Around 3:00 p.m., we top out on a ten-thousand-plus-foot pass and read the name proudly proclaimed by a big wooden trail sign.

"Jackass Pass. Yup, that pretty much sums it up," I quip, out of breath.

Jackass Pass, where the vistas are stunning and the name of the landmark—well, it speaks for itself. After all, what could be more fitting than naming a pass after the arduous experience of hauling gear up a steep ascent, feeling every bit like a stubborn pack mule?

We still have ten miles to go to camp, and as we begin our descent into the Cirque of the Towers, the landscape unfolds in breathtaking splendor. Towering granite peaks pierce the sky, their jagged edges framing the horizon like ancient sentinels. The air is crisp and invigorating, carrying the scent of pine and wildflowers.

Lonesome Lake, in the heart of the cirque, shimmers below like shards of turquoise glass, reflecting the clouds above. The surrounding pine trees, dark green in color, have settled as close as they can get to the lake, seeking hydration.

Clusters of evergreen carpet the meadows, which are dotted with granite boulders. Streams cascade from the snowcapped peaks, carving intricate patterns into the rocky landscape. Down and left, a waterfall sits in the center of a long slab that resembles a dam. As we traverse the trail, I glimpse playful marmots darting between boulders.

So, this is the Cirque of the Towers.

What a sight! It's like stepping into some long-forgotten realm that holds thousands of years of secrets. We descend, traversing part of Lonesome Lake over boulders, the scenery just as alluring up close as from above.

It's no surprise that we must ascend out of the valley, and we begin to climb again. This side is noticeably busier, featuring a grassier terrain speckled with red and white wildflowers. Zigzagging up, we cross streams rushing like liquid ribbons over stair-stepped rocks. I enjoy the dynamic nature of watching my footfalls, navigating around boulders, and finding ways to avoid hiking on the patches of snow I always seem to encounter. It's a welcome change from hiking straight up a plain trail and solely focusing on the exertion needed to keep going.

Fuego leads the way, with Master Chef bringing up the rear. It's been the same climbing formation all day. Fuego prefers to navigate, a role I gladly relinquish. Master Chef struggles with the climbs, so she trails a few hundred feet behind me.

By 7:30 p.m., the landscape has leveled out, and the jagged granite pinnacles now surround us. Despite still being four miles from our intended campsite, we're depleted. The rain throughout the day had eased off at opportune moments, allowing us to appreciate the scenery, but not enough to keep us dry. But like beggars, thru-hikers can't be choosers.

We finally make it back to the CDT, and a man on horseback passes by, leading two other horses. He politely asks the three of us to stand on the same side of the trail to avoid startling the horses.

Approaching dark clouds and thunder prompt a change of camping plans. Instead of going on to the campsite we planned, the three of us hurriedly set up our tents near a small lake just before the rain pours down.

The next day around 1:00 p.m., we arrive in the cowboy/outfitter town of Pinedale and reunite with Nature and Chee Mack. After a rejuvenating night's sleep and a refreshing shower, we collect our resupply packages from the post office. Following our immersion in the town vortex, we casually set off again around 5:00 p.m., having hitched a ride back to the trail from a hiker known as Golden.

The CDT has its fair share of animal droppings, with none more prevalent than flat cow dung. In New Mexico, it seemed like every few steps we encountered these hardened, pastry-looking piles. Lately, however, I've noticed a different kind of feces: fluffy and unusual. I guess that it originates from an animal that recently ingested a furry creature, and the enzymes and acids in its digestive system failed to fully break down the fur. It's a wild hypothesis; perhaps it's just waste filled with berries that have begun to mold, like strawberries forgotten in the back of the refrigerator.

There must be an app that can identify the animal responsible for the fluffy poop. If I was an app developer, I would call it Dookie Duty. "This here is the Sphincter Souvenir. See the blackberries, and smell the waft of honey? And here, feel how warm it is. It's a young vintage," my imaginary poop connoisseur says as he rubs the berry-filled scat between his fingers and thumb.

"There's all kinds of scat out here," I tell Nature as we hike on, riffing on my app idea. "There's hard poop, soft poop, wet poop, dry poop, pancake poop, pastry poop, fried poop, berry poop of assorted colors, steamed poop, petrified poop, poop in a blanket, nutty poop, two-layer poop, three-layer poop, incognito poop, splattered poop, poop on a stick, poop kebab, and the poop marker, that's . . . that's about it."

Nature laughs at my take on Bubba's famous shrimp monologue from *Forrest Gump*. Maybe I'll call the app Bubba Poop.

CHAPTER 25

End of the Trail

"IS IT BELL BIV DEVOE?" I ask, trying to recall the acronym for the colors of the rainbow.

"You mean ROYGBIV?" Nature gives me a quizzical look.

"Oh, right. I always mix it up with the '90s new jack swing group."

"Red, orange, yellow, green, blue, indigo, and violet. Those are the colors of the rainbow," she explains.

"ROY . . . G . . . BIV! Ha-ha-ha-ha, now I know." I start singing my own version of Bell Biv DeVoe's "Poison," but Nature speeds up to get away from me.

The trail pierces through the middle of a grassy field, bordered by a band of white firs on our right, with more visible roughly a mile ahead. Once again, Nature and I find ourselves racing against an encroaching rain. This time, though, our goal is to seek refuge among the distant trees.

"We're not going to make it," Nature says.

"We can at least give it a shot." I gaze up at the dark clouds nearly upon us. "Nah, you're right, they're moving fast. How about we wait it out under these trees?" I point to the closer trees, just fifty yards away.

I'd prefer to keep moving, but if we do, staying dry will be out of the question.

After an hour of waiting out the storm under the umbrella of the trees, we hike three more miles to Highway 26. Dubois, our next resupply town, lies about thirty miles away. Walking is out of the question—it would cost us another day without contributing to our progress north. Our only option is to hitch a ride.

Few cars are on the road, though, and after forty-five minutes, we hear more hikers arriving from the CDT. Nature and I share a knowing look. Adding more thru-hikers to an already difficult hitchhiking situation means that no one will stop—trail-weary and filthy, we'll look like a jug band from the 1920s.

Fab and the Ragtags would be our stage name.

I hear a curse said under someone's breath, followed by mumbled epithets I don't need to repeat. Nature is not happy with our predicament. Still, she pops her thumb up, and after almost an hour, someone pulls over, only to tear off with a screech after spotting the rest of the untidy band. Had that car arrived fifteen minutes earlier, I'm sure Nature and I would be on our way to town.

"This isn't going to work," I calmly say. "Let's camp and try tomorrow."

I hate to give up a spot we claimed an hour ago, but there's no sense in staying here wasting time.

Nature and I surrender our hitching post and walk toward an RV camp, and I begin to wonder why it wasn't obvious to the other hikers that there were too many of us on the road. Why didn't they hang back, especially after finding out that Nature and I had been waiting for almost an hour? Did we not have first dibs at a ride? There should be a hitchhiking etiquette that thru-hikers adhere to.

The next day, and after another hour of trying, Nature and I finally secure a ride to Dubois, a small town in Fremont County known for its log architecture and connection to the Old West.

Still a bit damp from the rain, we're relieved to have reached town. However, it appears that our wait is far from over. At The Trails End motel, the owner proves to be quite the chatterbox, spinning lengthy tales in response to every question posed by the couple checking in at the counter. And with another couple waiting behind them, it seems patience will have to be our greatest virtue here.

I use the time to take in the motel's curious décor. Behind the front desk, in a rather unconventional spot, hangs a shoulder wall mount of a buck. The buck is positioned just inches above the floor and its enormous antlers dominate a substantial portion of the workspace. I can't fathom the rationale for placing it there. A single misstep by the clerk could result in at least a rather painful eye-poking, if not a goring, though at least the fish just above it is displayed at a logical height. There are also a dozen fox skins dangling from a single hook, suspended by their noses. Additional fox furs and more fish decorations adorn the side wall behind the desk.

On the opposite side wall, I notice what appears to be an ice cream–dipping cabinet. While I'm tempted to lift one of the lids, my intuition suggests that I won't discover frozen treats within—probably just game meat.

In the waiting area, a white leather lounge with imprints of chuck wagons sits next to a coffee table with reading material: a Wyoming trivia book and, to my surprise, a book entitled *The Great Wyoming Whorehouses.*

"That's hysterical," Nature says.

The cover displays a painting of a woman seated in an armchair. She's wearing a red, multilayered dress with ruffles and frills. Her legs are draped over one of the armrests, and she holds a feather fan by her head. By today's standards, her garb seems innocent enough and could even make for a great Halloween costume. However, I assume that back in the Wild West, this might have been as scandalous as it got.

On another table, I see *Dubois Area History*, a hardcover encyclopedia. Thinking this would document a less salacious slice of history, I open the book to a random page, and there, in black and white, is a portrait of a young couple. A man in a military uniform sits behind his wife with his arm around her. He has a sly look, and she has a huge grin.

"Nature, look at this." I show her the photo. "What do you see?"

"That guy has his hand on her breast!"

"I thought I was seeing things," I say as I take another quick look, and then shut the book.

From there, my eyes are drawn to a large painting above the leather lounge. It depicts a Native American man, slumped over an exhausted horse. Initially, I think the man has been pierced by a spear, but then I realize he's holding it under his arm.

I pull out my phone and do a reverse image search on this weary-warrior painting. Although the painting has the signature "S. Ruddy" and is dated 1977, it's in fact taken from a famous sculpture called *End of the Trail*, first created by James Earle Fraser in 1894.

The work, I learn, represents the exhaustion and defeat Native American peoples felt in the face of the European colonizers' westward expansion across the United States. It's considered a poignant symbol of Indigenous life during this period. I gaze at the painting, which is framed by weathered wood and adorned with arrowheads. Its depiction resonates deeply within me. I can feel the weariness of the brave warrior, running on his last reserves. It makes me consider how the past few days have taken their toll on me—relentless rain dampening both body and spirit, and endless hours spent waiting as passing cars refuse to pick up this thru-hiker.

Following our check-in, I take a couple of hours to unwind before making my way to the Black Bear Inn next door. There, I catch up with Blister, the Netherlands thru-hiker I last saw in his tent during the final stretch of the Great Basin Divide. He tells me that he's considering ending his time on the CDT.

"Every day out there has started feeling like a chore," he explains as we sit in his motel room.

I understand that sentiment—I've experienced it myself. I'll admit, the weight of the rain can be burdensome, casting a shadow over the beauty of my thru-hike. At times, during *la brega,* it's easy to overlook the majestic mountain views, to ignore the sounds of nature, to lose sight of the charm of blooming wildflowers in favor of ruminations on your own suffering. Yet there's still no place I'd rather be right now.

If I were to lose this ardor, and if my mantra of Peace, Love & All That Good Stuff failed to sustain me, then perhaps it would be time to reconsider. If hiking the CDT becomes a chore, then it's time to leave the trail. It seems that Blister, whether reluctantly or not, has found peace with his decision. Like that famous sculpture, this moment, for him, marks the end of the trail.

CHAPTER 26

Smells Like Hard-Boiled Eggs

AFTER HIKING FORTY-ODD miles through the Bridger-Teton Wilderness, leaving behind the last of the Wind River Range, our trail fam stops at the Snake River Ranger Station at the southern border of Yellowstone National Park. There, I'm hit with a surprise: Bears are attracted to human urine.

I'm baffled. I always thought pee marked our territory, and bears would think twice before trespassing into our camp. Yet the short instructional video we watch reveals that bears are attracted to urine for its salts and minerals, especially in areas where natural salt licks are scarce. The video suggests we urinate on rocks instead of the ground.

Grizzity-dang-blasted bears.

Due to the extra water I drink daily, I have a habit of crawling out of my tent at night to relieve myself more frequently than others. I doubt I'll have much luck finding a rock in my groggy, half-asleep state. If anything, I'll probably end up alerting the bears to my presence by bumping into the trees and bushes.

The two rangers assisting us assure me that I'll be safe from bears.

"I'm not so sure about that. Fab has a knack for attracting bears, especially when he's trying not to," Nature tells the rangers. I've told her about how I narrowly avoided a couple of potentially dangerous moments with black bears on the AT. Both times, I happened upon bears while they were feeding, and the one thing you never want to do is startle a bear while it's eating. They don't take kindly to that. Both followed me—whether out of curiosity or annoyance, I'm not sure. Thankfully, I was far enough away to avoid a bluff charge from one, and I managed to outpace a curious bear that eventually lost interest. I always got away safely, but those moments were unnerving.

Nature's comment heightens my caution and contradicts the reassurances from Ranger Matys and Ranger Stewart, who have more Yellowstone bear experience than she does and were very close to putting me at ease.

"Great, Nature. Way to announce it to any bear within earshot."

"Listen," Ranger Matys begins with a chuckle. "Bear attacks are rare as long as you're cautious with your food at camp, and from what I understand about thru-hikers, you're pretty diligent."

I quickly express my gratitude to Ranger Matys before Negative Nature can say another word.

Ranger Stewart assigns us campsites based on the miles we plan to hike through Yellowstone, averaging about twenty miles a day. We again express our gratitude for the rangers' patience and kind words. I falsely assumed they might be grumpy, given the number of hikers they deal with. However, they were nothing but pleasant and even indulged my overly nonsensical questions, like my concern about smarter-than-average bears invading camp to look for picnic baskets. They graciously explained that this is Yellowstone National Park, not Jellystone Park, and reassured me that their bears don't wear bow ties—unless, of course, they happen to ingest one along with a tourist.

Nature and I thank them and then head out, following the Snake River to our first campsite, West Shore.

"Between the cold and the crappy attitude, I had a hard time gettin' out of the sleeping bag," Nature grumbles the next day.

"You struggled, huh?" I laugh.

"Yes," she responds.

I empathize. The most challenging aspect of this thru-hike is the struggle to peel oneself away from the warmth of a sleeping bag and confront the biting cold. This morning feels like the coldest yet—even worse than those freezing thirteen-thousand-foot mornings in Colorado. This is only the second week of August, not quite cold enough to freeze our water bottles, but cold enough for the meadow we're crossing to be shrouded in mist.

Yet, with each frigid morning, I remind myself that it's temporary. The thought "Once I start moving, I'll warm up" has been my source of comfort. Today, however, each step is a jolt of pain, and I walk as if the next step will be the one that shatters my frozen pinky toes. The cold is so intense it gnaws at my very bones. Adding to the discomfort, the trail seems scarcely traveled, with knee-deep, dew-covered grass in some sections that soaks my pants and shoes, intensifying the chill. Nevertheless, I press on, accompanied by the muffled expletives of a certain thru-hiker ahead of me.

Apart from generating body heat, I'm relieved that we're moving. Just before nightfall yesterday, Nature and I spotted creatures with four-foot wingspans soaring above camp, emitting deep, unfamiliar, *Jurassic Park*-ian sounds. It wasn't my imagination this time. Nature was as bewildered at the birds' size and eerie calls as I was. The thought of those flying dinosaurs makes me want to shout, "Must go faster!" But moving quickly doesn't pair well with this wet, freezing cold.

This is my first visit to Yellowstone, and I find it incredible that the CDT passes through this national treasure. As a child, I dreamed of witnessing it. Young Derick envisioned Yellowstone, with its geysers and hot springs, as the most iconic natural wonderland on the planet, and I'm elated that our route will take us right past the geyser.

"Does Yellowstone smell like hard-boiled eggs, or is it just me?" I wrinkle my nose and wave my hand, as if dispersing an altitoot.

"It's the sulfur," Nature responds.

There was no mention of this in the instructional video, but I'll gladly take the scent of hard-boiled eggs, even if bordering on rotten eggs, over New York City sewage. Just then, I inadvertently take a deep sniff, triggering olfactory memories—urine, feces, and the aftermath of drunken mistakes—of the local stations on the A/C trains.

As I later learn from a park employee, the park's unique hydrogen sulfide smell comes from its geothermal features—hot springs, geysers, and mud pots. Beneath the surface, there's a huge reservoir of magma that's constantly bubbling and steaming. Yellowstone's actual natural beauty is the source of the stench. It's like dating the most attractive person in town, only to realize they have excessive flatulence.

A staff member at the Old Faithful Basin store assures me that while it might be unpleasant, the smell is not harmful in the park's low concentrations. However, she also discreetly informs us that a human foot had been discovered recently in the Abyss Pool, a hot spring more than fifty feet deep with 140-degree water.

"Come again?" I ask, convinced that the sulfur was affecting my hearing.

She explains that a few days earlier, a park visitor had noticed a floating foot still wearing a size 8.5 black shoe. Investigators determined that a man had fallen in the water during the last week of July. No other human remains had been found, but fatty deposits were seen floating on the surface.

Damn!

However, she adds that deaths are still incredibly rare in Yellowstone. Prior to this incident, a man had died in 2016 after falling into a boiling spring; his body was dissolved by the acidic water.

Needless to say, swimming in Yellowstone's hot springs is illegal, yet some visitors are unaware of this regulation.

"How is that even possible? There should be graphic warning signs everywhere!" I protest.

I wouldn't consider doing it now, but I can envision an impulsive, unknowing teenage Derick attempting a cannonball into a geyser. I can already imagine the headlines: "Young Black Hispanic Male Chased by Park Rangers Jumps into Boiling Water to Avoid Capture." "No, wait, it didn't happen like that," I'd yell from the afterlife.

Nature and I do come across a few small signs that read DANGER—Fragile Thermal Area—Stay on Officially Marked and Maintained Trails. In my opinion, there should be larger signs depicting a melting body part next to a pool of steaming water, with a skull and crossbones. I recognize the importance of maintaining the park's family-friendly image, but sometimes you must be explicit to drive a point home.

Nature and I grab breakfast at the Old Faithful Basin restaurant before we make our way to the geyser. There's a big screen inside with a timer for the next eruption, which will happen in ten minutes.

According to FarOut, Old Faithful erupts every 60 to 110 minutes, shooting about five thousand gallons of water up to 130 feet high. According to the National Park Service, the famous geyser erupts around seventeen times a day and can be predicted with a 90 percent confidence rate within a ten-minute variation.

The dining room staff kindly allow Nature and me to store our backpacks in the employee area while we head out to see the eruption. While a crowd is gathering, there's still ample space for us to stand at the front and enjoy an unobstructed view. As we wait, I overhear a guide sharing details with a group of tourists.

"Yellowstone National Park is renowned for its breathtaking natural landscapes, including Yellowstone Lake and Yellowstone Caldera, sometimes referred to as the Yellowstone Supervolcano."

Supervolcano—I need to know more!

While I wait, I do a quick Google search. Turns out a Yellowstone eruption would be pure chaos: ash clouds choking the sky, wildlife wiped out, and states like Montana and Idaho getting wrecked. Air travel, agriculture, and water? All in trouble. But my next search is reassuring—the odds of it happening anytime soon are basically nonexistent. Scientists keep a close eye on it, and if it were about to blow, we'd get plenty of warning.

With that out of the way, I settle in and wait for the show. It's like watching a diva preparing for her big moment: The anticipation builds, the crowd hushes in reverence, and then, with all the drama of a seasoned performer, Old Faithful bursts forth like a giant sneeze. It's nature's way of saying, "Ta-da!" in the most spectacularly splashy manner possible. A towering column of steam and water rockets skyward, shimmering in the sunlight before cascading back down in a misty curtain. The spray lingers, hanging in the air like a fading firework, as the geyser keeps surging, defying gravity for what feels like an impossibly long moment. The sheer force of the eruption is impressive, but the fact that it started precisely on time is mind boggling.

The entire spectacle lasts about ten minutes, and then it's over. Akin to a roller-coaster ride, it was brief yet exhilarating.

Nature and I grab our packs, and despite having reserved a camp spot at Yellowstone, we opt to pass it, leave the park, and hike farther on the CDT instead. As we distance ourselves from Old Faithful, I notice that whenever the path veers off the boardwalk, the ground beneath my feet feels oddly hollow. It's difficult to convey how this feels, but after trekking over two thousand miles in the past few weeks, I've developed an intuition for the terrain beneath me.

Midday, we encounter our first SOBO thru-hiker, heading south on the CDT. I inquire whether the mosquitoes are less bothersome farther north. He jokes that there are no more mosquitoes, because he inadvertently ate them all while hiking with his mouth open. As we bid farewell, I express gratitude for his pest-control efforts.

Nature and I pause at a lake for a late lunch. Having completed about 15 miles, and with the Idaho border only 5.5 miles ahead, we resolve to push on and search for a suitable camping spot.

Two hikers pass us as we eat. One holds a whiskey bottle, as if just taking a swig. The other looks familiar—I think he was at Doc Campbell's Post back in New Mexico. We didn't exchange words, just a nod of hello. Today, I ask for his trail name.

"It's Blackout."

However, says Blackout, other thru-hikers have been calling him Mr. Fabulous. While he doesn't express annoyance, and he seems to have a chill demeanor, I can sense his bemusement at being continually mistaken for me.

"Hey, it's meant as a compliment," I quip.

"Yeah, I've heard nothing but positive remarks," he replies.

Later, I express to Nature, "Sure, Blackout is a handsome, charismatic BIPOC, but that's where our similarities end." I'm aiming for suave but probably land somewhere between awkward and cringe.

She reminds me of how a fellow CDT thru-hiker once called me Blackalachian—the trail name for a Black hiker friend who also thru-hiked the AT—and how the guy later apologized to me when we ran into him a few days later.

Despite the passage of time, being a person of color on the trail is still regarded as unusual. I didn't see another person of color on the entire AT. On the CDT, Blackout is only the second person of color I've come across.

Sometimes, it seems to me that we're lumped together as one, singular thru-hiker, rather than recognized as the distinct individuals we are. I don't think anyone is being flippant about it; it's just the way it is.

An hour later, we reach the two-thousand-mile mark and Wyoming's border with Idaho, our fourth state. With approximately one thousand miles remaining, Nature and I pause to reflect on the journey so far.

Two-thirds of the way in, the trail has become a blur—at this point, even the trees have started to look like old friends. I caught myself chatting to one of them the other day, asking it for advice on how to handle the rest of this journey. It didn't respond, but it did offer a nice, shady spot to rest. Maybe that's the secret to this whole thing: When you can't find the answers, the trail will give you the shade to sit with your thoughts long enough to find them yourself. Or maybe the trees just know when to keep their mouths shut.

While it took us four months to traverse the first three states, we set our sights on completing the last two states—Idaho and Montana—quickly, in the next month. Why? To beat the weather. The clock's ticking, and I'm determined to make it through before winter catches up with us, which can come as early as late September in Montana. The next thousand miles will throw a bit of everything at us—rocky trails, some steep climbs, and weather that's as unpredictable as a toddler on a sugar high.

CHAPTER 27

Salty by Nature

NATURE AND I are over one hundred miles north of the Idaho border, spending the entire day stepping off the dirt road as damn all-terrain vehicles (ATVs) zip by, leaving dust confetti in their wakes. We can practically taste the earth, and it's not a culinary flourish I particularly savor. Move over, Michelin stars; we're diving into the world of Michelin tires, where the menu includes subtle notes of a freshly plowed field with an aftertaste of, well, everything dusty.

"Here comes another freakin' four-wheeler," Nature exclaims.

We cover our faces to shield ourselves from the ensuing storm. Some drivers slow down as they approach, but most speed by without so much as a glance. Nature and I now sport a hiker's tan that resembles a farmer's tan, but is composed primarily of dirt.

"Enjoying your birthday dirt cake?" I ask Nature.

"I hate those fuc—" she starts. Just then, the roar of another passing ATV drowns out her words, though I can guess what she's saying. I'm not thrilled either, and relief washes over us as the CDT veers off the dirt road and into wild grasses and knee-high green foliage, leading into a thick forest of pine trees. However, as we begin to ascend a mountain with a steep drop, that sense of relief on Nature's part dissipates. She might detest an uphill trail even more than inhaling ATV dust.

The trees here are so close to the narrow trail that their branches scrape against my backpack, as if to say, "If you fall this way, we've got you. No need to worry about vertigo!"

We come upon an ATV flipped on its side, dangling precariously off the trail, its torn-off seat lying in the dirt. It's partially obstructing the path; were it not for two trees that it rests against, it would have surely tumbled down the mountainside. Karma certainly had its way with the driver, though I'm assuming no one was hurt, since there's no blood or other signs of injury.

There's clearly no safe way to retrieve this machine from its precarious position without additional equipment. I wonder how the driver is explaining this mishap to their friends. Will they admit it was a foolish mistake to attempt a trail clearly meant for foot traffic only, or will they concoct a wild tale of an animal attack? Personally, I'd embellish the story, claiming I was ambushed by a cryptic creature that grabbed a tire and then flung me off the trail.

Coming across the broken machine on this remote trail is bizarre, as unexpected as stumbling upon a tarnished pay phone tucked into a forgotten corner of a New York City alley, a relic from another time.

As we approach camp for the night, the distant bleating of sheep fills the air. A few miles back, we passed a sign for something called the Sheep Experiment Station, run by the Agricultural Research Service. They focus on sheep grazing, genetics, and sustainable land use in high-altitude environments. There are plenty of sheep around, and they're making sure we know it.

It's initially endearing, but after setting camp, eating, and hearing three hours of constant "baaaah," my brain is short-circuiting. I shake my head, futilely attempting to blot out the ruckus. What on earth could be so urgent that they must express it to each other so loudly? Are they hard of hearing, or perhaps trying to communicate with a sheep that's fifty deep in the flock?

"Baaaaxter!" bleats Fluffy McFlufferson.

"Yeah? Is that you, Fluffy?"

"Yes! Did you hear about Ramington ramming his head up the farmer's arse, knocking him into the fodder? We all laughed and laughed."

"Baaaah, that is funny! There's some scandal in these parts," bleats Baaaaxter.

"Naaaah, really?" bleats Fluffy. "Do go on."

"Woolly Wonka ran off after getting caught fooling around with his girlfriend Baaaabra's twin sister, Aaaamy."

"Baaaad Woolly."

I wrap my fleece around my head, covering my ears. Whoever suggested counting sheep to fall asleep clearly never attempted it within earshot of hundreds of actual, gossiping sheep.

"I hope they don't keep this up all night. What an unconventional sixty-fourth-birthday lullaby for you," I jest to Nature, who grumbles something from her tent and then seems to promptly conk out.

Exhaustion from the day's hike overtakes me, and I begin to drift into a deep sleep, though it might as well be a sheep sleep, with the bleating accompanying dreams I can barely recall.

We're up and hiking before dawn, donning our headlamps. Guided by the cries of the busybody sheep, we ascend again. After a ten-minute climb, we spot the flock a mere ten feet from our path, standing shoulder to shoulder, sleepy and bleating more softly now. The animals blanket a meadow as vast as a football field. It's a wall-to-wall carpet of sheep, their muted bleating carrying a strangely soothing rhythm—if such a clamor can be called soothing.

I hear a dog bark. I'm not concerned. Yesterday, a dude on horseback, trailed by five friendly sheepdogs, trotted by our camp and asked if we'd spotted a renegade sheep.

My money's on Woolly Wonka; he's probably skulking around, embarrassed about his affair.

"I haven't," I admitted. "Those darn sheep, always thinking the grass is greener on the other side."

My attempt at humor fell flat. The cowboy just nodded and went on his way. As he left, one dog sniffed around us, seeking attention, while another—with quills protruding from all around its mouth and a hangdog look on its face—had clearly had a porcupine encounter. The dogs soon moved on in search of the runaway sheep.

This morning, as we pass the flock, the barking grows louder. An angry sheepdog emerges through the cloud of wool. It's the same one that approached me last night, wagging its tail as it sniffed my hand. But now the dog seems ready to chase us away, its eyes narrowed into a glare that could pierce steel.

"Talk about taking your job seriously. Let's get moving before this dog decides to take a chunk out of you, Nature."

"Me?"

"Yeah, someone needs to slow it down while I make my escape."

The advantage of starting before sunrise and trekking across mostly flat terrain becomes clear when we reach Interstate 15 by 10 a.m., covering an impressive twelve miles in four hours. While our pace is not exactly record breaking, our sense of accomplishment feels well earned.

The CDT took us alongside wooden property posts and through expansive stretches of dry grass dotted with the occasional pine tree. Cows lingered on the trail as we approached, and for a moment, it felt like they were challenging us to a game of chicken—a game I'd gladly lose by walking around them. But they always scurried away when we got within several yards, except for one black bull that lingered as, this time, *I* was the one to scurry past, keeping a wary eye on him.

We've already arranged for a shuttle to Lima, nineteen miles north into Montana, since Idaho law prohibits standing on a highway to solicit a ride—there's no hitchhiking allowed. Although we're technically hiking in Idaho on an established trail, it skirts so closely along the border that a brief ride effortlessly whisks us across the state line.

We've reserved space at the Mountain View RV Park and Guest Motel. With a name like that, my expectations are pretty low. Even if it's haunted by the ghosts of truck drivers past and the TV in my room turns itself on to say, "Get out!" as long as there is a hot shower, I'll still give it five stars and a Yelp review worthy of the Ritz-Carlton.

Lima, it turns out, is more of a rest stop than a town. I've seen bigger Walmart parking lots. The motel, a gas station, and an old café that I don't expect will serve vegan dishes are a hop, skip, and a jump from one another.

We climb out of the pickup that shuttled us and grab our gear. As I wait to thank the driver, I see him backing away from his truck as if it's on fire. I look at Nature, whose back is to me as she struggles with her backpack. She sneezes.

"Did it get you?" asks the driver.

I see Nature adjusting her bear spray on her backpack and it quickly becomes clear to me: While pulling her backpack out of the truck, she accidentally triggered the bear spray attached to the pack's strap, spraying it right onto her face.

"Did you just nail yourself with bear spray?" I ask. I don't show my amusement until I see that she's OK.

"I did, but I'm fine—it was just a little."

"Are you sure?"

"Yeah, one hundred percent."

I must admit, I was hoping for a bit more drama. If this bear spray doesn't elicit convulsions from a sixty-four-year-old hiker, how would it deter an angry quarter-ton grizzly from charging for my jugular?

Nature insists that only a small amount of spray escaped the canister, so I suggest we test a full spray on her. She wisely refuses to volunteer, assuring me that the spray isn't just a breath freshener for bears, as I jokingly suggest.

After a night in town and dinner at the diner—a contradictory huge plate of french fries and a side salad, the only vegan options—we venture back onto the trail the next day. Our next destination is the tiny town of Leadore, Idaho, a distant 103 miles away. This leg will involve plenty of ridge walking with gradual elevation gains, offering us sweeping, uninterrupted views of the landscape.

Nature, presumably still shaking off the lingering taste of red pepper, resumes her vigilant stride. As we begin to climb, her focus intensifies, her gaze fixed steadfastly on the ground ahead. As I've learned over the miles, Nature can't afford to look up, to the sides, or around while hiking, lest she veer off the trail and into the mountainside. She enters a zone of focus in which the world around her fades away; she won't talk to anyone, and you can't talk to her. If there's a scenic vista to admire, she must come to a complete stop or risk losing her balance entirely.

Her obliviousness to her surroundings has led to some amusing incidents on the trail. Nature has collided with children, had dogs dart between her legs, bumped into fellow hikers, and stumbled over fallen trees, and she's constantly startled by birds, passersby, and even me. Today, she hikes ahead of me with her head down like a determined bull. Soon I hear a scream. I look up and find her entangled in branches from a tree that's fallen across the trail.

"Great, perfect! Bring on the hail, Mother," Nature shouts, looking up at the dark clouds releasing rain, as she untangles herself from the branches. She has her own unique way of reacting to whatever her namesake, Mother Nature, throws at her. But this time, I'm unsure if this "Mother" was directed at Mother Nature or was instead a curse she halted midway. I glance up at the sky and remark that I'd like to be judged separately; Nature doesn't speak for both of us.

"Why does it always rain when I'm going uphill?" she shouts.

Not sure how true that is, but it ain't far off. Colorado, at least, felt that way.

"That meadow just did me in. I hate those plants. I gotta put my poles in the ground. 'Hellllooo, plants.' . . . Damn plants didn't answer," Nature says to no one in particular.

"What's going on, Nature?" I ask.

"My trekking poles are bouncing back up at me!"

"Oh, really?"

"Yeah, 'cause they snag on a branch like this," she says with a sigh, her trekking poles catching once again on the foliage lining our path.

"So, you hate these bushes?" I ask.

"They need to back off the trail."

I laugh. Although she's genuinely mad at the plants, my laughter lightens her mood—or at least stifles any more potential curse words.

There are times when I think it might be nice if Nature softened a bit. Later that day, I pause to admire a lake's reflection of the trees, perfect and clear like a mirror.

"Yeah, well, I think we made a wrong turn—we're still in Colorado. I'm getting tired of this mud. I hope the whole trail today is not like this, but I suspect that it is," she pouts, eyeing the rough and wet terrain from last night's rain.

I suspect she's feeling what we all feel at times during this thru-hike after the trip over a rock, the wet socks from rain and puddles, or the wildflowers' colors glaring too brightly for sensitive eyes. Well, I imagine the latter is just another of Nature's complaints, right before she snaps a photo. Her outsized reactions to whatever the day sends her way are her way of navigating through it.

I can't imagine the Nature I would witness if she didn't take her special gummies that help her sleep through the night.

"What kind of stupid cow would walk up here. You don't have enough pasture? You're gonna walk up here? That's a dumbass cow. Why would a cow climb up to eleven thousand feet for a strand of grass?" Nature rants. We are actually not that high in elevation, maybe nine thousand feet. I do see a half dozen black cows grazing by a cluster of pine trees. The slopes beyond them and around us roll like fondant icing draped over a cake, before being sculpted into decorative shapes.

Nature continues, throwing in more swear words for emphasis. With all her colorful, salty-sailor language, I sometimes wonder if she has coprolalia.

"Wait, you did what?!" I ask her a few miles later, after she mentions yet another random "Act of Nature."

"I licked it to see if it was really salt," Nature replies matter-of-factly.

"You put your tongue on a livestock salt block?!"

"Yeah. How else was I supposed to find out?" She is unfazed.

"Nature, that's nasty. It's been sitting out in the elements, surrounded by animal waste, and most importantly, licked by cows. You didn't just lick salt; you licked something that could cause explosive diarrhea. Have you ever heard of foot-and-mouth disease, bovine tuberculosis, or anthrax?"

She brushes me off with a laugh, as if what she did was akin to licking a salt lamp to test its authenticity, except salt lamps aren't coated in cow saliva. Fortunately, she has no adverse consequences—perhaps she's protected by her own saltiness.

All this talk of salt is making me thirsty, and I'm low on water. I check a comment in FarOut indicating that a spring up ahead is maintaining a flow rate of about 1 liter per minute.

The idea of measuring the time it takes to fill a water bottle never crossed my mind, but a minute per liter seems like a sensible metric. I suppose it's an improvement over Nature's measurement system: "Freakin' floaties, dumbass drip, slow as . . . " You get the idea.

That said, we all cope in our own way. When I feel some form of discomfort, whether it's caused by the trail or by interactions with another person, I tend to withdraw, not curse. If I go quiet, something's off, and I'm retreating into a defense mechanism I've had since childhood.

My first memory of creating protective space happened when I was about eight years old. While waiting in line for the school bus, I'd chased after a handball my classmate had dropped, intending to return it to her. A teacher assumed I'd been disruptive, took the ball, and scolded me. At home, surrounded by my family's laughter, I felt distant, not wanting to stir things up, simply staying quiet until I was ready to speak, as I still do to this day. Silence, I've learned, is sometimes the only thing I can control.

Our idiosyncrasies—my own, Nature's, all of ours—are what make us who we are. Embracing them is essential for understanding ourselves and others better. At least that's what I read on a social media post.

CHAPTER 28

The Good Days

PEACE, LOVE, & ALL That Good Stuff has been my motto for ten years. It's my salutation after every trail-register entry and my mantra when things aren't going well. It shifts a bad day into a good one. Whether I write it, say it, or just think it, Peace, Love & All That Good Stuff always gives me good vibes.

When I thru-hiked the AT, I wore a silver necklace that hung just below my chest, holding three pendants I've had for years: a silver peace sign bought at a market in New York City when I was a teen, seeking balance in the chaos of life; an ankh found at an antique store in Madrid, sitting forgotten in a dusty vintage curio cabinet; and a four-leaf clover encased in clear resin, given to me by an old friend. Each pendant had found its way to me at a significant moment in my life, and all three were with me from the start of the AT until the end. However, after years of moving, my necklace ended up in a crowded storage unit, and I couldn't find it before my Long Trail hike. When I ended up leaving that trail after just two days, I began to realize those pendants might have had a more protective and luck-creating role than I had suspected.

I come from a culture rich in superstitions—where leaving your shoes on their side invites bad luck, letting a tree or pole pass between you while walking with someone is ominous, and saying "rabbit, rabbit, rabbit" first thing on the first day of the month brings good fortune for the entire month.

Do I adhere to these beliefs? I'm not sure, but it doesn't hurt to be mindful.

This brings me back to my pendants, which I most certainly needed to wear on the CDT. Before I took a step on the trail, I researched the deeper meanings of the four-leaf clover. We all know that four-leaf clovers are associated with good luck, but that's just one aspect. Each leaf also symbolizes something different: One represents luck, another faith, the third hope, and the fourth love.

Love? I can see that—the leaves on a four-leaf clover are heart-shaped.

It all made sense. Maybe I wasn't just a charm carrier, hex fearer, and myth follower after all. Perhaps there was a deeper meaning to it. After all, my pendants seemed to embody my *Peace*—the peace symbol; *Love*—the clover; and *All That Good Stuff*—the ankh, a symbol used in ancient Egyptian hieroglyphs to represent eternal life.

Bam! 'Nuff said!

I've noticed that hikers from the West Coast love the open trails out here and aren't as enthusiastic about the densely forested AT. However, I have a strong affinity for hiking in the woods. Perhaps it's because my first hiking experience immersed me in thick forests. Whenever I encountered the rare open fields or reached elevations above the tree line, my excitement would soar.

On the CDT, there's minimal tree cover. The trail often stretches across the desert or along mountain ridges, leaving me exposed to the elements. So, on the rare occasions when the trail leads me into a dense forest, as it does in Idaho, my heart swells with joy. *Now this is my kind of thru-hiking.*

Because the CDT's skies are not blocked by the canopy, I also have the enchanting night view of the Milky Way, a luminous river of light stretching across the night sky, a cosmic city teeming with celestial wonders.

Still, not every day is all cotton-candy skies, wildflower meadows, sun-kissed trails, and sleeping under the Milky Way. There have been, as you've seen, plenty of challenges. But to find the littlest pleasures of the trail and call it a good day—no matter what—is what Peace, Love, & All That Good Stuff embodies.

We're in tiny Leadore, with a population of barely over a hundred. The whole town could fit in less than half a square mile. Highway 28 (Railroad Street) cuts through the main stretch, which features a gas station, a community library next door, the post office across the street, and a restaurant a block down. There's also the Mustang Inn, where we stayed last night, but not much more except an expansive landscape and a backdrop of the Lemhi and Beaverhead mountain ranges.

"I love the smell of new shoes," I say as I lift a new pair of Oboz up to my face. I swirl the inside around my nose as if aerating a glass of wine. "This 2022 vintage is a good year," I say, before putting them on.

A new pair of shoes means good trail days ahead. Plus, we're getting closer to Bozeman, the town on the CDT I've been excited to visit. It's the only place along this trail I'd heard of before starting. Salgado, the photographer, lives there, and he described his town as a vibrant, picturesque place, nestled in the Gallatin Valley and surrounded by majestic mountain ranges. I need to see that for myself and find out if it's the kind of place where I could spend hours at a café, reading, writing, and chatting with artsy locals. Yeah, that's the vibe I'm after.

We still have around a hundred miles to go until our Bozeman pickup spot, however. Nature and I have been doing some steady miles the last few days, high twenties and a few thirties. I suspect we'll be at the Chief Joseph Pass parking lot before long, where we'll get a ride to Bozeman from Baggins, who also lives there.

For the next few days, we hike among trees, more grasslands, and up small climbs, but don't encounter other hikers. It's like that sometimes, especially when we're moving at such a fast pace. It's reassuring to realize that my body has adjusted and strengthened from the daily hiking workouts.

A couple of years ago, I strained my back sweeping the floor of my New York City apartment. It was a rough year, with everything going awry due to the pandemic. I wasn't hiking, and my body wasn't happy about it. Ever since, my lower back felt different—strained, tight, and occasionally hit with sharp spasms. Before the CDT, I worried that carrying a backpack for several months would be too much. I kept that concern to myself and decided to take it one day at a time. To my surprise, from the beginning, daily hiking relieved my pain, most likely by strengthening the muscles around my midsection and back. In fact, after four months of hiking, the only pain I have is hunger pain, which, for a thru-hiker, is par for the course.

I don't always pay close attention to my hiking speed. Nature normally hikes several yards ahead of me, serving as a steady pacesetter. Even if I don't see her, I know she's close. Sometimes, when I'm not lost in thought, I'll pick up my pace and make sure I'm not miles behind. It's a nice gig, this thru-hiking.

These are the things I'm thinking about as I move along the trail. Nature is, as usual, up ahead. Suddenly, I hear a flapping of wings, and then Nature yelling, "Stupid mountain chicken!"

She must have gotten startled again.

I nearly collapse with laughter, and as tears begin to fall, I realize that moments like this make it a good day.

PART 4

MONTANA

CHAPTER 29

Outside Bozeman

FOR DAYS, the trail followed the border of Idaho and Montana, dipping into and out of each state as it continued northbound. However, today we have finally settled into Montana, the last state on the CDT. It's August 22, and day 133, and we have just over six hundred miles remaining.

"Here in Montana, the summer sun offers a delightful warmth, complimented by a rejuvenating cool breeze," I read Nature a text from Abigail, another Oboz friend and Bozeman resident.

"Good to hear," says Nature.

"Finally, a state with weather that's ideal for us."

We're perched on our backpacks at the Chief Joseph Pass parking lot, eagerly awaiting Baggins's arrival. He's making a four-hour round-trip from Bozeman just to pick us up.

"Speak the truth, Baggins. How awful is this place?" I ask as he drives us toward the town where we plan to zero at for a few days.

"Dude, Bozeman is a pretty special town," he admits.

"Hmmm, you've been talking to Salgado."

"It's true. What did he already tell you?"

"He said Bozeman has the perfect mix of natural beauty, adventure, and cultural richness. It's an outdoor paradise with activities like climbing, hiking, fishing, skiing, and wildlife viewing. Plus, the downtown area is full of charming shops and eateries, and has a vibrant, intellectual vibe." I pause and glance over at Baggins and at Nature in the back seat.

"Well, that sounds about—" Baggins begins, but I cut him off.

"He also mentioned that the city's focus on sustainability, the arts scene, and friendly community all add to its allure. That's it."

"Did you just read all of that from your cell?" Baggins asks.

"OK, it wasn't Salgado. It's from a travel website," I confess. "Come on, we need distractions." I click around for a few more minutes and then say, "Baggins, you have to hear this!"

The video on my phone captures the unearthly call from the dinosaur-looking bird Nature and I heard that first morning in Yellowstone. It trills a haunting symphony of high-pitched warbles that bounce off the surrounding pine-covered cliffs.

"Oh, that's a sandhill crane," Baggins says.

"Really? I've never heard anything quite like it. It's what I'd imagine a pterodactyl sounds like."

"Well, sandhill cranes are one of the oldest bird species," Baggins says.

"I can believe that. They had me thinking we'd stumbled into Jurassic Park instead of Yellowstone," I say, feigning distress.

Highway 43 winds through the Pioneer Mountains, showcasing granite peaks, alpine meadows, and lodgepole pine forests. Expansive grasslands and the occasional ranch fly past the car window. I spot a sign reading SET, with an arrow pointing left and a familiar-looking *Y* beneath it.

"Aww snap! This is the set for that Kevin Costner show, *Yellowstone*," I say. I'm used to seeing sets on the streets of New York City, especially in Harlem, but I'm ecstatic to see this one.

Baggins pulls the car over and hands me binoculars, as if he was expecting this moment.

I see a group of cowboys and cowgirls spread out, some under a canopy, others lined shoulder to shoulder looking over at two cowboys on horseback racing through a river with a helicopter close behind. It must have been the last take, because the helicopter disappears behind some trees, and the actors gather in small groups.

"Well, be on the lookout for a helicopter scene next season," I say, handing Nature the binoculars.

After we've all had a look, we move on, and I can tick "movie set" off my CDT bucket list. It wasn't originally on there, but it should have been, and it certainly is now.

I slowly open my eyes, greeted by darkness. As my sleep-heavy lids struggle to adjust, I peer toward the tent entrance. I'm bewildered by its distance. I close my eyes again, attempting to comprehend my dream-state surroundings. When I reopen them, the tent entrance transforms into sliding closet doors, and the cozy tent interior becomes a spacious bedroom.

I'm not in the wilderness, snug in my trusty tent. Instead, I'm in Salgado's guest bedroom. After nearly five months of camping, I've grown so accustomed to the comfy confines of my tent that this room feels oddly vast. It took a moment for my brain to catch up and remind me that I'm back in civilization.

Much of Bozeman feels like a dreamscape. I'm spending three days here, enough to pull me out of my thru-hiking routine but not enough to erase my body's familiarity with hiking, camping, and living in the outdoors. That part clings to my soul like body art. As I ride Salgado's bicycle around town, I don't feel entirely present; the tattooed part of me is still out there, thru-hiking.

In the evening, I have dinner at the vegan-friendly MacKenzie River Pizza Co. with Salgado; his girlfriend, Emma; and a few peeps from Oboz. I discover that Oboz stands for "outside Bozeman." It feels perfect in so many ways. Earlier in the day, I had been given a tour of the Oboz headquarters. The staff was incredibly friendly, establishing a connection so genuine it's no wonder I'm now hanging out with many of them here.

Emma starts to share her thoughts on how thru-hikers talk: "Hanging around these people, if you listen for long enough—"

"'These people'?" I jokingly cut her off.

"Yeah, what does that mean?" Salgado chimes in.

There's a break for laughter, and then Emma emphasizes, "This community, this outdoor community." She continues, "Most of my life, I've been in corporate settings that aren't related to this hiking world. I had to learn how to decipher inanimate objects from human beings. Like, last night we were talking, and Kenny asked Fab, 'What day are you headed out?' And Fab says, 'You know, whenever me and nature . . . '" Emma begins to wave her arm, as if taking in the atmosphere. "And I thought, that's a very spiritual answer, but I can track with you, I'm following. I can meet you there . . . and then I realized that Nature is a person, not the entity."

She continued, "Or Fab would start a story, 'Sidetrack, yada, yada, yada,' and I thought Sidetrack meant 'sidenote,' like as a way to start a new part of his story. But once again, it was a person."

It's hilarious to think that we thru-hikers have our own special language. However, I can understand how it might also all seem rather perplexing. It's a reminder that, seen from an outsider's perspective, things can often seem baffling or irrational.

Here are a few of my favorite linguistic quirks:

Blister Collection: The act of comparing blisters with fellow hikers as if they were badges of honor: "Oh, you've got one on your heel? Cute. Wait 'til you see this beauty on my pinky toe."
Hiker Box Gourmet: The art of creating a meal from random items left in a hiker box. That was me in Pie Town, my culinary playground.
Pink Blazing: When a hiker adjusts their pace or route to follow or meet up with someone they're romantically or socially interested in. I haven't fallen victim to it, but I've seen others practically turn their trek into a rom-com with extra miles.
Dirtbag Shower: A quick rinse in a stream or lake, or even with just wet wipes, to freshen up. Not sure who'd do that . . . oh wait, it's me, all day, every day.
Hiker Funk: The unique aroma of hikers after they've gone several days without a shower or laundry. But not me, I've mastered the art of the dirtbag shower.

The next day, I head to Country Bookshelf, a local independent bookstore where warm wooden shelves, packed with books, stretch endlessly in a colorful mosaic of spines. The space feels intimate, with cozy nooks and alcoves inviting me to linger. Upstairs, the balcony offers a perfect perch for reading in solitude.

I've been without books for nearly five months. While I could read one on my phone, call me old-fashioned, but I prefer a physical book. Plus, I need to conserve my phone battery for my navigation app.

Today, I pick up a book called *Merle's Door*, written by Ted Kerasote about his relationship with his best friend Merle, a Labrador mix.

Ever since I started this journey, I've been thinking about Magic, the dog I hiked with for a few days on the AT. I've missed that dog for ten years. As a child, I was afraid of dogs. They always seemed to chase me, but that might have been because I used to run whenever I saw one. As an adult, I was mostly indifferent to dogs; I didn't run from them, but I also didn't feel compelled to pet them. However, Magic changed things, and I developed a newfound fondness for canines.

After the AT, I was gifted a vizsla I named Naomi, but with all my hiking and lack of a permanent residence, I had to give her to someone who could provide her with more stability. Naomi is still in my life, but not the way I wish her to be, though I know I made the responsible choice.

All that being said, in the bookstore I think reading a memoir featuring a dog might ease my dog melancholy. I'm not sure where the logic is in that, but I'm going with it.

I spend much of my Bozeman time hanging with Salgado. He's a chill dude. He leans casually against his kitchen counter, a half-empty coffee cup in hand, when he talks about his favorite local trails. He laughs often—the kind of deep, unhurried laugh that makes you feel like there's nowhere else he'd rather be. We reminisce about our early days on the CDT, including the time Salgado ran out of toilet paper and had to use dried cordgrass.

"Bro, did you get any dookie on your hand? Actually, don't—I'd rather not know," I say.

Instead, he shares another nasty moment.

"I dropped an ibuprofen down my shorts. I didn't want to take it, but it was my last one. I had to do it—I was sore from hiking more miles in a day with you than I have ever done," Salgado says with zero shame.

I get it. If I dropped an Oreo in my shorts, even with all the sweat and whatever other trail funk is collected down there, I wouldn't hesitate to grab that Oreo, lift it up to the sky, have the universe bless it, kiss it, and quickly pop it in my mouth with a self-satisfied smile.

"I'll be sure to have extra ibuprofen when I meet up with you on your last week," he adds. Salgado joined me for my first week on the CDT and now plans on doing the last week with me in Glacier National Park. It's a fine way to finish—with a good friend.

After three days in Bozeman, Nature and I return to Chief Joseph Pass. Baggins opts to join us for our first day and night back on the trail. Rather than the 20 miles we planned, we cover 13.6—a choice that proves to be the right call. The next day, Baggins texts me, "I got back to my truck at 11:45 a.m. yesterday, and my legs were pretty wrecked."

"I bet you're glad we didn't do a twenty-mile day," I respond.

"Haha, yes!"

Coming from a Triple Crowner, this is a testament that there's such a thing as "trail legs." A thru-hiker's adaptation to daily hiking helps them tackle challenging terrain more efficiently and with less fatigue. Give Baggins a few weeks out here, and I bet he'd be leading the charge on a thirty-miler.

CHAPTER 30

The Evolution of Evergreens

IN THE COOL shadows cast by towering conifers, I find a profound sense of peace. These silent poets of the wild tell stories of endurance and adaptation, their sturdy trunks etched by time. From the gentle quivering of the aspens to the stiller needles of the Douglas-firs, every tree adds its own note to the grand symphony of nature.

When setting up camp amid the trees, I always search for the oldest one among them. The one that stands the tallest and largest, having stood watch over the forest for the longest time. I acknowledge this tree's presence and ask for its protection throughout the night. This act is a small token of my respect, gratitude, and surrender to the elements, and it brings me comfort, particularly when I'm alone in the wilderness.

As we continue through the Northern Rockies, many miles unfold in a landscape shaped by the capricious hand of wildfire. What was once a dense canopy of evergreens now gives way to a surreal tableau of charred trunks and ash-laden air. Towering skeletons with blackened bark and bare branches reach toward the sky, leaving the landscape a raw, tortured network of scorched trunks and twisted limbs.

Hearing about past forest fires is one thing, but seeing the aftereffects up close along the CDT is truly heart-wrenching. The vague scent of burned wood still hangs in the breeze, a powerful reminder of the recent dance between flames and forest. As I hike, the sun feels more intense, as if absorbing residual heat from the fire's aftermath.

Yet, amid the desolation, signs of rebirth emerge. Small, resilient shoots push through the ash-covered ground, and later, we see emerging trees up to three feet tall. The contrast between scorched earth and black trunks and the vivid green shoots is both stark and mesmerizing—it's life itself, seeking to reclaim the terrain. These fire-scarred Northern Rockies tell a tale of destruction and renewal, a narrative that unfolds beneath my hiking shoes with each passing mile.

When Baggins was hiking with us, he described how fire plays a crucial role in the life cycle of evergreens in the Northern Rockies. Certain species depend on fire for seed release and regeneration, enabling them to utilize the cleared areas and nutrient-rich soil left behind.

That's absolutely remarkable, I muse.

As I hike, I reflect on how some seeds actually need intense heat to germinate. The lodgepole pines rely on wildfires to stimulate new tree growth, their resilience allowing them to regenerate and thrive in the wake of destruction. Even though the forest I'm in now shows signs of past fires, it also holds the promise of renewal.

In a way, I see my own journey reflected in these trees. Growing up in a lower-class household, raised by a single mother, was like navigating my own "wildfire" environment full of challenges that could have easily consumed me. But instead, those trials cleared the way for growth I didn't know I was capable of. They forced me to adapt, root myself in resilience, and find strength in the face of adversity. The fires we face may shape us, I thought, but they also prepare the ground for something stronger to emerge.

In the same way, the evergreens in the Northern Rockies have adapted to survive their harsh environment, finding strength in what might seem like an inhospitable landscape. Another interesting point is how some evergreens in the region have developed needle-like leaves to minimize water loss and endure the cold winters and dry summers.

"Here's a fun fact," Baggins told us. "You can differentiate fir trees from pine trees by their twigs. If the twig feels soft and friendly, it's likely a fir. However, if it causes discomfort or pain when you squeeze it, it's likely a pine."

There are exceptions and variations among different species of fir and pine trees, he explained, so it may not always be true. There are other characteristics, like needle arrangement, cone shape, and bark texture that are also important.

"Are you some kind of tree sage?" I asked him, surprised by my own interest.

"No, just a Baggins," he replied with a smile.

"I'm drawn to the super-skinny, tall trees. They bring to mind those slender Santa figurines," I mentioned.

"Oh, those are probably lodgepole pines," Baggins said, earning himself the nickname "Tree Whisperer" in my mind.

To test his knowledge, I asked about the pine bark beetle, a topic I'd heard others mention.

"These little guys are called mountain pine beetles." He pointed to a nearby tree. "When there's an outbreak, beetles go after pines in particular. They burrow under the bark, creating tunnels that slowly dehydrate the tree from the inside out. What's worse is they introduce fungi that mess with the tree's ability to transport water and nutrients, pretty much shutting it down. You can spot their work by looking for pitch tubes, boring dust around the bark, or staining inside the tree."

"Can you show me?" I asked.

"Look over here," Baggins replied, pointing to a fallen tree off the trail that had been cut down, likely because of a beetle infestation. "See this ring? This is where they infested the tree."

The distinctive blue-green ring contrasted markedly with the noninfested sections—which lacked the ring—indicating where the tree's health had been compromised.

He continued, "They consume the tree at a certain rate until it eventually dies. This area here is where the fluid flows through the tree's xylem layers. When these layers become dead like this, the fluid can't flow, causing the tree to weaken and fall. This ring is a telltale sign of pine beetle blight."

Yeah, I fall over too when dehydrated.

Baggins went on to explain that while the beetles' activity is a natural aspect of forest ecosystems, extensive infestations can lead to substantial ecological and economic consequences, resulting in widespread tree loss and impacting forest landscapes.

This concerns me even more than wildfire. The trees have coexisted somewhat harmoniously with wildfires, but I'm unsure how they can adapt to the beetles desiccating them. Still, the evolution of trees shouldn't be underestimated. Also, forest workers are planting more trees and offering some extra care.

The more time I spend among trees, the more I feel like a "tree hugger," though I'd prefer the more impactful "eco-tree warrior."

A mile ahead on the trail, I see an impressive stand of evergreens, their dark silhouettes rising against the horizon. My best days out here are always spent among these trees, where every step feels like a passage deeper into nature's haven.

CHAPTER 31

An Ode to Peanut Butter

IN MY THRU-HIKING odyssey, a steadfast comrade has unfailingly commanded my attention, and by the time I reach Montana, it has become a beacon of solace on the trail, a remedy for yearning taste buds. This unrivaled protagonist is none other than peanut butter.

Peanut butter is not only a source of sustenance but also a versatile and beloved staple that transforms mundane moments into trailside triumphs in the heart of the CDT's rugged landscapes.

A simple spoonful, scooped from a compact jar nestled in my pack, becomes an instant energy elixir during arduous ascents and endless stretches between resupply points. The dense amalgamation of healthy fats and protein is my secret weapon against the fatigue that looms over every uphill battle. A solitary spoonful becomes a momentary escape, a sensory indulgence that temporarily transports me from the rigors of the trail to a realm of gastronomic delight.

However, peanut butter refuses to be relegated to just a snack; it also asserts itself in various culinary concoctions. A hiker friend enlightened me by demonstrating how a spoonful stirred into her morning oatmeal adds a creamy indulgence. This left me pondering why I hadn't considered it before, and I exclaimed, perhaps overdramatically, "Oh, oh, oh . . . the cosmic enigma unveiled. I now possess the universe's secrets," before going on to add peanut butter to various dehydrated dinners as a fortifying and seasoning agent.

As the miles stack up, peanut butter has assumed an increasingly vital role as a protein powerhouse, fortifying my body against the physical demands of the trail, transforming simple trail fare into a nutrient-dense feast. Whenever I have a "snaccident" (all my snacks have been "accidentally" eaten), peanut butter comes to the rescue.

While resupplying in the town of Lima, Montana, I chance upon a small bottle labeled Skrewball Peanut Butter Whiskey. Initially, I have to do a double take, half expecting it to vanish like a mythical creature. Whiskey isn't my typical choice, but hey, when it (or anything!) is infused with peanut butter, I'm game. Plus, this whiskey comes in a petite 50-milliliter bottle, light enough for this thru-hiker.

At our first campsite out of town, I sample the whiskey. Two observations: First, unsurprisingly the whiskey lacks noticeable peanut butter notes. Second, it surprisingly becomes my preferred whiskey. Perhaps it's the sweetness that appealed to me.

If this ode to peanut butter hasn't made it abundantly clear, my affection for the stuff knows no bounds. Safe to say, it's left its mark—on my taste buds and perhaps even my soul.

CHAPTER 32

As the Crow Flies

I LOOK UP from the steep climb, and as usual, Nature has her head down, trudging along. She's moving slowly but steadily, focused on her feet. I'm too far back to catch her words, but she's surely murmuring something that might offend delicate sensibilities as she struggles to catch her breath. To my right, a steep 45-degree slope descends, covered in pine trees. A few yards of dry grass buffer the edge, keeping the drop far enough away to ward off my vertigo. When I turn my gaze upward, I see two hikers about a hundred feet away, standing on a flat section of the trail.

Both gaze down at us, but Nature, true to form, remains oblivious to their presence. She'll stay like that until she inadvertently collides with them, threatening to send them tumbling down the mountain.

One hiker videos our ascent while providing a running commentary. I recognize the duo.

"Pirate and Dan!" I shout.

"What?" Nature responds, her forward momentum uninterrupted, head still lowered like a horse with blinders.

"Nature, lift your head before you send the Brits into a nosedive!"

She pauses, looks up, and is startled into letting loose a curse and then a joyful scream.

It's nice to see the Brits, though I'm puzzled how they managed to catch up to us. Given Dan's unplanned naps and his tendency to bushwhack in the wrong direction when he's awake, I would have thought they'd be at least a week behind.

"We decided on an alternate trail out of Yellowstone," Dan clarifies.

Ah-hah! They cut several hundred miles from their thru-hike, a necessary adjustment to avoid still being on the CDT in winter. In any case, we hike together like old times, as Dan fills in me and Nature.

"At Yellowstone, we took a route north to Gardiner to shave some miles. We got to Mammoth, but the rangers wouldn't let us proceed north, as the road had been washed out in the flooding earlier this year. They wanted us to head back south and leave via West Yellowstone, a significant retreat we weren't keen on.

"Eventually, the last remaining ranger relented and said that it was possible for us to cut across private land to get to Gardiner, but we had to wait for the ranger to leave before starting, since they could not officially allow our route."

Had the ranger noticed their desperation? Either way, it was a solid move.

Love me some Yellowstone rangers; they are decent people.

"It was pitch black when we got to Gardiner," Dan tells us, "and there were a few steep hills that were tough to traverse. We crossed the Montana border to little fanfare on the private land before we hit Gardiner." The hikers joined the official road just before hitting the town and had to sneak past a staffed ranger station, but nobody noticed them.

We continue hiking closely together for the rest of the climb, enjoying lunch on a mountaintop, discussing how we plan to approach the remainder of our thru-hike. I hope we can stick together for the rest of the day, but shortly after we resume hiking, I notice Pirate, who was right behind me moments ago, falling farther behind, possibly waiting on Dan.

Nature and I pull ahead, then wait at a trail junction where we will turn left onto an alternate trail toward the town of Lincoln for a needed resupply—I'm down to my last energy bar and no peanut butter. The Brits will continue toward High Divide Outfitters near the Stemple Pass trailhead. I pull out my phone and see that we still have ten miles to Lincoln, yet it looks shorter on the app.

"It's as the crow flies," Nature explains.

It's a term I've heard a lot out here on the CDT, one I never used before my time on this trail, but it has a rhythm I like. The words flow with a certain simplicity and elegance, echoing the directness—the proverbial crow flying between two points—that they describe. Out here on the CDT, it's fitting—practical yet poetic, with a cadence that sticks in my mind.

After twenty minutes of waiting, and with ten trail miles, not crow miles, still ahead, we reluctantly press on before the Brits appear. I glance back a couple of times before the trail curves and obscures the view of the junction, half expecting those chuckleheads to appear behind us for a proper farewell. But nothing. I turn one last time.

"Good luck, guys," I whisper before turning back and following Nature.

By 8:00 p.m., we find a side trail that leads to a stream with a grassy spot to camp, six miles from town. While pitching our tents, we receive a group text from Pirate that reads, "Sorry we couldn't keep up. Dan Colorado-ed again."

I shake my head. Yeah, they're going to need a lot of luck and trail magic to finish. And they'll also probably need the CDT to be as straight as the crow flies.

Nature and I arrive in Lincoln by midmorning, checking in to the Blue Sky Motel by 11:00 a.m. It's one of those quintessential roadside motels you find scattered across the CDT's tiny towns, a relic from a time when family road trips ruled and big-box hotels hadn't yet taken over. The wood-paneled walls give off a faint whiff of pine and nostalgia, the kind where you half expect to find a rotary phone on the nightstand. The sign outside proudly advertises "Cable TV!" as if it's still a novelty. But after weeks on the trail, this little one-star wonder feels like pure luxury—a bed, a roof, and a moment of stillness before the next stretch of wilderness.

However, town days are seldom merely for rest; laundry, resupplying, and, most importantly, a shower are top priorities. We empty our backpacks, scattering items across the beds and floor, creating a chaotic scene suggestive of a police raid. Pausing to take in our impressive "packsplosion," I catch Nature reaching into her pockets. She reveals a handful of rocks, which she delicately arranges on the bed like precious gems.

What in the wacky Fraggle Rock *world is all this?*

It's as if Nature has multiple personalities, and one is playing the old practical joke in which a hiker secretly stashes a rock in their friend's backpack. I'm no psychiatrist, but I'm going to go ahead and diagnose Nature with dissociative identity disorder, because no sane thru hiker would continue filling their own pockets with rocks.

But there is a more prosaic explanation. Sofia, Nature's granddaughter, has a deep fondness for rocks with classic geometric shapes. So, Nature collects various stones for her and mails them from the next post office she finds. I suspect the shapes might not be exactly what Sofia expects.

"This is round, right?" Nature asks.

"Well, that's more like an oval," I truthfully answer. "And that's not a cube, it's a cuboid, and that one looks more like a bumpy rock with a side point, instead of a triangle."

Can a person have shape blindness, in the same way they might have color blindness? If not, I'm pretty sure I've stumbled upon the first-ever case. I'm totally going to publish this in a medical journal and become the geometric-figure sensation of the scientific world.

"Fab?"

I come out of my daydream.

"Fab, these shapes are close enough," she assures me.

"OK, what do I know?" I say as I grab my notebook-turned-medical journal and begin jotting down notes.

By evening, Nature and I are joined by Gluten Puff, a friend who thru-hiked the AT the same season I did. We also did some trail maintenance on the AT that same season. She has kindly offered to provide support for the next sixty-odd miles, as she lives in the area. While Nature and I carry only water and energy bars, Gluten Puff will drive ahead, find a short side trail, and have our tents set up and ready by the time we reach camp. This sweet and generous hookup will significantly speed up our thru-hike, shaving off a day or two. Our goal is to finish the CDT in just over two weeks. That should put us in a great position to avoid any harsh winter weather in Montana.

Gluten Puff earned her moniker from a hiker unwilling to share his snack by claiming it contained puffs made of gluten, to which she is allergic. Not the most generous move, but the nickname turned out to be both fitting and helpful, helping her avoid constantly explaining her gluten-free status.

The next morning, Gluten Puff drives us to the Rogers Pass access point on Highway 200, where Nature and I will start a 28.5-mile hike to the Dearborn River.

As we start hiking away, I discreetly snap a photo of Gluten Puff's license plate. Nature shoots me an inquisitive glance.

"I haven't seen her in ten years, and we didn't really hike together. Do I really know her well enough? What if she takes off with everything we need to finish this thru-hike?" I voice my concerns.

"Wait, *now* you tell me?" Nature responds.

It will probably be fine, but the New Yorker in me can't shake these suspicious thoughts. Some old habits are harder to break than others.

"It's fine, I'm just playin'," I say to reassure Nature, though I wonder if it really *is* fine.

Yeah, I'm sure it is. Absolutely probably, or maybe just verging on probably sure.

I check to make sure the license plate number is clear in the photo. I also took a photo of Gluten Puff, cleverly disguised as a group selfie, just in case. If she doesn't change her hair color and leave the state, we should be covered if she absconds with our things.

An hour into our hike, we come across a yurt so close it's practically on the trail. I've never been inside one, so I don't hesitate to offer Nature the chance to walk in first when I see that the door is unlocked. I follow her once it's clear that no one is inside waiting to attack us with a fire poker.

To this native New Yorker who has lived in small apartments his entire life, even this tiny yurt looks fancy-big. It's like a round, portable house for people who are tired of living in shoebox-sized apartments. I'd live here. It has everything my last studio apartment had: a cot, a functional kitchenette, storage space, electricity, and natural lighting from several windows—all part of its serene vibe. There are even stairs up to a second floor. I could totally picture myself sitting in here sipping artisanal coffee and reading an issue of *This Old House: Tiny Home Edition*.

"Come on, Fab. We still have about twenty-five more miles," Nature informs me, ending our open-house tour.

"Twenty-five miles? Is that as the hiker hikes?" I ask.

It takes Nature a moment to grasp what I'm asking before she responds, "No, as the crow flies."

Son of a crow's nest.

A few hours later, we approach 6,500-foot Lewis and Clark Pass, where a sign tells us that, on his return journey, Meriwether Lewis crossed the Continental Divide on July 7, 1806. During their westward journey to the Pacific, Lewis and Clark were unaware of the pass. However, by the time of their return, local Native Americans had informed them about it. The pass had been a key part of the network of trails used by Indigenous peoples long before European explorers ventured into the area.

I wonder if Lewis was crushin' miles like we are. With lighter packs, we're moving swiftly. Now I understand why those ultralighters insist on making their packs as small as possible, cutting corners in ways Lewis and Clark couldn't have dreamed of. I think there's something obsessive about how ultralighters shave off every ounce, from cutting toothbrushes in half to swapping out heavier gear for ultralight alternatives like titanium stoves and dehydrated meals. Even the weight of a tent can be trimmed down with newer, high-tech materials. When you hike like that, every detail matters. You move faster, conserve more energy, and make better time.

As for me, I guess I'm just too attached to my luxury items—if I could, I would carry a portable espresso maker, an inflatable camp couch, and maybe a compact fan to keep things breezy.

By 8:30 p.m., the sun has nearly set. I notice white rocks arranged on the ground spelling out "FAB." It's clearly a sign from Gluten Puff, signaling that she is camped nearby. After half a mile, and having completed our goal of 28.5 miles, I climb down a hill. Through the trees, I spot three tents and someone heating a meal at a campsite.

"Woot woot," I call out.

"Woot woot," I hear in response.

I embrace Gluten Puff, not only because I'm relieved she didn't pilfer our gear, but also because she took the time to set up our tents. Plus, she's the first familiar face I've seen all day since Nature and I separated after I missed a turnoff for a water source.

Nature arrives thirty minutes later.

"I told you she wouldn't plunder and pillage us," I say with glee.

"That was all you, Fab," Nature retorts.

I glance at our trail angel with a shy smirk and a shrug, as if to say, "Oops, my bad."

Gluten Puff laughs it off, but I can't tell if it's a forgiving laugh or a mischievous I'm-going-to-get-you laugh. The silly thought fades quickly as the three of us prepare dinner and describe our days.

The following day, Nature and I cover 28.9 miles, reaching the Benchmark trailhead by 5:00 p.m., where Gluten Puff has set up camp at South Fork, a frontcountry campground right off the CDT. Spread out before us on a picnic table we find chips, bananas, cherries, hummus, bell peppers, and to top it off, Oreos and Dr. Pepper. Once again, Gluten Puff outdid herself. If there was ever any doubt that she would look out for us, she squashed it.

Besides a tinge of guilt for even thinking she had nefarious designs on our battered and stinking backpacking gear, I'm feeling beyond grateful. These last two days, with a total of 57.4 miles hiked with support, have been the break we needed to make it to the end on time. With just over 220 miles left on this thru-hike, it certainly feels like we've moved as swiftly as the crow flies.

CHAPTER 33

Atmospheric Perspective

A YEAR AGO, while I was on a short day hike with my friend Ruth, a landscape painter, she completely shifted my perspective on how I see the shades and colors of nature. She referred to this as "atmospheric perspective."

"It's this cool thing you notice," she began, "when you're looking at stuff that's far away. It's all about how things change in appearance as they recede, and it's influenced by Earth's atmosphere."

To me, it seemed like a refined skill for creatively observing and interpreting the visual world. I was instantly captivated.

"Now, there are a few key things that happen with this perspective magic," Ruth continued. "First off, there's a color shift. You might notice that scenery way in the back starts looking lighter, with a bluish or grayish tint. That's because our atmosphere loves to play with light, scattering it around, and shorter wavelengths like blue get scattered more than the longer ones.

"Then there's the contrast-reduction party. As stuff moves farther away, the difference between light and shadow starts to chill out. It's like nature hits the dimmer switch, giving those distant things a softer, less in-your-face look.

"And last but not least, there's the detail-fading act. Fine details—those little things that make stuff look sharp up close—well, they start getting a bit shy as things go off into the distance. Blame it on the scattering of light and the bits and pieces floating in the atmosphere between your eyes and the object. Artists love to play with these effects to create depth and make things look real in their paintings. It's like they're bringing the outdoors into their studio by mimicking how our eyes see the natural world. Pretty neat, right?"

Wow, talk about having an artist's eye.

I realize that atmospheric perspective goes beyond simple observation; it's also about perceiving the nuances of light, shadow, color, form, and composition. It surpasses what I ever imagined my eyes could notice. Capturing the essence of a scene—understanding the interplay of meadows, mountain shapes, and tree lines, and recognizing subtleties that might escape a casual observer—is a cultivated way of seeing that develops with practice and with a childlike sense of wonder.

My experience on the CDT has been filtered through this idea of atmospheric perspective, and I've maintained a curiosity about what lies at the edge of my sight while traversing the trail. As I draw closer to the distant, monolithic Rocky Mountains, they start to reveal themselves to be an imposing limestone escarpment, gradually dominating the horizon. The air becomes crisper, and the anticipation builds with each step. As I emerge from the forested path, the full grandeur of a massive vertical cliff of craggy rocks comes into view. The Chinese Wall stretches unbroken for roughly a dozen miles and averages one thousand feet tall. It's an ancient geological marvel rising majestically against the backdrop of the Bob Marshall Wilderness, a.k.a. the Bob.

As I approach the Chinese Wall, I attempt to observe this landscape through the eyes of an artist. The limestone formations closest to me reveal a mosaic of deep browns and greens, like a weathered canvas brought to life by sunlight, with sharp details and rugged textures reminiscent of crumpled parchment or the rough skin of an ancient tree.

As my gaze moves, the midrange sections subtly shift into cooler tones of greenish gray and pale brown, softened by a gentle haziness, imparting a sense of distance. Notably, these jagged sections take on the appearance of massive steps; the wall itself seems pieced together, with distinct separations creating a mesmerizing visual of two and sometimes three connected layers. I can see waterlines etched into the rock, evidence of the enduring forces of nature that have shaped this geological wonder. The atmospheric perspective not only adds realism to this scene but also accentuates its grandeur, offering a captivating visual journey through the Chinese Wall's varied colors, jagged precipices, and geological singularity.

This atmospheric perspective has me sounding like an art critic, but not your average art critic. I'm more like a detective with a monocle, hunting for meaning in a painting like it's the last clue to crack the case of *What's Really Going On Here?* Armed with a thesaurus and a skeptical smirk, I'd stalk through art galleries like a cat burglar, ready to pounce on any canvas that dares defy my interpretation. With a flair for the dramatic and a knack for turning a simple brushstroke into a philosophical debate, I'd be the Sherlock Holmes of the art world, solving mysteries such as "Is this a masterpiece or just a mess?" All while sipping on espresso and wearing a beret, of course.

CHAPTER 34

Dreadlocks and the Three Bears

IT'S UNCANNY HOW often I'll chance upon an ideal campsite miles before concluding my day's journey or discover picturesque spots just beyond where I settled the previous night. A mischievous woodland sprite toys with me, rearranging the forest's layout and teasing me with these elusive, perfect campsites.

In my quest for the ideal place to sleep, I often find myself echoing the sentiments of Goldilocks from the classic tale *Goldilocks and the Three Bears*: "This location is too uneven. That one is too strewn with rocks. Ah, but this spot, it's just right." Perhaps my version should be *Dreadlocks and the Three Bears*, though without the three bears, an especially prudent choice in the grizzly-infested terrain of northern Montana.

The size and unpredictable nature of grizzly bears make them far more hazardous than the black bears I saw on the AT. Grizzlies can weigh up to fifteen hundred pounds and stand eight to ten feet tall, while black bears typically reach six hundred pounds and five to seven feet. Grizzlies are stronger, with powerful limbs, two- to four-inch claws, and a shoulder hump for digging and tearing prey. They can run thirty-five miles per hour. In confrontations, grizzlies are more likely to be aggressive, especially if surprised or with cubs, making them potentially deadly, whereas black bears are more likely to flee than fight unless provoked.

I learned from one of my favorite TV shows, the survival-competition series *Alone*, that a bear can detect a carcass from as far as twenty miles and may ambush camps in pursuit of food. This means that in bear country we always eat away from camp, or even before setting up camp, and hang our food bags or use bear canisters. Absolutely no food should be left in a tent.

Ever since leaving Lander a month ago, I've also had my bear spray strapped to my chest while I hike. It reminds me of the time my brother strongly suggested that I carry a machete on the AT for protection from animals and human animals alike. He mentioned they come in sizes small enough to be easily attachable to my chest—right about where my bear spray is now strapped.

Carrying a machete on a thru-hike always felt like a bad idea, so I never added it as part of my gear. There's a big difference in the woods between a thru hiker and a guy wielding a machete. Throw in a hockey mask, and I'd be all set to terrorize fellow hikers. I also feel more reassured by the potential range of bear spray than that of a machete.

I've never actually used bear spray, but I studied a poster I saw at a trailhead that illustrated how to use it. There was a diagram with a silhouette bear charging toward a silhouette person. The person aimed their bear spray downward, about ten feet in front of them. As the bear silhouette charged, its head was low, ensuring that it would run into the cloud of spray and be stopped in its tracks before it gobbled up the silhouette person. To me, this looked way more effective than trying to swing a machete at an attacking beast that weighs ten times more than me.

Especially after witnessing the brutal bear attack in the movie *The Revenant*, I have zero desire to engage in a hands-on battle with a grizzly, even with the help of a machete or bear spray. Heck, I might accidentally injure myself. I imagine the bear observing me as I swing the blade and miss the bear, cutting my own leg off instead. It would likely sit back and chuckle, eagerly anticipating sharing the tale with its bear buddies over a meal—which would, of course, be me.

Nature also carries bear spray and has added finger cymbals to her arsenal. The zills are strapped to the sides of her backpack, ringing like bells as she hikes—no chance of us surprising a bear with all this noise. In addition to warning bears of her approach, she believes they will bring beautiful music to her steps. Plus, she can practice zilling when in camp.

"Oh, we got this," I assure Nature as I walk behind her along the trail, hearing the cymbals clash.

At that moment, she lets out a burp, and for a fleeting moment, I think it's the rumbling growl of a grizzly bear.

Despite all of our preparations, I have another bear encounter. I'm on a trail, northbound, when a hundred yards down a slope to the left of the trail, a black bear catches sight of me. It regards me with curiosity and then proceeds to ascend in my direction, as though I beckoned it like a dog with a "Come, boy." I'm relieved that it's not a grizzly, but this black bear is still a stocky creature whose coat shimmers faintly in the dappled sunlight. Its rounded ears twitch, and its nose, dark and glistening, sniffs the air as if trying to discern the intention behind my frozen stance.

I hasten up the trail, around a boulder, and out of the bear's sight. I stop, and then peek back around the rock. The bear has halted. I watch as it rises onto its hind legs and extends its neck, as though peering up at a high shelf. It spots me once more and starts to move in my direction again. If this bear possessed the power of speech, it would say, "Hold on, I'll be right there." However, whether it harbors a desire for a game of fetch or to gnaw on my limbs, I don't really care to stick around to find out.

I launch into a sprint up the trail. Frustration courses through me for having stopped. It's unfathomable—I'm usually the one vociferating at the screen during horror movies, chastising the characters who inexplicably halt mid-chase to gauge if the axe-wielding killer remains in pursuit. The better strategy is simple: Run until your lungs burn, then continue until the metallic taste of blood fills your mouth. The real challenge lies in not stumbling over a twig or stone, like these small rocks on the trail that are now, damnably, slowing my pace. If I stumble, I suppose I'll have little grounds for complaint; it would be a just consequence of my belated dash to safety.

I catch up to Nature and try to put on an air of composure.

"You know, that bear started climbing toward us. Might be wise to pick up the pace," I suggest, my tone urgent.

We move as quickly as the uphill climb allows. The trail slants slightly to the left, clinging to the gradient. However, it doesn't slow me down. I press on, leaning right, toward the rock outcrops that line the trail.

"We lost it," I finally inform Nature, who is walking in front of me.

As she turns back, I scream, "Oh snap, it's on the trail in front of you!" and dart in the opposite direction.

Amid my laughter, I can't tell if my childish prank has worked.

"Not funny, Fab," she scolds.

"Yeah, let's just keep going in case it actually does catch up," I suggest.

Normally, I let Nature take the lead with her noisemakers so she can scare off any predators—or be the first to be attacked, giving me a chance to escape. However, this time around, I charge ahead, trying to put distance between us and the bear I know is still somewhere behind us.

CHAPTER 35

Hike, Climb, Repeat

AS I NEAR the end of my time on the CDT, I've come to see thru-hiking as a rugged and rhythmic dance with nature. Each day unfolds with the same routine—hike, climb, repeat—the days out here are stripped down to their core elements. We wake with the sun, put one foot in front of the other, ascend towering peaks, and descend into serene valleys. Each step becomes a meditation, each climb a new challenge, and each repetition of the ritual a testament to our ever-increasing endurance. Through it all, I find solace in the simplicity, the raw attachment with the land, and the profound sense of accomplishment that comes from completing miles of rigorous terrain. Thru-hiking is not just a physical feat; it's a soul-stirring experience.

I am trudging along the dusty trail just south of Glacier County, my trusty backpack strapped on securely, as I struggle with an annoying sensation that has been bothering me for several miles: a wedgie.

It's not just any wedgie; this one is a relentless, persistent, and determined wedgie that seems to have made it its life's mission to torture me. With each step, I awkwardly attempt to discreetly dislodge it, but this wedgie refuses to give up its grip. I attempt the speed-walking-and-hoping-it-vanishes approach, but that appears to push it deeper into my crevice.

"This damn wedgie. I can't get rid of it," I mutter.

"Yeah, I've seen you going at it for a while now," says Nature.

Guess I wasn't so discreet after all.

"It must be glued to my butt," I say in frustration as I try yet again to wiggle it loose.

I thought about stopping, stripping down, and readjusting, but the idea quickly passed—I really want to keep moving. Plus, I have a feeling my underwear will crawl right back up as soon as I start hiking again. In fact, I've begun to wonder if this wedgie aspires to become a thru-hiker itself; I can hear it saying, "Hey, I hiked the Continental Divide Trail too—one chafe at a time."

As I march along the crystal-clear waters of Dean Lake, its surface reflecting the pine trees that skirt its edge and the craggy peaks of the towering Pentagon Mountain, I grin at the absurdity of my situation—and at my new archnemesis, the Wicked Wedgie of the West.

It's a reminder that even in a majestic landscape like the Flathead National Forest, life's little nuisances have a way of keeping me humble, distracted, and engaged. So onward I hike, wedgie and all, accepting the hilarity wrought by this new and unexpected companion.

We've established camp just a few yards off the trail, beside the peaceful flow of Benson Creek. Large rocks form a circle around a firepit, and five tree stumps serve as seating. The cleared area is spacious enough for three, maybe four tents, and the surrounding conifers add a cozy, sheltered feel to the spot, perfect for an evening under the stars. Tomorrow, we anticipate reaching East Glacier Park by midafternoon, our final rest and resupply town on the CDT before the last hundred miles. Knowing this rejuvenates me, liberating me from the discomfort of the underwear yank.

Nestled in my tent, I write in my journal by headlamp, earbuds in, grooving to '90s R&B while jotting down a rush of thoughts. I'm typically cautious about conserving battery life on my phone, as it serves as my primary navigation tool, but the assurance of charging all my devices in town tomorrow leaves me unconcerned about running out of juice.

I sing Maxwell's song "Sumthin' Sumthin'" in my best sultry voice. Right now, everything feels copacetic.

Suddenly I feel my tent abruptly shake and shift off the ground. I quickly remove my earbuds.

"What the . . . ?"

I pop my head up and stretch my neck like an animal, scanning for danger. Frozen, I strain to hear. Silence surrounds me.

"Nature!" I shout.

"Yeah," she says from her tent.

"Did you hear that?"

"What, your scream?"

I didn't realize I had made a sound. I hope it wasn't a high-pitched scream. Explaining that away would be tricky.

"Uh, yeah, but what else did you hear? My tent just shook!"

"Well," she calmly says, "I did hear something walking past my tent."

"What-the-what!" I exclaim.

I wonder if that exuberant, fetching bear I encountered the other day has finally tracked me down. If only thru-hiking came with a bailout option like on *Alone*. This would be the moment I'd grab the satellite phone and calmly utter, "I'm officially tapping out."

Make sure the extraction team has tranquilizer darts potent enough to take down a bear.

All these thoughts cross my mind, yet here I am in the wilderness with a phone boasting zero bars. On the plus side, I'm not alone—I figure I have a 50/50 chance of surviving, maybe 70/30 since I'm optimistic I can outpace Nature, especially in the dire circumstance of fleeing for our lives. Realistically, our chances of survival would be better together, facing down and trying to scare off a bear. Also, the way Nature is so chill after hearing something walk past our tents is eerie in itself—she's the calm, cool, and collected person in those horror movies who always seems to find their way to safety.

I dim my headlamp, wondering if the bright light attracted an animal (bear!) that then leaned against my tent, accidentally slipped down, and then had to lift my tent to free itself. Regardless, I'm feeling too apprehensive to poke my head out and have a look.

This is going to keep me up all night is my last thought as I drift into my thru-hiker slumber, marshaling my energy for tomorrow's thirty-miler.

The next day Nature and I pause for a break at Summit Campground, located near Highway 2. The town of East Glacier is just eleven miles away.

"By the way, Fab, I spoke to my son this morning," Nature begins as she puts her phone into her front pants pocket. "He thinks that it was a Bigfoot that shook your tent last night." Nature nonchalantly says this as if a Sasquatch was an everyday occurrence.

"Hold on a sec," I respond, adopting the tone of a receptionist taking a call. I wish everything around me would freeze, giving me time to ponder this. The jolt to my tent, the leisurely stroll past Nature's tent. She described the sound as like a human stride, but on a grander scale.

"Eureka, that's what it was!" I exclaim.

It was a hairy cryptid. I'm sure of it now.

How thrilling to have survived a Bigfoot encounter. Although I didn't see or hear anything, I did feel something large shake and push into my tent that I'm guessing wasn't a bipedal circus bear. It's funny how, now that I've seen a moose, all sorts of creatures seem to present themselves to me. What's next, aliens?

Do I truly believe in Bigfoot? While there are numerous anecdotal stories about Bigfoot sightings on all three major long-distance hiking trails in the United States—the AT, PCT, and CDT—the most prominent tales tend to come from the more remote and forested sections of the PCT and the northern stretches of the CDT, where dense wilderness provides a suitable habitat for such a legendary creature. Stories frequently emerge from the rugged Wyoming and Montana sections, where the remote and mountainous terrain is believed to be a potential Bigfoot habitat.

I want to believe, just like I want to believe in mermaids, fairies, the Mothman, and that ugly creature from Puerto Rico, the chupacabra. My fascination with cryptids stems from their inherent mystery—they linger in my mind unchallenged and can be as grand as I make them. And maybe, just maybe, the world is a bit more magical with these mysteries left unsolved.

CHAPTER 36

Through with This Thru-Hike

WE CONTINUE HIKING and talking, riffing on how much Nature's granddaughter, Sofia, would love it out here if there were fairies. Our goal is to complete the CDT on September 16, Sofia's birthday and nine days away. It would be incredibly special for Nature to mark the occasion with her granddaughter—she could proudly say she completed her toughest hike on Sofia's special day.

We arrive in East Glacier around 5:00 p.m. This tiny village, nestled on the eastern edge of Glacier National Park, serves as a gateway to the park's exquisite wilderness and breathtaking mountain landscapes. From town, we take in views of the rugged Lewis Range, its peaks etched sharply against the sky and dusted with snow, with more snow predicted in the next day or so.

At the Looking Glass Basecamp hostel, Will, the owner, greets us warmly. He and his wife, Luna, recently purchased the former restaurant, which they've transformed into a cozy hostel.

After checking in, our next stop is, of course, lunch. We go to Two Medicine Grill, a local diner with a classic setup. The front half features a counter with stools that face the open kitchen. Toward the back, a dining area is arranged with booths and small tables. The hardwood-paneled walls are adorned with work from local artists, creating a cozy, hometown vibe. Behind one of the booths, an open door leads directly into the Glacier Park Trading Company, conveniently stocked with groceries, hiking gear, souvenirs, and even a deli counter.

On our way back to our hostel, we pass a train station. I'm surprised, but shouldn't be by now, to see three cows standing right by the tracks, looking like the neighborhood stray dogs. All along the CDT, I've seen cows. Cows rule the CDT. It's their territory, and they don't care one bit how you feel about that.

At a Native American art gallery shop, Nature and I learn that this area is the traditional territory of the Blackfeet tribe. The Blackfeet live in the northern Great Plains, primarily in present-day Montana and Alberta, Canada. They are part of the Blackfoot Confederacy, which includes three closely related tribes: the Siksika, Kainai, and Piikani.

Historically, the Blackfeet were nomadic bison hunters who followed herds across the plains. Over centuries, they developed a rich cultural heritage and complex societal structures. That way of life was significantly affected by European colonization, the introduction of horses, and later, the depletion of bison due to overhunting by fur traders and settlers. Today, the Blackfeet Nation works to preserve their culture, language, and traditions while navigating the challenges of the modern world.

Doing my own research, I find that there was a well-known member of the Blackfeet tribe called Running Eagle, or Pi'tamaka. She lived at the end of the nineteenth century and held a prominent position as a skilled warrior and leader, earning admiration for her bravery and strategic acumen. Notably, Running Eagle embraced a Two-Spirit identity, embodying both masculine and feminine qualities. Despite her unique identity, Running Eagle commanded great respect within the tribe.

A lot of the CDT goes through or near traditional Native American lands and reservations. Many times, when hiking along high ridges, I would lose myself in thoughts of how the Indigenous people once roamed free here—until the Europeans came along.

After coordinating our camping plans and schedule with the Glacier National Park rangers, we start our final days. Months ago, when the border was still closed in many places because of Covid-19, I had to choose to take the Chief Mountain alternate trail instead of the Waterton Lake trail, which is the CDT's red line, or official path. The border has recently reopened, but my plans to meet up with friends who'll be my ride back to civilization are already set in motion and can't be changed. So, Chief Mountain remains our route.

Because of recent bear activity, the Glacier rangers inform me that no one's allowed to camp at the first designated campground, Two Medicine.

It's a nice day for a hike, so Nature and I don't mind the extra miles. In fact, our first two days are weather perfect.

Twenty-six miles into Glacier, we begin to skirt around Red Eagle Lake. We pass by a guy who looks like a hippie Jesus, wearing nothing but his undershorts. He's so transfixed by the lake, lost in a moment of communion, that he doesn't acknowledge us as we hike by. Respecting his spiritual moment, I move on, tapping my bear spray for reassurance—I'm ready for curious bears or "curious" people.

Our designated campground for the night awaits on the northern side of the large lake. From a distance, we see a bear near the campground, but it meanders toward the other side of the lake.

As night falls, I realize I haven't used the privy today. This is a big deal—I'm usually as regular as clockwork. Not wanting to break a long-running streak, I get out of my tent at 10:00 p.m. and behold a clear night sky, the moon just coming up over the surrounding silhouette of the mountains.

I walk to the privy in the dark with one trekking pole and my bear spray, making enough noise to make myself known in case the bear we saw earlier is lingering. At the privy, I handle my business quicker than a race car pit stop, and then make it back to my tent without incident.

The next few days pass quietly, which suits me just fine. I spend my time mentally capturing the landscape, the trees, and the surrounding mountains. While I do take some actual photos—I'd be a fool not to—I focus primarily on using all my senses to fully absorb the experience.

Today, the trail is overgrown, with underbrush that reaches our shoulders and, at times, completely covers our path. I watch as Nature, ahead of me, is swallowed by thimbleberry bushes. As she steps into them, they close behind her like a revolving door. I step into them and hold my breath, as if jumping into a wave.

When not submerged in foliage, we glimpse Saint Mary Lake—the second-largest lake in Montana, lined with spectacular, castellated mountains—to our right. Nature draws my attention to movement across the lake, about half a mile away, where cars glide along the scenic Going-to-the-Sun Road.

Four days in, we make it to Many Glacier, a public campground inside Glacier National Park run by the National Park Service. It's a frontcountry campground, with trappings like fire rings, picnic tables, restrooms, and potable water. These differ from backcountry camping sites, which are more remote, less accessible, and with few or no amenities—the kinds of sites we've become used to.

It feels disorienting to have the comforts of civilization so close while we camp, the hum of distant engines reminding us of a world that's been mostly distant for months. There's a strange comfort in the familiarity of paved paths and clean restrooms, but also a subtle discomfort. The buzz of nearby campers, the casual chatter over campfires, the ease of it all is almost too safe, too predictable. The open skies, the wind whispering through the trees, and the relentless rhythm of the wilderness feel miles away, already part of a vanishing dream. The clink of a metal pot, the hiss of a stove, the clatter of a cooler lid—it's a different vibe here, the kind that comes not from isolation but from surrender to convenience and comfort.

We initially intend to spend one night, but the weather forecast calls for rain the next day, and Salgado is supposed to join us but hasn't arrived yet. Nature and I decide to stay at Many Glacier for an extra day, then hike the few additional miles to our designated campground tomorrow.

I hope Salgado is ready to hike.

"Hey, is that him?" Nature asks. She has been looking for Salgado's car all morning, and has been calling out every car that passes. After a half dozen false alerts, this time she seems to have found him.

The slow-moving car comes to a stop, then reverses. I see the broad smile of the guy who, five months ago, witnessed me vomit into the bushes on my first day on the CDT.

"Fab!"

"Salgado, you made it." I'm happy to see my guy again, and we hug when he gets out of the car.

"Dude, I thought I was going to have to drive through this huge campground for hours looking for you."

Yeah, with over a hundred campsites, that may have taken him a while.

"You can thank Nature's eagle eyes for that. She was on the lookout."

I help him unload gear, and we set out on a short hike from the Swiftcurrent Pass trailhead, which starts right at the parking lot. A quarter mile in, we round a bend and spot a moose bathing at Fishercap Lake.

Now that I've finally seen a moose, they appear to me so frequently it's like I have the power to summon them at will.

We join other people standing by the lake, taking pictures of the bathing moose.

I notice it moving toward us.

"No way, that moose is headed our way," I say with my phone still recording. "Oh, it's moving toward us—time to move, everyone!" I begin to back up, planning to scamper off into the woods.

Chaos erupts, like something from a Godzilla movie. Everyone is stumbling, tripping over one another. Amid the commotion, I hear a baby wailing. We're having a doomsday moment. I half expect a tree to be flung past me by some colossal monster or perhaps to be knocked down by someone in the crowd.

To my right, I see Salgado entangled in branches and vines, scrambling through thick undergrowth. It strikes me as odd that he's not staying on the trail. I catch sight of others just behind me.

I continue running, relieved that I'm still on the trail with a clear path ahead for a swift escape. I anticipate a scream from Salgado, who I assume will be trampled at any moment, but no such sound reaches my ears. I risk a quick glance back, only to realize that Salgado is now running close behind me. Before I can ask him how he managed to extract himself from the slender trees, the massive moose thunders across the trail right in front of us. Its hooves slam against the earth, echoing like drums as it vanishes into the dense woods. We're rooted in place, hearts pounding like we've just dodged a freight train.

"That was nuts!" exclaims Salgado.

I agree. That was exhilarating and dangerously awesome, yet a surefire way to age prematurely—my heart is still pounding as I stand there and pant.

"Hey, you won't believe what just happened," I exclaim to a hiker who's arrived amid the post-moose-attack chaos.

I eagerly show her my video capturing the moment the moose initiated its charge.

"It was total mayhem," I recount, with my words speeding out. "I saw parents sprinting with their toddler, passing him back and forth like a football, like a quarterback handoff. I'm not exactly sure why, though."

"Really?" the hiker responds circumspectly.

"Nah," I admit with a chuckle. "I was too busy running for my life. Honestly, I thought this guy here"—pointing to Salgado—"was a goner."

"So did I," Salgado says with a sigh.

More people arrive to hear the moose-stampede story, which becomes more outrageous with each retelling. Someone claims the moose spit at them as it ran past. I call malarkey on that one, but then, not to be outdone, add, "Well, the moose winked at me and let me touch its antlers before galloping off toward the UFO it came from," keeping a straight face until I break into a smile.

"I can't believe that happened. I need to rewrite a letter," I say.

"What's that, Fab?" Salgado asks.

"Oh, nothing," I say, brushing it off, but I'm mentally adding to my Dear Moose II letter:

PPS. Scratch that. I was chased.

Nature and I are currently opting for short miles on the trail. We could have wrapped up the last three legs of our thru-hike—a ten-miler, a three-miler, and a six-miler—in a single day. However, we want to stick to our plan to finish on September 16, Sofia's birthday.

We're on the Chief Mountain Trail, a mere twenty-seven miles from the Canadian border and the completion of this five-month journey. As my days here grow fewer, I'm more resolved than ever to soak in as much of Mother Nature's classic quirkiness as my senses can hold. With only two days left, we traverse the vast, untamed landscapes of northern Montana, where a sensory orchestra unfolds before us. The air is full of a refreshing bouquet of lupines, beargrass, and Indian paintbrush. Their subtle sweetness mingles with the mountain breezes. The temperature is just right—that perfect equilibrium where the warmth of the sun meets the cool caress of mountain air. Add to that the endless azure skies, and what you have is the ideal weather for a hike.

In this immersive tapestry, time loses its grip, and I am left to revel in the exquisite details of the trail, savoring the crisp, woody fragrances of lodgepole pines, Douglas-firs, and Engelmann spruce. Their scents are sharp, fresh, and grounding. Under my shoes, the trail changes texture, the soft embrace of pine-needled paths giving way to the earthy crunch of gravel, producing a rhythmic and hypnotic cadence of footfalls.

"Are you seeing this?" Nature asks me about the scenery.

"What, the pink elephants?" I say.

"Huh?"

Of course I see it.

It's day 158, our last morning on the CDT. We begin at Gable Creek Campground. Our tents rest on some of the flattest ground we've found on this trail, nestled among pine trees that block much of the morning light. We sit on six-foot-long log benches, arranged in two squares of four logs each, side by side, creating plenty of spaces to prepare and eat breakfast before starting the final six miles of our thru-hike. It should be a straightforward, uneventful day . . . or so I'm thinking, until Nature approaches me as I grab our hung food bags.

"Sit down. I want to tell you something, and don't say anything," Nature demands.

Oh no, she's really going to let me have it.

I'm not sure what I did, but she's never used such a serious tone with me before—except for that time we were climbing in the heat and then the rain, and she snapped at me for something I don't recall. Maybe I deserved it, maybe not, but it obviously wasn't serious enough to cause a rift, because here we are, all these miles later. Yet, maybe she somehow knows about my early hesitation about hiking with her, way back in Silver City. Much has happened since then. I've come to see how strong of a hiker she is—stronger than most who are much younger.

Couldn't she have waited until we finished this last hike to bring this up, whatever it is?

"Look, if you ever need anything, if you need a mom to be proud of what you're doing—because you're a nice guy, a good guy, and you have so much to be proud of—I'm here for you," she says solemnly.

I'm touched yet surprised at what I'm hearing. Throughout this entire journey, Nature has kept insisting she's no one's trail mother. She is very adamant about that.

"Hey, I thought you said you weren't anyone's mom out here?"

"I will be for you," she says.

I stand there, fighting back tears. I give Nature a hug, and then she walks away.

This woman is really trying to make me cry.

What a turn of events. Not only is she not mad at me, but she wants to adopt me. It just goes to show you that the most foulmouthed, toughest-exterior people are often the sweetest inside.

"F'ing yeah. I hiked the CDT, and I'll never have to do it again," Nature remarks, sounding like a disgruntled cashier on her last day on the job.

I continue hiking ahead, listening to Nature's unique brand of sentimental musings behind me. I want a solitary and nostalgic farewell, distancing myself from Nature's cranky monologue.

Salty by Nature to the end.

I smile at the thought, reminiscing about all the outrageous remarks this diminutive sixty-three-year-old has made in the past five months. Thoughts of my CDT journey sway in my mind like the branches of a weeping willow tree. No single moment dominates, but many vie for my attention. I transition from recalling my time in the New Mexico desert those first days, to crossing the Gila River multiple times within a few days, to trekking to the highest altitude I've ever reached, summiting Grays Peak in Colorado.

I'm aware that I'm pulling farther and farther away from not just Nature, but Salgado, who is finding it difficult trying to keep up with two fit thru-hikers. As I hike on, the boundary between nature and myself blurs. I realize that I was not just a visitor in the wilderness, but an integral part of it. This experience has taught me that the greatest rewards often lie just beyond the edge of my comfort zone.

And then there was that killer wedgie.

Caught in a maze of thoughts, I teeter on the brink of introspection, lost amid the majestic peaks stretching endlessly before me.

"Derick!"

I snap back to reality. My eyes are open, but I'm not really seeing what's in front of me. I shake my head to clear my thoughts.

"Fam!"

My two close friends from Asheville, Shirley and Gary, approach with open arms. They've come to support, congratulate, and join me for these last few miles. I'm thrilled to see them, but it also hits me that we're nearing the end. This thought, along with their presence, makes my eyes well up.

"We were hoping to catch you farther down the trail, but we got caught in traffic," Shirley announces.

"How close are we?" I ask.

"About a half a mile," Gary says.

"Oh, that close. I thought we had a bit farther," I softly say.

"Yeah, we wanted to hike at least the last three miles with you," Shirley shares.

"Hey, I'm just grateful you're here to celebrate this moment," I say.

We wait for Nature, I do the introductions, and then we begin the last half mile together. We reach the Chief Mountain trailhead and parking area—less than a quarter mile from the border—where Nature's son, Kyle, is waiting with a big grin.

We chat for a bit, savoring the last few steps. I see a US Border Patrol car just south of the lot. I sense that he's watching us, waiting for us to make our move toward the border so he can jump into action—and probably not with celebratory balloons.

We move toward the line between the countries, with me leading and Nature, Kyle, Gary, and Shirley following. I expect a bullhorn warning from the patrol car, but instead I hear the car engine start and drive toward us as we begin leaving the lot. I keep my eyes on the two metal barrier gates that mark the entry to Canada; there's a stop sign posted on one. Between them sits a round, raised-stone garden bed, about two feet high and five feet in diameter. None of this is meant to be difficult to pass—that's what the Border Patrol is for. Just beyond the gates, on the Canadian side, stands a border inspection building.

I refuse to tear my eyes away from the border, even when I hear the agent step out of his patrol car.

"Hi, we just hiked the entire Continental Divide Trail!" Nature gleefully says.

"Well, I woke up this morning," the Border Patrol agent shoots back, in a failed attempt at wit.

I'm wary of saying something snarky and confrontational that might put the final steps of my thru-hike in jeopardy. I also consider the kind of day this agent is having and the countless times he's probably heard the CDT spiel before.

He tells us that we can approach the international boundary monument, which looks identical to the one at the southern terminus of the CDT—a four-foot-tall stone obelisk set on a two-foot-square base—a few hundred feet away, but go no farther. It goes unsaid that Nature and I will approach the monument independently. We give each other space to finish alone, with our feelings, thoughts, and emotions. Then we can all celebrate together.

Oddly, I'm not filled with emotion, as I was when hiking alone three miles back. In fact, I feel as if I'm not physically here. I touch the monument, lean my forehead against it, and whisper a thank you. I stay in that position, unaware for how long.

I must look like I'm praying to this thing.

I pull back as soon as the thought pops into my head and walk a few feet away to give Nature her moment.

Once we all have our time with the stone, the photo shoot begins. We pose together by the monument. Our friends ask questions about our CDT experience. Nature and I share a few stories and spend some time reminiscing. We talk of Nature's hiking pants, and how they have more patches than a quilt made by my grandma.

As we celebrate our completion, I receive a text from Verizon "congratulating" me on my thru-hike.

Welcome to Canada.
As talk, text and data
is included in your
domestic plan you'll
have no additional
charges while roaming.
Enjoy your trip.

What a trip it was. I wasn't sure what to expect, but I knew I wouldn't find out unless I took those initial steps. As the American poet Theodore Roethke once said, "I learn by going where I have to go."

At the beginning, in the New Mexico desert, it would have been reasonable to assume from my faltering first steps that I'd quit within days. Yet, like Frodo in *The Lord of the Rings*, I somehow defied expectations and reached the journey's end. Although I feel a bit weathered, I conceal it. I savor the moment like I would a chilled bottle of champagne.

Nature's smile is radiant, bigger than I have ever seen. I sense the joy behind that smile is the one of a castaway spotting a rescue ship. Salvation has come, and returning home is paramount. She completed the CDT and is now a Triple Crowner. She will sit back and take it all in one day, but for now, she's through with this thru-hike.

We walk back to the parking area. I wave at the Border Patrol guy standing at his car. He waves back. Not a bad chap after all. He watched every minute of our celebration, and I sense that he at least acknowledges that this is a special moment for us all.

Before Nature leaves with Kyle, we compare our sun gloves, still on our hands, noting how dirty and torn they've become. I'm not much for goodbyes, and I can tell Nature isn't either. We promise to stay in touch; she lives just an hour from the Long Trail in Vermont, so we agree to connect if I ever attempt that trail again. And just like that, she and Kyle are off on their long drive to Denver.

Salgado and I ride with Gary and Shirley, who have rented a cabin. On our way, we pick up Salgado's car. When morning comes, we say our goodbyes, and Salgado and I drive through East Glacier to pick up an extra resupply box I left at the Looking Glass.

When we arrive, the owner tells us that Dan and Pirate are staying there—and that a black bear pounced on Pirate's tent, and he punched it in the nose. When we see the Brits, Pirate says that he inadvertently punched it, but I think the story is much cooler if he leaves "inadvertently" out.

I wonder if what happened to Pirate is what happened to me when I felt something large land on my tent. I push the thought aside—my story's way cooler if I stick with Bigfoot.

Our catch-up is brief, as Pirate, distracted, walks away—either after a female hiker I've never seen before or to the free breakfast buffet in town. I'm guessing the breakfast.

Dan tells us, "Just because I don't want to seem like less than a man, and I don't have a cool story, I feel like I should add that I did give a mouse a light slap. It was in the inner lining of my tent. It wouldn't go away."

"Mouse, bear—same difference," I respond.

"Yeah, that's how I feel."

"OK, I'll let you go. Get you some of that breakfast," I say with a wave.

"OK, congrats, Fab," he says, heading off toward the free food.

"Congrats, Buck," I say, finally using Dan's absurd trail name.

Dan turns toward me. I see a glint in his eyes, a smile on his face, and he sighs, relieved that the showdown is over. With my having finally embraced his trail name—a perfect fit for his wry, ironic British sense of humor—we part ways. Ahead, he and Pirate still have over ninety miles to complete, while all my miles are now behind me.

What a fabulous thru-hike.

I shake my head in disbelief. Another unlikely adventure completed, a feat I never imagined I'd achieve. Initially, I thought my first thru-hike would be a singular experience, a one-time adventure. Yet, here I am, drawn back to the long-distance trail. It called out to me, and I answered, hiking farther and experiencing more than I ever thought possible. I wasn't sure how I'd pull it off, but deep down, I sensed that this was how my time on the CDT would conclude. It's astonishing to reflect upon and realize what it took to complete the CDT.

As I anticipated, my 158-day, nearly 3,100-mile thru-hike wasn't without its challenges. But smooth sailing? Where's the adventure in that? It unfolded precisely as it was meant to: a period of self-discovery and acceptance, sprinkled with lessons learned and humor shared with friends. The CDT presents countless extremes, yet if approached with an understanding of what awaits at the finish line, it offers the right blend of the good, the bad, and the fab.

Having said that, I now grasp why Triple Crowners opt for this trail as their final one—completing the grueling CDT might leave one with scant inclination to embark on another thru-hike. As for whether I have another thru-hike in me, I'll refrain from saying *never*, except when I'm absolutely certain. And I won't shut any doors—especially if they lead to the great outdoors.

Epilogue

SALGADO ONCE SHARED with me a quote by C. S. Lewis from his novel *Out of the Silent Planet*: "A pleasure is full grown only when it is remembered." This thru-hike, along with the remarkable people I met, will be etched in my memory forever.

When I thru-hiked the AT in 2012, something changed in me that I didn't completely understand. I went from city life to craving the trail every day. I couldn't stop talking about my AT thru-hike, and soon people were asking me to share my story. An overzealous guy with dreadlocks, passionately praising the outdoors, caught attention and led to my first book.

For years, I toured with my first book, *The Unlikely Thru-Hiker,* and shared all my wacky stories at middle schools, high schools, colleges, bookstores, libraries, outfitters, outdoor events, and even a few times at the Javits Center in New York City. I was hooked. If I wasn't hiking, I was talking about it, and if I wasn't doing either, I was writing about hiking. Hiking is now ingrained in me, like the rhythm of my own heartbeat.

Yet, it wasn't until I completed the CDT and delved into speaking and writing *this* book that I realized storytelling is more than just my interest—it is my full-time calling. To fully commit to this new direction, I left the fast-paced life of New York City and moved to the mountain town of Asheville, North Carolina, a place that offers both inspiration and practicality for my new chapter. Focusing on sharing the outdoors comes with sacrifices, including a significant financial adjustment. New York City, as vibrant as it is, no longer aligned with the life I envisioned, so I committed, in my new home, to making writing, speaking, and hiking not just my work, but the very essence of my life's purpose.

On several occasions, I've been told that when it comes to the AT, CDT, and PCT, I can do one or all three, but stopping at two isn't an option. I'm not thrilled by that pressure, especially since I've never felt a personal need to complete all three. Hiking long trails isn't about ticking off boxes or meeting some arbitrary standard; it's about the journey, the moments that unfold along the way, and the personal growth that comes with each step. The idea of being bound to a checklist felt limiting, the real value of the experience being lost in the expectation to finish them all.

Thru-hiking requires commitment, resources, and, above all, time. If all three of these factors align for me, who knows—the PCT might be in my future. For now, though, my focus is on writing, speaking, and deepening my connection with this incredible outdoor community.

Plot Twist: By the time this book is in your hands, I will have attempted to thru-hike the PCT. Did I actually finish? Well, that's classified information. Maybe I crushed it. Maybe I took a side trip to Los Angeles, got caught up in the Hollywood scene, and now I'm moonlighting as a stunt double. Chances are, if you follow me on social media you already know whether I made it—but for the rest of you, guess you'll have to wait and see—who knows, there might just be a PCT book in the works. *Cue mysterious eyebrow raise.*

I toyed with the idea of naming this book *Type-Two, Teetering on Type-Three, Fun* because that was the essence of most of this thru-hike. I can write and talk about the CDT now with a smile, but damn if I didn't think I was in over my head more times than I can count. However, "Peace, Love & All That Good Stuff" got me through. An optimistic mindset will always go farther than a pessimistic one.

Now, living in North Carolina, I've been leaning on that same optimism as I rebuild my life after the devastation wrought by Hurricane Helene. Asheville's tight-knit community has been a source of strength, and I've found purpose in lending a hand wherever I can—helping neighbors clear debris, supporting local organizations, and simply showing up for others. It's a grounding reminder of how resilience, whether on the trail or in everyday life, can turn chaos into connection. Balancing my new life here with writing and speaking has been its own kind of thru-hike, one step at a time, with gratitude ever my guide.

Acknowledgments

SO MANY PEOPLE to thank. Here we go!

To all my beta readers, who were so valuable in helping me refine this story, your insights, encouragement, and honesty have been indispensable:

Mark Slotoroff, my dude! We go way back. I love your kind soul and the honest opinions you gave on my rough draft.

Jennifer McManus, I deeply appreciate that, despite knowing nothing about me or my first book, you offered invaluable feedback tailored to help newcomers understand this nutty yet fabulous thru-hiking world.

Sue Schleh, you went above and beyond with your feedback and edits. You are one heck of an awesome person.

Alasdair and Katherine Green—schoolteachers give some of the best feedback. Love you both!

Abigail Coyle was the editor of my first book, *The Unlikely Thru-Hiker*, and when I asked if she would be a beta reader, she did not hesitate. Abigail, you gave me insight into my work that I would have paid for—but I'm thankful you didn't charge me.

Solo, Tie, and Sidetrack, the beginning of my thru-hike would have been completely different without you three. I truly appreciate everything you did to help me get started. Big hugs to all of you—you're an absolute blast to be around!

To all my sponsors, thank you—without your support, another thru-hike wouldn't have been possible.

Sven Brunso from Leki, who was the first to build a friendship with me and make me a sponsored athlete.

Farm to Feet, though we didn't know each other long, you didn't hesitate to sponsor this thru-hike.

Rob Peterson, from the jump, I thought you were one cool dude. I thank you and the entire Big Agnes crew for supplying me with the best tent, sleeping bag, and pad—oh, and an air pillow I didn't know I needed on a thru-hike. Special thanks to Kate Wingrove for the ride into Steamboat Springs, Colorado, and a tour of the Big Agnes headquarters and the repair shop.

Rob Coughlin, owner of Granite Gear, you're like the big brother I always wanted. Even before we met, I've only used your backpack, and I never turned back. Thank you, Granite Gear team, for making sure I had a new backpack for this thru-hike.

To the entire Oboz Footwear Fam: Regan Betts, who started the ball rolling on this CDT thru-hike idea. Kenny "Salgado" Gamblin, thank you for capturing my good side on the trail. Martijn Linden and Abigail Cook, our brainstorming Zoom meetings are my fav. And to the rest of the Oboz crew, thank you all for embracing me and making me your first-ever sponsored athlete.

The Mountaineers Books team: Emily White, acquisitions editor—thank you for always being willing to hop on a Zoom call and answer my many questions. You did it with a smile and were as enthusiastic as I was about tackling this CDT project. Matt Samet, developmental editor—your notes throughout the revision process were the key to unlocking the best story I could tell. Theresa Winchell, copy editor—your insight and writing expertise are impeccable. It's clear that words are your thing. Beth Jusino, project editor—as I navigated the publishing process, which some writers may find tedious, I found myself looking forward to your notes. Your input wasn't just valuable; it was something I truly wanted to see and learn from. It didn't feel like work at all—more like a conversation with a friend about the words I created.

Jon LaValley, cover illustrator, I knew you were going to create another piece of art that would make it hard for eyes to tear away from. Thank you! Melissa McFeeters, interior designer, thank you for giving the readers a map they can follow along and for giving this book a fabulous and sleek look. Big thanks to creative director Jen Grable and to Kate Jay, publicist extraordinaire, whose enthusiasm for sharing this book had no limits—thank you!

To the CDTC, thank you for your unwavering support and dedication to preserving and promoting the Continental Divide Trail. Your efforts make it possible for hikers like me to experience this incredible journey, and your passion for the trail is truly inspiring. Thank you for all you do to protect and enhance this beautiful route.

A big hug to Nancy and Richard Cobb, my neighbors, who checked on me during my secluded writing time in a small cabin in Tuscaloosa, Alabama.

Yesenia, since we were kids, you've always believed in me. Selling my drawings to your elementary school classmates for a quarter—that was a hustler move, though I can't recall ever seeing a cent of the profits. Love ya, Sis!

To my social media peeps, who never doubted that I would not only complete the CDT but also write another book for you. I love you all.

About the Author

DERICK LUGO, a native of New York City, is an accomplished and acclaimed storyteller, best known for his captivating first memoir, *The Unlikely Thru-Hiker*. This compelling book takes readers on a remarkable six-month journey along the Appalachian Trail, weaving humor and vivid narratives into a tale that has captured the hearts of readers worldwide.

Recognized for his exceptional ability to engage and entertain, Derick has made significant contributions to various outdoor magazines and journals. He has also penned short stories for *Campfire Stories II*, a Mountaineers Books publication, and *Stories from the Trail*, a Wayfarer Books outdoor anthology. Through his writing, he transports readers into the heart of the wilderness, bringing the outdoors to life on the page.

Derick is a highly sought-after keynote speaker, sharing inspiring stories of adventure and resilience. His infectious enthusiasm for outdoor adventure and his unwavering spirit make him an engaging presence on stage. Derick also hosts the popular *Unlikely Stories* podcast, in which he invites listeners to join him on an audio journey filled with unexpected tales and thought-provoking conversations with notable guests.

You can find Derick on Instagram, Threads, X, and TikTok @dericklugo; connect with him on Facebook @TheUnlikelyThruHiker; and visit his official website at dericklugo.com.

recreation • lifestyle • conservation

MOUNTAINEERS BOOKS, including its two imprints, Skipstone and Braided River, is a leading publisher of quality outdoor recreation, sustainability, and conservation titles. As a 501(c)(3) nonprofit, we are committed to supporting the environmental and educational goals of our organization by providing expert information on human-powered adventure, sustainable practices at home and on the trail, and preservation of wilderness.

Our publications are made possible through the generosity of donors, and through sales of 700 titles on outdoor recreation, sustainable lifestyle, and conservation. To donate, purchase books, or learn more, visit us online:

MOUNTAINEERS BOOKS

1001 SW Klickitat Way, Suite 201 • Seattle, WA 98134

800-553-4453 • mbooks@mountaineersbooks.org

www.mountaineersbooks.org

An independent nonprofit publisher since 1960

YOU MAY ALSO ENJOY:

MORE PRAISE FOR *A FABULOUS THRU-HIKE*

"*A Fabulous Thru-Hike* gives you the feeling of traversing the Continental Divide Trail with a storyteller, comedian, and friend. It's a lighthearted and uplifting read from one of the most challenging trails in North America—a tale that instills the significance of adventure and human kindness."

—JENNIFER PHARR DAVIS, AUTHOR, SPEAKER, AND NATIONAL GEOGRAPHIC ADVENTURER

"Through his witty observations and vivid depictions of the CDT, Mr. Fabulous will make you feel like you are one of his trail mates, like the loveable Tie or supportive Sidetrack. Fortunately, as a filmmaker, I get to sit in my trailer with my feet up and enjoy the journey like it's my new favorite movie, while Derick does all the work. Sometimes arduous (*la brega* is real), triumphant, and always entertaining, this adventure picks up where his first memoir, *The Unlikely Thru-Hiker,* leaves off.

—EUGENE ASHE, EMMY-NOMINATED WRITER/DIRECTOR OF *SYLVIE'S LOVE*